ROADS OF DESTINY

BY

O. HENRY

Author of " The Voice of the City," " The Trimmed Lamp," " Strictly Business," " Whirligigs," " Sixes and Sevens," Etc.

PUBLISHED BY

DOUBLEDAY, PAGE & COMPANY

FOR

REVIEW OF REVIEWS CO.

1915

"The old medical outrage . . . had a nigger along."

CONTENTS

I.

ROADS OF DESTINY

I go to seek on many roads
    What is to be.
True heart and strong, with love to light —
Will they not bear me in the fight
To órder, shun or wield or mould
    My Destiny?
        Unpublished Poems of David Mignot.

THE song was over. The words were David's; the air, one of the countryside. The company about the inn table applauded heartily, for the young poet paid for the wine. Only the notary, M. Papineau, shook his head a little at the lines, for he was a man of books, and he had not drunk with the rest.

David went out into the village street, where the night air drove the wine vapour from his head. And then he remembered that he and Yvonne had quarrelled that day, and that he had resolved to leave his home that night to seek fame and honour in the great world outside.

"When my poems are on every man's tongue," he told himself, in a fine exhilaration, "she will, perhaps, think of the hard words she spoke this day."

Except the roysterers in the tavern, the village folk were abed. David crept softly into his room in the shed of his father's cottage and made a bundle of his small store of clothing. With this upon a staff, he set his face outward upon the road that ran from Vernoy.

He passed his father's herd of sheep huddled in their nightly pen — the sheep he herded daily, leaving them to

3

scatter while he wrote verses on scraps of paper. He saw a light yet shining in Yvonne's window, and a weakness shook his purpose of a sudden. Perhaps that light meant that she rued, sleepless, her anger, and that morning might — But, no! His decision was made. Vernoy was no place for him. Not one soul there could share his thoughts. Out along that road lay his fate and his future.

Three leagues across the dim, moonlit champaign ran the road, straight as a ploughman's furrow. It was believed in the village that the road ran to Paris, at least; and this name the poet whispered often to himself as he walked. Never so far from Vernoy had David travelled before.

THE LEFT BRANCH

Three leagues, then, the road ran, and turned into a puzzle. It joined with another and a larger road at right angles. David stood, uncertain, for a while, and then took the road to the left.

Upon this more important highway were, imprinted in the dust, wheel tracks left by the recent passage of some vehicle. Some half an hour later these traces were verified by the sight of a ponderous carriage mired in a little brook at the bottom of a steep hill. The driver and postilions were shouting and tugging at the horses' bridles. On the road at one side stood a huge, black-clothed man and a slender lady wrapped in a long, light cloak.

David saw the lack of skill in the efforts of the servants. He quietly assumed control of the work. He directed the outriders to cease their clamour at the horses and to exercise their strength upon the wheels. The driver alone urged the animals with his familiar voice; David himself heaved a powerful shoulder at the rear of the carriage, and with one harmonious tug the great vehicle rolled up on solid ground. The outriders climbed to their places.

David stood for a moment upon one foot. The huge gentleman waved a hand. " You will enter the carriage," he said, in a voice large, like himself, but smoothed by art and habit. Obedience belonged in the path of such a voice. Brief as was the young poet's hesitation, it was cut shorter still by a renewal of the command. David's foot went to the step. In the darkness he perceived dimly the form of the lady upon the rear seat. He was about to seat himself opposite, when the voice again swayed him to its will. " You will sit at the lady's side."

The gentleman swung his great weight to the forward seat. The carriage proceeded up the hill. The lady was shrunk, silent, into her corner. David could not estimate whether she was old or young, but a delicate, mild perfume from her clothes stirred his poet's fancy to the belief that there was loveliness beneath the mystery. Here was an adventure such as he had often imagined. But as yet he held no key to it, for no word was spoken while he sat with his impenetrable companions.

In an hour's time David perceived through the window that the vehicle traversed the street of some town. Then it stopped in front of a closed and darkened house, and a postilion alighted to hammer impatiently upon the door. A latticed window above flew wide and a nightcapped head popped out.

" Who are ye that disturb honest folk at this time of night? My house is closed. 'Tis too late for profitable travellers to be abroad. Cease knocking at my door, and be off."

" Open ! " spluttered the postilion, loudly; " open for Monseigneur the Marquis de Beaupertuys."

" Ah ! " cried the voice above. " Ten thousand pardons, my lord. I did not know — the hour is so late — at once shall the door be opened, and the house placed at my lord's disposal."

Inside was heard the clink of chain and bar, and the door was flung open. Shivering with chill and apprehension, the landlord of the Silver Flagon stood, half clad, candle in hand, upon the threshold.

David followed the marquis out of the carriage. " Assist the lady," he was ordered. The poet obeyed. He felt her small hand tremble as he guided her descent. " Into the house," was the next command.

The room was the long dining-hall of the tavern. A great oak table ran down its length. The huge gentleman seated himself in a chair at the nearer end. The lady sank into another against the wall, with an air of great weariness. David stood, considering how best he might now take his leave and continue upon his way.

" My lord," said the landlord, bowing to the floor, " h-had I ex-expected this honour, entertainment would have been ready. T-t-there is wine and cold fowl and m-m-maybe —"

" Candles," said the marquis, spreading the fingers of one plump white hand in a gesture he had.

" Y-yes, my lord." He fetched half a dozen candles, lighted them, and set them upon the table.

" If monsieur would, perhaps, deign to taste a certain Burgundy — there is a cask —"

" Candles," said monsieur, spreading his fingers.

" Assuredly — quickly — I fly, my lord."

A dozen more lighted candles shone in the hall. The great bulk of the marquis overflowed his chair. He was dressed in fine black from head to foot save for the snowy ruffles at his wrist and throat. Even the hilt and scabbard of his sword were black. His expression was one of sneering pride. The ends of an upturned moustache reached nearly to his mocking eyes.

The lady sat motionless, and now David perceived that she was young, and possessed of pathetic and appealing beauty. He was startled from the contemplation of her forlorn loveliness by the booming voice of the marquis.

"What is your name and pursuit?"

"David Mignot. I am a poet."

The moustache of the marquis curled nearer to his eyes.

"How do you live?"

"I am also a shepherd; I guarded my father's flock," David answered, with his head high, but a flush upon his cheek.

"Then listen, master shepherd and poet, to the fortune you have blundered upon to-night. This lady is my niece, Mademoiselle Lucie de Varennes. She is of noble descent and is possessed of ten thousand francs a year in her own right. As to her charms, you have but to observe for yourself. If the inventory pleases your shepherd's heart, she becomes your wife at a word. Do not interrupt me. To-night I conveyed her to the *chateau* of the Comte de Villemaur, to whom her hand had been promised. Guests were present; the priest was waiting; her marriage to one eligible in rank and fortune was ready to be accomplished. At the altar this demoiselle, so meek and dutiful, turned upon me like a leopardess, charged me with cruelty and crimes, and broke, before the gaping priest, the troth I had plighted for her. I swore there and then, by ten thousand devils, that she should marry the first man we met after leaving the *chateau,* be he prince, charcoal-burner, or thief. You, shepherd, are the first. Mademoiselle must be wed this night. If not you, then another. You have ten minutes in which to make your decision. Do not vex me with words or questions. Ten minutes, shepherd; and they are speeding."

The marquis drummed loudly with his white fingers upon the table. He sank into a veiled attitude of waiting. It was as if some great house had shut its doors and windows against approach. David would have spoken, but the huge man's bearing stopped his tongue. Instead, he stood by the lady's chair and bowed.

"Mademoiselle," he said, and he marvelled to find his

words flowing easily before so much elegance and beauty. "You have heard me say I was a shepherd. I have also had the fancy, at times, that I am a poet. If it be the test of a poet to adore and cherish the beautiful, that fancy is now strengthened. Can I serve you in any way, mademoiselle?"

The young woman looked up at him with eyes dry and mournful. His frank, glowing face, made serious by the gravity of the adventure, his strong, straight figure and the liquid sympathy in his blue eyes, perhaps, also, her imminent need of long-denied help and kindness, thawed her to sudden tears.

"Monsieur," she said, in low tones, "you look to be true and kind. Hs is my uncle, the brother of my father, and my only relative. He loved my mother, and he hates me because I am like her. He has made my life one long terror. I am afraid of his very looks, and never before dared to disobey him. But to-night he would have married me to a man three times my age. You will forgive me for bringing this vexation upon you, monsieur. You will, of course, decline this mad act he tries to force upon you. But let me thank you for your generous words, at least. I have had none spoken to me in so long."

There was now something more than generosity in the poet's eyes. Poet he must have been, for Yvonne was forgotten; this fine, new loveliness held him with its freshness and grace. The subtle perfume from her filled him with strange emotions. His tender look fell warmly upon her. She leaned to it, thirstily.

"Ten minutes," said David, "is given me in which to do what I would devote years to achieve. I will not say I pity you, mademoiselle; it would not be true — I love you. I cannot ask love from you yet, but let me rescue you from this cruel man, and, in time, love may come. I think I have a future; I will not always be a shepherd. For the present

I will cherish you with all my heart and make your life less sad. Will you trust your fate to me, mademoiselle?"

"Ah, you would sacrifice yourself from pity!"

"From love. The time is almost up, mademoiselle."

"You will regret it, and despise me."

"I will live only to make you happy, and myself worthy of you."

Her fine small hand crept into his from beneath her cloak.

"I will trust you," she breathed, "with my life. And — and love — may not be so far off as you think. Tell him. Once away from the power of his eyes I may forget."

David went and stood before the marquis. The black figure stirred, and the mocking eyes glanced at the great hall clock.

"Two minutes to spare. A shepherd requires eight minutes to decide whether he will accept a bride of beauty and income! Speak up, shepherd, do you consent to become mademoiselle's husband?"

"Mademoiselle," said David, standing proudly, "has done me the honour to yield to my request that she become my wife."

"Well said!" said the marquis. "You have yet the making of a courtier in you, master shepherd. Mademoiselle could have drawn a worse prize, after all. And now to be done with the affair as quick as the Church and the devil will allow!"

He struck the table soundly with his sword hilt. The landlord came, knee-shaking, bringing more candles in the hope of anticipating the great lord's whims. "Fetch a priest," said the marquis, "a priest; do you understand? In ten minutes have a priest here, or —"

The landlord dropped his candles and flew.

The priest came, heavy-eyed and ruffled. He made David Mignot and Lucie de Varennes man and wife, pocketed a gold piece that the marquis tossed him, and shuffled out again into the night.

"Wine," ordered the marquis, spreading his ominous fingers at the host.

"Fill glasses," he said, when it was brought. He stood up at the head of the table in the candlelight, a black mountain of venom and conceit, with something like the memory of an old love turned to poison in his eye, as it fell upon his niece.

"Monsieur Mignot," he said, raising his wineglass, " drink after I say this to you: You have taken to be your wife one who will make your life a foul and wretched thing. The blood in her is an inheritance running black lies and red ruin. She will bring you shame and anxiety. The devil that descended to her is there in her eyes and skin and mouth that stoop even to beguile a peasant. There is your promise, monsieur poet, for a happy life. Drink your wine. At last, mademoiselle, I am rid of you."

The marquis drank. A little grievous cry, as if from a sudden wound, came from the girl's lips. David, with his glass in his hand, stepped forward three paces and faced the marquis. There was little of a shepherd in his bearing.

"Just now," he said, calmly, " you did me the honour to call me ' monsieur.' May I hope, therefore that my marriage to mademoiselle has placed me somewhat nearer to you in — let us say, reflected rank — has given me the right to stand more as an equal to monseigneur in a certain little piece of business I have in my mind? "

"You may hope, shepherd," sneered the marquis.

"Then," said David, dashing his glass of wine into the contemptuous eyes that mocked him, " perhaps you will condescend to fight me."

The fury of the great lord outbroke in one sudden curse like a blast from a horn. He tore his sword from its black sheath; he called to the hovering landlord: "A sword there, for this lout!" He turned to the lady, with a laugh that chilled her heart, and said: "You put much labour upon me, madame. It seems I must find you a husband and make you a widow in the same night."

"I know not sword-play," said David. He flushed to make the confession before his lady.

"'I know not sword-play,'" mimicked the marquis. "Shall we fight like peasants with oaken cudgels? *Hola!* François, my pistols!"

A postilion brought two shining great pistols ornamented with carven silver, from the carriage holsters. The marquis tossed one upon the table near David's hand. "To the other end of the table," he cried; "even a shepherd may pull a trigger. Few of them attain the honour to die by the weapon of a De Beaupertuys."

The shepherd and the marquis faced each other from the ends of the long table. The landlord, in an ague of terror, clutched the air and stammered: "M-M-Monseigneur, for the love of Christ! not in my house! — do not spill blood — it will ruin my custom —" The look of the marquis, threatening him, paralyzed his tongue.

"Coward," cried the lord of Beaupertuys, "cease chattering your teeth long enough to give the word for us, if you can."

Mine host's knees smote the floor. He was without a vocabulary. Even sounds were beyond him. Still, by gestures he seemed to beseech peace in the name of his house and custom.

"I will give the word," said the lady, in a clear voice. She went up to David and kissed him sweetly. Her eyes were sparkling bright, and colour had come to her cheek. She stood against the wall, and the two men levelled their pistols for her count.

" *Un — deux — trois!* "

The two reports came so nearly together that the candles flickered but once. The marquis stood, smiling, the fingers of his left hand resting, outspread, upon the end of the table. David remained erect, and turned his head very slowly, searching for his wife with his eyes. Then, as a garment falls from where it is hung, he sank, crumpled, upon the floor.

With a little cry of terror and despair, the widowed maid ran and stooped above him. She found his wound, and then looked up with her old look of pale melancholy. " Through his heart," she whispered. " Oh, his heart! "

" Come," boomed the great voice of the marquis, " out with you to the carriage! Daybreak shall not find you on my hands. Wed you shall be again, and to a living husband, this night. The next we come upon, my lady, highwayman or peasant. If the road yields no other, then the churl that opens my gates. Out with you to the carriage! "

The marquis, implacable and huge, the lady wrapped again in the mystery of her cloak, the postilion bearing the weapons — all moved out to the waiting carriage. The sound of its ponderous wheels rolling away echoed through the slumbering village. In the hall of the Silver Flagon the distracted landlord wrung his hands above the slain poet's body, while the flames of the four and twenty candles danced and flickered on the table.

THE RIGHT BRANCH

Three leagues, then, the road ran, and turned into a puzzle. It joined with another and a larger road at right angles. David stood, uncertain, for a while, and then took the road to the right.

Whither it led he knew not, but he was resolved to leave Vernoy far behind that night. He travelled a league and then passed a large château which showed testimony of recent entertainment. Lights shone from every window; from the great stone gateway ran a tracery of wheel tracks drawn in the dust by the vehicles of the guests.

Three leagues farther and David was weary. He rested and slept for a while on a bed of pine boughs at the roadside. Then up and on again along the unknown way.

Thus for five days he travelled the great road, sleeping upon Nature's balsamic beds or in peasants' ricks, eating of their black, hospitable bread, drinking from streams or the willing cup of the goatherd.

At length he crossed a great bridge and set his foot within the smiling city that has crushed or crowned more poets than all the rest of the world. His breath came quickly as Paris sang to him in a little undertone her vital chant of greeting — the hum of voice and foot and wheel.

High up under the eaves of on old house in the Rue Conti, David paid for lodging, and set himself, in a wooden chair, to his poems. The street, once sheltering citizens of import and consequence, was now given over to those who ever follow in the wake of decline.

The houses were tall and still possessed of a ruined dignity, but many of them were empty save for dust and the spider. By night there was the clash of steel and the cries of brawlers straying restlessly from inn to inn. Where once gentility abode was now but a rancid and rude incontinence. But here David found housing commensurate to his scant purse. Daylight and candlelight found him at pen and paper.

One afternoon he was returning from a foraging trip to the lower world, with bread and curds and a bottle of thin wine. Halfway up his dark stairway he met — or rather came upon, for she rested on the stair — a young woman of a beauty that should balk even the justice of a poet's imagination. A loose, dark cloak, flung open, showed a rich gown beneath. Her eyes changed swiftly with every little shade

of thought. Within one moment they would be round and
artless like a child's, and long and cozening like a gypsy's.
One hand raised her gown, undraping a little shoe, high-
heeled, with its ribbons dangling, untied. So heavenly she
was, so unfitted to stoop, so qualified to charm and command!
Perhaps she had seen David coming, and had waited for his
help there.

Ah, would monsieur pardon that she occupied the stairway,
but the shoe! — the naughty shoe! Alas! it would not remain tied. Ah! if monsieur *would* be so gracious!

The poet's fingers trembled as he tied the contrary ribbons.
Then he would have fled from the danger of her presence,
but the eyes grew long and cozening, like a gypsy's, and held
him. He leaned against the balustrade, clutching his bottle
of sour wine.

"You have been so good," she said, smiling. "Does monsieur, perhaps, live in the house?"

"Yes, madame. I — I think so, madame."

"Perhaps in the third story, then?"

"No, madame; higher up."

The lady fluttered her fingers with the least possible gesture of impatience.

"Pardon. Certainly I am not discreet in asking. Monsieur will forgive me? It is surely not becoming that I should
inquire where he lodges."

"Madame, do not say so. I live in the —"

"No, no, no; do not tell me. Now I see that I erred. But
I cannot lose the interest I feel in this house and all that is
in it. Once it was my home. Often I come here but to
dream of those happy days again. Will you let that be my
excuse?"

"Let me tell you, then, for you need no excuse," stammered the poet. "I live in the top floor — the small room
where the stairs turn."

"In the front room?" asked the lady, turning her head sidewise.

"The rear, madame."

The lady sighed, as if with relief.

"I will detain you no longer, then, monsieur," she said, employing the round and artless eye. "Take good care of my house. Alas! only the memories of it are mine now. Adieu, and accept my thanks for your courtesy."

She was gone, leaving but a smile and a trace of sweet perfume. David climbed the stairs as one in slumber. But he awoke from it, and the smile and the perfume lingered with him and never afterward did either seem quite to leave him. This lady of whom he knew nothing drove him to lyrics of eyes, chansons of swiftly conceived love, odes to curling hair, and sonnets to slippers on slender feet.

Poet he must have been, for Yvonne was forgotten; this fine, new loveliness held him with its freshness and grace. The subtle perfume about her filled him with strange emotions.

On a certain night three persons were gathered about a table in a room on the third floor of the same house. Three chairs and the table and a lighted candle upon it was all the furniture. One of the persons was a huge man, dressed in black. His expression was one of sneering pride. The ends of his upturned moustache reached nearly to his mocking eyes. Another was a lady, young and beautiful, with eyes that could be round and artless, like a child's, or long and cozening, like a gipsy's, but were now keen and ambitious, like any other conspirator's. The third was a man of action, a combatant, a bold and impatient executive, breathing fire and steel. He was addressed by the others as Captain Desrolles.

This man struck the table with his fist, and said, with controlled violence:

"To-night. To-night as he goes to midnight mass. I am

tired of the plotting that gets nowhere. I am sick of signals and ciphers and secret meetings and such *baragouin*. Let us be honest traitors. If France is to be rid of him, let us kill in the open, and not hunt with snares and traps. To-night, I say. I back my words. My hand will do the deed. To-night, as he goes to mass."

The lady turned upon him a cordial look. Woman, however wedded to plots, must ever thus bow to rash courage. The big man stroked his upturned moustache.

"Dear captain," he said, in a great voice, softened by habit, "this time I agree with you. Nothing is to be gained by waiting. Enough of the palace guards belong to us to make the endeavour a safe one."

"To-night," repeated Captain Desrolles, again striking the table. "You have heard me, marquis; my hand will do the deed."

"But now," said the huge man, softly, "comes a question. Word must be sent to our partisans in the palace, and a signal agreed upon. Our stanchest men must accompany the royal carriage. At this hour what messenger can penetrate so far as the south doorway? Ribout is stationed there; once a message is placed in his hands, all will go well."

"I will send the message," said the lady.

"You, countess?" said the marquis, raising his eyebrows. "Your devotion is great, we know, but —"

"Listen!" exclaimed the lady, rising and resting her hands upon the table; "in a garret of this house lives a youth from the provinces as guileless and tender as the lambs he tended there. I have met him twice or thrice upon the stairs. I questioned him, fearing that he might dwell too near the room in which we are accustomed to meet. He is mine, if I will. He writes poems in his garret, and I think he dreams of me. He will do what I say. He shall take the message to the palace."

The marquis rose from his chair and bowed. "You did not permit me to finish my sentence, countess," he said. "I would have said: 'Your devotion is great, but your wit and charm are infinitely greater.'"

While the conspirators were thus engaged, David was polishing some lines addressed to his *amorette d'escalier.* He heard a timorous knock at his door, and opened it, with a great throb, to behold her there, panting as one in straits, with eyes wide open and artless, like a child's.

"Monsieur," she breathed, "I come to you in distress. I believe you to be good and true, and I know of no other help. How I flew through the streets among the swaggering men! Monsieur, my mother is dying. My uncle is a captain of guards in the palace of the king. Some one must fly to bring him. May I hope —"

"Mademoiselle," interrupted David, his eyes shining with the desire to do her service, "your hopes shall be my wings. Tell me how I may reach him."

The lady thrust a sealed paper into his hand.

"Go to the south gate — the south gate, mind — and say to the guards there, 'The falcon has left his nest.' They will pass you, and you will go to the south entrance to the palace. Repeat the words, and give this letter to the man who will reply 'Let him strike when he will.' This is the password, monsieur, entrusted to me by my uncle, for now when the country is disturbed and men plot against the king's life, no one without it can gain entrance to the palace grounds after nightfall. If you will, monsieur, take him this letter so that my mother may see him before she closes her eyes."

"Give it me," said David, eagerly. "But shall I let you return home through the streets alone so late? I —"

"No, no — fly. Each moment is like a precious jewel. Some time," said the lady, with eyes long and cozening, like a gipsy's, "I will try to thank you for your goodness."

The poet thrust the letter into his breast, and bounded down the stairway. The lady, when he was gone, returned to the room below.

The eloquent eyebrows of the marquis interrogated her.

"He is gone," she said, "as fleet and stupid as one of his own sheep, to deliver it."

The table shook again from the batter of Captain Desrolles's fist.

"Sacred name!" he cried; "I have left my pistols behind! I can trust no others."

"Take this," said the marquis, drawing from beneath his cloak a shining, great weapon, ornamented with carven silver. "There are none truer. But guard it closely, for it bears my arms and crest, and already I am suspected. Me, I must put many leagues between myself and Paris this night. To-morrow must find me in my *château*. After you, dear countess."

The marquis puffed out the candle. The lady, well cloaked, and the two gentlemen softly descended the stairway and flowed into the crowd that roamed along the narrow pavements of the Rue Conti.

David sped. At the south gate of the king's residence a halberd was laid to his breast, but he turned its point with the words: "The falcon has left his nest."

"Pass, brother," said the guard, "and go quickly."

On the south steps of the palace they moved to seize him, but again the *mot de passe* charmed the watchers. One among them stepped forward and began: "Let him strike —" but a flurry among the guards told of a surprise. A man of keen look and soldierly stride suddenly pressed through them and seized the letter which David held in his hand. "Come with me," he said, and led him inside the great hall. Then he tore open the letter and read it. He beckoned to a man uniformed as an officer of musketeers, who was passing. "Captain Tetreau, you will have the guards at the south entrance and the south gate arrested and confined. Place men known to be loyal in their places." To David he said: "Come with me."

He conducted him through a corridor and an anteroom into a spacious chamber, where a melancholy man, sombrely dressed, sat brooding in a great, leather-covered chair. To that man he said:

"Sire, I have told you that the palace is as full of traitors and spies as a sewer is of rats. You have thought, sire, that it was my fancy. This man penetrated to your very door by their connivance. He bore a letter which I have intercepted. I have brought him here that your majesty may no longer think my zeal excessive."

"I will question him," said the king, stirring in his chair. He looked at David with heavy eyes dulled by an opaque film. The poet bent his knee.

"From where do you come?" asked the king.

"From the village of Vernoy, in the province of Eure-et-Loir, sire."

"What do you follow in Paris?"

"I — I would be a poet, sire."

"What did you in Vernoy?"

"I minded my father's flock of sheep."

The king stirred again, and the film lifted from his eyes.

"Ah! in the fields!"

"Yes, sire."

"You lived in the fields; you went out in the cool of the morning and lay among the hedges in the grass. The flock distributed itself upon the hillside; you drank of the living stream; you ate your sweet, brown bread in the shade, and you listened, doubtless, to blackbirds piping in the grove. Is not that so, the shepherd?"

"It is, sire," answered David, with a sigh; "and to the

bees at the flowers, and, maybe, to the grape gatherers singing on the hill."

"Yes, yes," said the king, impatiently; "maybe to them; but surely to the blackbirds. They whistled often, in the grove, did they not?"

"Nowhere, sire, so sweetly as in Eure-et-Loir. I have endeavoured to express their song in some verses that I have written."

"Can you repeat those verses?" asked the king, eagerly. "A long time ago I listened to the blackbirds. It would be something better than a kingdom if one could rightly construe their song. And at night you drove the sheep to the fold and then sat, in peace and tranquillity, to your pleasant bread. Can you repeat those verses, shepherd?"

"They run this way, sire," said David, with respectful ardour:

> "'Lazy shepherd, see your lambkins
> Skip, ecstatic, on the mead;
> See the firs dance in the breezes,
> Hear Pan blowing at his reed.
>
> "Hear us calling from the tree-tops,
> See us swoop upon your flock;
> Yield us wool to make our nests warm
> In the branches of the—'"

"If it please your majesty," interrupted a harsh voice, "I will ask a question or two of this rhymester. There is little time to spare. I crave pardon, sire, if my anxiety for your safety offends."

"The loyalty," said the king, "of the Duke d'Aumale is too well proven to give offence." He sank into his chair, and the film came again over his eyes.

"First," said the duke, "I will read you the letter he brought:

"'To-night is the anniversary of the dauphin's death. If he goes, as is his custom, to midnight mass to pray for the soul of his son, the falcon will strike, at the corner of the Rue Esplanade. If this be his intention, set a red light in the upper room at the southwest corner of the palace, that the falcon may take heed.'

"Peasant," said the duke, sternly, "you have heard these words. Who gave you this message to bring?"

"My lord duke," said David, sincerely, "I will tell you. A lady gave it me. She said her mother was ill, and that this writing would fetch her uncle to her bedside. I do not know the meaning of the letter, but I will swear that she is beautiful and good."

"Describe the woman," commanded the duke, "and how you came to be her dupe."

"Describe her!" said David with a tender smile. "You would command words to perform miracles. Well, she is made of sunshine and deep shade. She is slender, like the alders, and moves with their grace. Her eyes change while you gaze into them; now round, and then half shut as the sun peeps between two clouds. When she comes, heaven is all about her; when she leaves, there is chaos and a scent of hawthorn blossoms. She came to me in the Rue Conti, number twenty-nine."

"It is the house," said the duke, turning to the king, "that we have been watching. Thanks to the poet's tongue, we have a picture of the infamous Countess Quebedaux."

"Sire and my lord duke," said David, earnestly, "I hope my poor words have done no injustice. I have looked into that lady's eyes. I will stake my life that she is an angel, letter or no letter."

The duke looked at him steadily. "I will put you to the proof," he said, slowly. "Dressed as the king, you shall, yourself, attend mass in his carriage at midnight. Do you accept the test?"

David smiled. "I have looked into her eyes," he said. "I had my proof there. Take yours how you will."

Half an hour before twelve the Duke d'Aumale, with his own hands, set a red lamp in a southwest window of the palace. At ten minutes to the hour, David, leaning on his arm, dressed as the king, from top to toe, with his head bowed in his cloak, walked slowly from the royal apartments to the waiting carriage. The duke assisted him inside and closed the door. The carriage whirled away along its route to the cathedral.

On the *qui vive* in a house at the corner of the Rue Esplanade was Captain Tetreau with twenty men, ready to pounce upon the conspirators when they should appear.

But it seemed that, for some reason, the plotters had slightly altered their plans. When the royal carriage had reached the Rue Christopher, one square nearer than the Rue Esplanade, forth from it burst Captain Desrolles, with his band of would-be regicides, and assailed the equipage. The guards upon the carriage, though surprised at the premature attack, descended and fought valiantly. The noise of conflict attracted the force of Captain Tetreau, and they came pelting down the street to the rescue. But, in the meantime, the desperate Desrolles had torn open the door of the king's carriage, thrust his weapon against the body of the dark figure inside, and fired.

Now, with loyal reinforcements at hand, the street rang with cries and the rasp of steel, but the frightened horses had dashed away. Upon the cushions lay the dead body of the poor mock king and poet, slain by a ball from the pistol of Monseigneur, the Marquis de Beaupertuys.

THE MAIN ROAD

Three leagues, then, the road ran, and turned into a puzzle. It joined with another and a larger road at right angles.

David stood, uncertain, for a while, and then sat himself to rest upon its side.

Whither those roads led he knew not. Either way there seemed to lie a great world full of chance and peril. And then, sitting there, his eye fell upon a bright star, one that he and Yvonne had named for theirs. That set him thinking of Yvonne, and he wondered if he had not been too hasty. Why should he leave her and his home because a few hot words had come between them? Was love so brittle a thing that jealousy, the very proof of it, could break it? Mornings always brought a cure for the little heartaches of evening. There was yet time for him to return home without any one in the sweetly sleeping village of Vernoy being the wiser. His heart was Yvonne's; there where he had lived always he could write his poems and find his happiness.

David rose, and shook off his unrest and the wild mood that had tempted him. He set his face steadfastly back along the road he had come. By the time he had retravelled the road to Vernoy, his desire to rove was gone. He passed the sheepfold, and the sheep scurried, with a drumming flutter, at his late footsteps, warming his heart by the homely sound. He crept without noise into his little room and lay there, thankful that his feet had escaped the distress of new roads that night.

How well he knew woman's heart! The next evening Yvonne was at the well in the road where the young congregated in order that the *curé* might have business. The corner of her eye was engaged in a search for David, albeit her set mouth seemed unrelenting. He saw the look; braved the mouth, drew from it a recantation and, later, a kiss as they walked homeward together.

Three months afterward they were married. David's father was shrewd and prosperous. He gave them a wedding that was heard of three leagues away. Both the young people were favourites in the village. There was a procession in the streets, a dance on the green; they had the marionettes and a tumbler out from Dreux to delight the guests.

Then a year, and David's father died. The sheep and the cottage descended to him. He already had the seemliest wife in the village. Yvonne's milk pails and her brass kettles were bright — *ouf!* they blinded you in the sun when you passed that way. But you must keep your eyes upon her yard, for her flower beds were so neat and gay they restored to you your sight. And you might hear her sing, aye, as far as the double chestnut tree above Père Gruneau's blacksmith forge.

But a day came when David drew out paper from a long-shut drawer, and began to bite the end of a pencil. Spring had come again and touched his heart. Poet he must have been, for now Yvonne was well-nigh forgotten. This fine new loveliness of earth held him with its witchery and grace. The perfume from her woods and meadows stirred him strangely. Daily had he gone forth with his flock, and brought it safe at night. But now he stretched himself under the hedge and pieced words together on his bits of paper. The sheep strayed, and the wolves, perceiving that difficult poems make easy mutton, ventured from the woods and stole his lambs.

David's stock of poems grew larger and his flock smaller. Yvonne's nose and temper waxed sharp and her talk blunt. Her pans and kettles grew dull, but her eyes had caught their flash. She pointed out to the poet that his neglect was reducing the flock and bringing woe upon the household. David hired a boy to guard the sheep, locked himself in the little room in the top of the cottage, and wrote more poems. The boy, being a poet by nature, but not furnished with an outlet in the way of writing, spent his time in slumber. The wolves lost no time in discovering that poetry and sleep are practically the same; so the flock steadily grew smaller. Yvonne's ill temper increased at an equal rate. Sometimes she would stand in the yard and rail at David through his high window. Then you could hear her as far as the double chestnut tree above Père Gruneau's blacksmith forge.

M. Papineau, the kind, wise, meddling old notary, saw this, as he saw everything at which his nose pointed. He went to David, fortified himself with a great pinch of snuff, and said:

"Friend Mignot, I affixed the seal upon the marriage certificate of your father. It would distress me to be obliged to attest a paper signifying the bankruptcy of his son. But that is what you are coming to. I speak as an old friend. Now, listen to what I have to say. You have your heart set, I perceive, upon poetry. At Dreux, I have a friend, one Monsieur Bril — Georges Bril. He lives in a little cleared space in a houseful of books. He is a learned man; he visits Paris each year; he himself has written books. He will tell you when the catacombs were made, how they found out the names of the stars, and why the plover has a long bill. The meaning and the form of poetry is to him as intelligent as the baa of a sheep is to you. I will give you a letter to him, and you shall take him your poems and let him read them. Then you will know if you shall write more, or give your attention to your wife and business."

"Write the letter," said David, "I am sorry you did not speak of this sooner."

At sunrise the next morning he was on the road to Dreux with the precious roll of poems under his arm. At noon he wiped the dust from his feet at the door of Monsieur Bril. That learned man broke the seal of M. Papineau's letter, and sucked up its contents through his gleaming spectacles as the sun draws water. He took David inside to his study and sat him down upon a little island beat upon by a sea of books.

Monsieur Bril had a conscience. He flinched not even at

a mass of manuscript the thickness of a finger length and rolled to an incorrigible curve. He broke the back of the roll against his knee and began to read. He slighted nothing; he bored into the lump as a worm into a nut, seeking for a kernel.

Meanwhile, David sat, marooned, trembling in the spray of so much literature. It roared in his ears. He held no chart or compass for voyaging in that sea. Half the world, he thought, must be writing books.

Monsieur Bril bored to the last page of the poems. Then he took off his spectacles and wiped them with his handkerchief.

"My old friend, Papineau, is well?" he asked.

"In the best of health," said David.

"How many sheep have you, Monsieur Mignot?"

"Three hundred and nine, when I counted them yesterday. The flock has had ill fortune. To that number it has decreased from eight hundred and fifty."

"You have a wife and a home, and lived in comfort. The sheep brought you plenty. You went into the fields with them and lived in the keen air and ate the sweet bread of contentment. You had but to be vigilant and recline there upon nature's breast, listening to the whistle of the blackbirds in the grove. Am I right thus far?"

"It was so," said David.

"I have read all your verses," continued Monsieur Bril, his eyes wandering about his sea of books as if he conned the horizon for a sail. "Look yonder, through that window, Monsieur Mignot; tell me what you see in that tree."

"I see a crow," said David, looking.

"There is a bird," said Monsieur Bril, "that shall assist me where I am disposed to shirk a duty. You know that bird, Monsieur Mignot; he is the philosopher of the air. He is happy through submission to his lot. None so merry or fullcrawed as he with his whimsical eye and rollicking step. The fields yield him what he desires. He never grieves that his plumage is not gay, like the oriole's. And you have heard, Monsieur Mignot, the notes that nature has given him? Is the nightingale any happier, do you think?"

David rose to his feet. The crow cawed harshly from his tree.

"I thank you, Monsieur Bril," he said, slowly. "There was not, then, one nightingale note among all those croaks?"

"I could not have missed it," said Monsieur Bril, with a sigh. "I read every word. Live your poetry, man; do not try to write it any more."

"I thank you," said David, again. "And now I will be going back to my sheep."

"If you would dine with me," said the man of books, "and overlook the smart of it, I will give you reasons at length."

"No," said the poet, "I must be back in the fields cawing at my sheep."

Back along the road to Vernoy he trudged with his poems under his arm. When he reached his village he turned into the shop of one Zeigler, a Jew out of Armenia, who sold anything that came to his hand.

"Friend," said David, "wolves from the forest harass my sheep on the hills. I must purchase firearms to protect them. What have you?"

"A bad day, this, for me, friend Mignot," said Zeigler, spreading his hands, "for I perceive that I must sell you a weapon that will not fetch a tenth of its value. Only last week I bought from a peddler a waggon full of goods that he procured at a sale by a *commissionaire* of the crown. The sale was of the *chateau* and belongings of a great lord — I know not his title — who has been banished for conspiracy against the king. There are some choice firearms in the lot. This pistol — oh, a weapon fit for a prince! — it shall be only forty francs to you, friend Mignot — if I lose ten by the sale. But perhaps an arquebuse —"

" This will do," said David, throwing the money on the counter. " Is it charged? "

" I will charge it," said Zeigler. " And, for ten francs more, add a store of powder and ball."

David laid his pistol under his coat and walked to his cottage. Yvonne was not there. Of late she had taken to gadding much among the neighbours. But a fire was glowing in the kitchen stove. David opened the door of it and thrust his poems in upon the coals. As they blazed up they made a singing, harsh sound in the flue.

" The song of the crow! " said the poet.

He went up to his attic room and closed the door. So quiet was the village that a score of people heard the roar of the great pistol. They flocked thither, and up the stairs where the smoke, issuing, drew their notice.

The men laid the body of the poet upon his bed, awkwardly arranging it to conceal the torn plumage of the poor black crow. The women chattered in a luxury of zealous pity. Some of them ran to tell Yvonne.

M. Papineau, whose nose had brought him there among the first, picked up the weapon and ran his eye over its silver mountings with a mingled air of connoisseurship and grief.

" The arms," he explained, aside, to the *curé*, " and crest of Monseigneur, the Marquis de Beaupertuys."

II

THE GUARDIAN OF THE ACCOLADE

Not the least important of the force of the Weymouth Bank was Uncle Bushrod. Sixty years had Uncle Bushrod given of faithful service to the house of Weymouth as chattel, servitor, and friend. Of the colour of the mahogany bank furniture was Uncle Bushrod — thus dark was he externally; white as the uninked pages of the bank ledgers was his soul. Eminently pleasing to Uncle Bushrod would the comparison have been; for to him the only institution in existence worth considering was the Weymouth Bank, of which he was something between porter and generalissimo-in-charge.

Weymouth lay, dreamy and umbrageous, among the low foothills along the brow of a Southern valley. Three banks there were in Weymouthville. Two were hopeless, misguided enterprises, lacking the presence and prestige of a Weymouth to give them glory. The third was The Bank, managed by the Weymouths — and Uncle Bushrod. In the old Weymouth homestead — the red brick, white-porticoed mansion, the first to your right as you crossed Elder Creek, coming into town — lived Mr. Robert Weymouth (the president of the bank), his widowed daughter, Mrs. Vesey — called " Miss Letty " by every one — and her two children, Nan and Guy. There, also in a cottage on the grounds, resided Uncle Bushrod and Aunt Malindy, his wife. Mr. William Weymouth (the cashier of the bank) lived in a modern, fine house on the principal avenue.

Mr. Robert was a large, stout man, sixty-two years of age,

with a smooth, plump face, long iron-gray hair and fiery blue eyes. He was high-tempered, kind, and generous, with a youthful smile and a formidable, stern voice that did not always mean what it sounded like. Mr. William was a milder man, correct in deportment and absorbed in business. The Weymouths formed The Family of Weymouthville, and were looked up to, as was their right of heritage.

Uncle Bushrod was the bank's trusted porter, messenger, vassal, and guardian. He carried a key to the vault, just as Mr. Robert and Mr. William did. Sometimes there was ten, fifteen, or twenty thousand dollars in sacked silver stacked on the vault floor. It was safe with Uncle Bushrod. He was a Weymouth in heart, honesty, and pride.

Of late Uncle Bushrod had not been without worry. It was on account of Marse Robert. For nearly a year Mr. Robert had been known to indulge in too much drink. Not enough, understand, to become tipsy, but the habit was getting a hold upon him, and every one was beginning to notice it. Half a dozen times a day he would leave the bank and step around to the Merchants and Planters' Hotel to take a drink. Mr. Robert's usual keen judgment and business capacity became a little impaired. Mr. William, a Weymouth, but not so rich in experience, tried to dam the inevitable backflow of the tide, but with incomplete success. The deposits in the Weymouth Bank dropped from six figures to five. Past-due paper began to accumulate, owing to injudicious loans. No one cared to address Mr. Robert on the subject of temperance. Many of his friends said that the cause of it had been the death of his wife some two years before. Others hesitated on account of Mr. Robert's quick temper, which was extremely apt to resent personal interference of such a nature. Miss Letty and the children noticed the change and grieved about it. Uncle Bushrod also worried, but he was one of those who would not have dared to remonstrate, although he and Marse Robert had been raised almost as companions. But there was a heavier shock coming to Uncle Bushrod than that caused by the bank president's toddies and juleps.

Mr. Robert had a passion for fishing, which he usually indulged whenever the season and business permitted. One day, when reports had been coming in relating to the bass and perch, he announced his intention of making a two or three days' visit to the lakes. He was going down, he said, to Reedy Lake with Judge Archinard, an old friend.

Now, Uncle Bushrod was treasurer of the Sons and Daughters of the Burning Bush. Every association he belonged to made him treasurer without hesitation. He stood AA1 in coloured circles. He was understood among them to be Mr. Bushrod Weymouth, of the Weymouth Bank.

The night following the day on which Mr. Robert mentioned his intended fishing-trip the old man woke up and rose from his bed at twelve o'clock, declaring he must go down to the bank and fetch the pass-book of the Sons and Daughters, which he had forgotten to bring home. The bookkeeper had balanced it for him that day, put the cancelled checks in it, and snapped two elastic bands around it. He put but one band around other pass-books.

Aunt Malindy objected to the mission at so late an hour, denouncing it as foolish and unnecessary, but Uncle Bushrod was not to be deflected from duty.

" I done told Sister Adaline Hoskins," he said, " to come by here for dat book to-morrer mawnin' at sebin o'clock, for to kyar' it to de meetin' of de bo'd of 'rangements, and dat book gwine to be here when she come."

So, Uncle Bushrod put on his old brown suit, got his thick hickory stick, and meandered through the almost deserted streets of Weymouthville. He entered the bank, unlocking the side door, and found the pass-book where he had left it, in the little back room used for private consultations, where he always hung his coat. Looking about casually, he saw that everything was as he had left it, and was about to start for home when he was brought to a standstill by the sudden rattle of a key in the front door. Some one came quickly in, closed the door softly, and entered the counting-room through the door in the iron railing.

That division of the bank's space was connected with the back room by a narrow passageway, now in deep darkness.

Uncle Bushrod, firmly gripping his hickory stick, tiptoed gently up this passage until he could see the midnight intruder into the sacred precincts of the Weymouth Bank. One dim gas-jet burned there, but even in its nebulous light he perceived at once that the prowler was the bank's president.

Wondering, fearful, undecided what to do, the old coloured man stood motionless in the gloomy strip of hallway, and waited developments.

The vault, with its big iron door, was opposite him. Inside that was the safe, holding the papers of value, the gold and currency of the bank. On the floor of the vault **was**, perhaps, eighteen thousand dollars in silver.

The president took his key from his pocket, opened the vault and went inside, nearly closing the door behind him. Uncle Bushrod saw, through the narrow aperture, the flicker of a candle. In a minute or two — it seemed an hour to the watcher — Mr. Robert came out, bringing with him a large hand-satchel, handling it in a careful but hurried manner, as if fearful that he might be observed. With one hand he closed and locked the vault door.

With a reluctant theory forming itself beneath his wool, Uncle Bushrod waited and watched, shaking in his concealing shadow.

Mr. Robert set the satchel softly upon a desk, and turned his coat collar up about his neck and ears. He was dressed in a rough suit of gray, as if for travelling. He glanced with frowning intentness at the big office clock above the burning gas-jet, and then looked lingeringly about the bank — lingeringly and fondly, Uncle Bushrod thought, as one who bids farewell to dear and familiar scenes.

Now he caught up his burden again and moved promptly and softly out of the bank by the way he had come locking the front door behind him.

For a minute or longer Uncle Bushrod was as stone in his tracks. Had that midnight rifler of safes and vaults been any other on earth than the man he was, the old retainer would have rushed upon him and struck to save the Weymouth property. But now the watcher's soul was tortured by the poignant dread of something worse than mere robbery. He was seized by an accusing terror that said the Weymouth name and the Weymouth honour were about to be lost. Marse Robert robbing the bank! What else could it mean? The hour of the night, the stealthy visit to the vault, the satchel brought forth full and with expedition and silence, the prowler's rough dress, his solicitous reading of the clock, and noiseless departure — what else could it mean?

And then to the turmoil of Uncle Bushrod's thoughts came the corroborating recollection of preceding events — Mr. Robert's increasing intemperance and consequent many moods of royal high spirits and stern tempers; the casual talk he had heard in the bank of the decrease in business and difficulty in collecting loans. What else could it all mean but that Mr. Robert Weymouth was an absconder — was about to fly with the bank's remaining funds, leaving Mr. William, Miss Letty, little Nan, Guy, and Uncle Bushrod to bear the disgrace?

During one minute Uncle Bushrod considered these things, and then he awoke to sudden determination and action.

"Lawd! Lawd!" he moaned aloud, as he hobbled hastily

toward the side door. "Sech a come-off after all dese here years of big doin's and fine doin's. Scan'lous sights upon de yearth when de Weymouth fambly done turn out robbers and 'bezzlers! Time for Uncle Bushrod to clean out some- body's chicken-coop and eben matters up. Oh, Lawd! Marse Robert, you ain't gwine do dat. 'N Miss Letty an' dem chillun so proud and talkin' 'Weymouth, Weymouth,' all de time! I'm gwine to stop you ef I can. 'Spec you shoot Mr. Nigger's head off ef he fool wid you, but I'm gwine stop you ef I can."

Uncle Bushrod, aided by his hickory stick, impeded by his rheumatism, hurried down the street toward the railroad station, where the two lines touching Weymouthville met. As he had expected and feared, he saw there Mr. Robert, standing in the shadow of the building, waiting for the train. He held the satchel in his hand.

When Uncle Bushrod came within twenty yards of the bank president, standing like a huge, gray ghost by the station wall, sudden perturbation seized him. The rashness and audacity of the thing he had come to do struck him fully. He would have been happy could he have turned and fled from the possibilities of the famous Weymouth wrath. But again he saw, in his fancy, the white, reproachful face of Miss Letty, and the distressed looks of Nan and Guy, should he fail in his duty and they question him as to his stewardship.

Braced by the thought, he approached in a straight line, clearing his throat and pounding with his stick so that he might be early recognized. Thus he might avoid the likely danger of too suddenly surprising the sometimes hasty Mr. Robert.

"Is that you, Bushrod?" called the clamant, clear voice of the gray ghost.

"Yes, suh, Marse Robert."

"What the devil are you doing out at this time of night?"

For the first time in his life, Uncle Bushrod told Marse Robert a falsehood. He could not repress it. He would have to circumlocute a little. His nerve was not equal to a direct attack.

" I done been down, suh, to see ol' Aunt M'ria Patterson. She taken sick in de night, and I kyar'ed her a bottle of M'lindy's medercine. Yes, suh."

" Humph! " said Robert. " You better get home out of the night air. It's damp. You'll hardly be worth killing to-morrow on account of your rheumatism. Think it'll be a clear day, Bushrod? "

" I 'low it will, suh. De sun sot red las' night."

Mr. Robert lit a cigar in the shadow, and the smoke looked like his gray ghost expanding and escaping into the night air. Somehow, Uncle Bushrod could barely force his reluctant tongue to the dreadful subject. He stood, awkward, shambling, with his feet upon the gravel and fumbling with his stick. But then, afar off — three miles away, at the Jimtown switch — he heard the faint whistle of the coming train, the one that was to transport the Weymouth name into the regions of dishonour and shame. All fear left him. He took off his hat and faced the chief of the clan he served, the great, royal, kind, lofty, terrible Weymouth — he bearded him there at the brink of the awful thing that was about to happen.

" Marse Robert," he began, his voice quavering a little with the stress of his feelings, " you 'member de day dey-all rode de tunnament at Oak Lawn? De day, suh, dat you win in de ridin', and you crown Miss Lucy de queen? "

" Tournament? " said Mr. Robert, taking his cigar from his mouth, " Yes, I remember very well the — but what the deuce are you talking about tournaments here at midnight for? Go 'long home, Bushrod. I believe you're sleep-walking."

" Miss Lucy tetch you on de shoulder," continued the old man, never heeding, " wid a s'ord, and say: ' I mek you a knight, Suh Robert — rise up, pure and fearless and widout reproach.' Dat what Miss Lucy say. Dat's been a long time ago, but me nor you ain't forgot it. And den dar's another time we ain't forgot — de time when Miss Lucy lay on her las' bed. She sent for Uncle Bushrod, and she say: ' Uncle Bushrod, when I die, I want you to take good care of Mr. Robert. Seem like '— so Miss Lucy say —' he listen to you mo' dan to anybody else. He apt to be mighty fractious sometimes, and maybe he cuss you when you try to 'suade him but he need somebody what understand him to be 'round wid him. He am like a little child sometimes '— so Miss Lucy say, wid her eyes shinin' in her po', thin face — ' but he always been '— dem was her words —' my knight, pure and fearless and widout reproach.' "

Mr. Robert began to mask, as was his habit, a tendency to soft-heartedness with a spurious anger.

" You — you old windbag! " he growled through a cloud of swirling cigar smoke. " I believe you are crazy. I told you to go home, Bushrod. Miss Lucy said that, did she? Well, we haven't kept the scutcheon very clear. Two years ago last week, wasn't it, Bushrod, when she died? Confound it! Are you going to stand there all night gabbing like a coffee-coloured gander? "

The train whistled again. Now it was at the water tank, a mile away.

" Marse Robert," said Uncle Bushrod, laying his hand on the satchel that the banker held. " For Gawd's sake, don' take dis wid you. I knows what's in it. I knows where you got it in de bank. Don' kyar' it wid you. Dey's big trouble in dat valise for Miss Lucy and Miss Lucy's child's chillun. Hit's bound to destroy de name of Weymouth and bow down dem dat own it wid shame and triberlation. Marse Robert, you can kill dis ole nigger ef you will, but don't take away dis 'er' valise. If I ever crosses over de Jordan, what I gwine to say to Miss Lucy when she ax me: ' Uncle Bushrod, wharfo' didn' you take good care of Mr. Robert?'"

Mr. Robert Weymouth threw away his cigar and shook free one arm with that peculiar gesture that always preceded his outbursts of irascibility. Uncle Bushrod bowed his head to the expected storm, but he did not flinch. If the house of Weymouth was to fall, he would fall with it. The banker spoke, and Uncle Bushrod blinked with surprise. The storm was there, but it was suppressed to the quietness of a summer breeze.

" Bushrod," said Mr. Robert, in a lower voice than he usually employed, " you have overstepped all bounds. You have presumed upon the leniency with which you have been treated to meddle unpardonably. So you know what is in this satchel! Your long and faithful service is some excuse, but — go home, Bushrod — not another word!"

But Bushrod grasped the satchel with a firmer hand. The headlight of the train was now lightening the shadows about the station. The roar was increasing, and folks were stirring about at the track side.

" Marse Robert, gimme dis 'er' valise. I got a right, suh, to talk to you dis 'er' way. I slaved for you and 'tended to you from a child up. I went th'ough de war as yo' body-servant tell we whipped de Yankees and sent 'em back to de No'th. I was at yo' weddin', and I was n' fur away when yo' Miss Letty was bawn. And Miss Letty's chillun, dey watches to-day for Uncle Bushrod when he come home ever' evenin'. I been a Weymouth, all 'cept in colour and entitlements. Both of us is old, Marse Robert. 'Tain't goin' to be long tell we gwine to see Miss Lucy and has to give an account of our doin's. De ole nigger man won't be 'spected to say much mo' dan he done all he could by de fambly dat

owned him. But de Weymouths, dey must say dey been livin'
pure and fearless and widout reproach. Gimme dis valise,
Marse Robert — I'm gwine to hab it. I'm gwine to take it
back to the bank and lock it up in de vault. I'm gwine to do
Miss Lucy's biddin'. Turn 'er loose, Marse Robert."

The train was standing at the station. Some men were
pushing trucks along the side. Two or three sleepy passengers got off and wandered away into the night. The
conductor stepped to the gravel, swung his lantern and called:
"Hello, Frank!" at some one invisible. The bell clanged,
the brakes hissed, the conductor drawled: "All aboard!"

Mr. Robert released his hold on the satchel. Uncle Bushrod hugged it to his breast with both arms, as a lover clasps
his first beloved.

"Take it back with you, Bushrod," said Mr. Robert, thrust-
ing his hands into his pockets. "And let the subject drop
— now mind! You've said quite enough. I'm going to take
this train. Tell Mr. William I will be back on Saturday.
Good night."

The banker climbed the steps of the moving train and
disappeared in a coach. Uncle Bushrod stood motionless, still
embracing the precious satchel. His eyes were closed and
his lips were moving in thanks to the Master above for the
salvation of the Weymouth honour. He knew Mr. Robert
would return when he said he would. The Weymouths never
lied. Nor now, thank the Lord! could it be said that they
embezzled the money in banks.

Then awake to the necessity for further guardianship of
Weymouth trust funds, the old man started for the bank with
the redeemed satchel.

Three hours from Weymouthville, in the gray dawn, Mr.
Robert alighted from the train at a lonely flag-station. Dimly
he could see the figure of a man waiting on the platform,

and the shape of a spring-waggon, team and driver. Half a dozen lengthy bamboo fishing-poles projected from the waggon's rear.

"You're here, Bob," said Judge Archinard, Mr. Robert's old friend and schoolmate. "It's going to be a royal day for fishing. I thought you said — why, didn't you bring along the stuff?"

The president of the Weymouth Bank took off his hat and rumpled his gray locks.

"Well, Ben, to tell you the truth, there's an infernally presumptuous old nigger belonging in my family that broke up the arrangement. He came down to the depot and vetoed the whole proceeding. He means all right, and — well, I reckon he *is* right. Somehow, he had found out what I had along — though I hid it in the bank vault and sneaked it out at midnight. I reckon he has noticed that I've been indulging a little more than a gentleman should, and he laid for me with some reaching arguments.

"I'm going to quit drinking," Mr. Robert concluded. "I've come to the conclusion that a man can't keep it up and be quite what he'd like to be —'pure and fearless and without reproach'— that's the way old Bushrod quoted it."

"Well, I'll have to admit," said the judge, thoughtfully, as they climbed into the waggon, "that the old darkey's argument can't conscientiously be overruled."

"Still," said Mr. Robert, with a ghost of a sigh, "there was two quarts of the finest old silk-velvet Bourbon in that satchel you ever wet your lips with."

III

THE DISCOUNTERS OF MONEY

THE spectacle of the money-caliphs of the present day going about Bagdad-on-the-Subway trying to relieve the wants of the people is enough to make the great Al Raschid turn Haroun in his grave. If not so, then the assertion should do so, the real caliph having been a wit and a scholar and therefore a hater of puns.

How properly to alleviate the troubles of the poor is one of the greatest troubles of the rich. But one thing agreed upon by all professional philanthropists is that you must never hand over any cash to your subject. The poor are notoriously temperamental; and when they get money they exhibit a strong tendency to spend it for stuffed olives and enlarged crayon portraits instead of giving it to the instalment man.

And still, old Haroun had some advantages as an eleemosynarian. He took around with him on his rambles his vizier, Giafar (a vizier is a composite of a chauffeur, a secretary of state, and a night-and-day bank), and old Uncle Mesrour, his executioner, who toted a snickersnee. With this entourage a caliphing tour could hardly fail to be successful. Have you noticed lately any newspaper articles headed, "What Shall We Do With Our Ex-Presidents?" Well, now, suppose that Mr. Carnegie should engage *him* and Joe Gans to go about assisting in the distribution of free libraries? Do you suppose any town would have the hardihood to refuse one? That caliphalous combination would cause two libraries to grow where there had been only one set of E. P. Roe's works before.

But, as I said, the money-caliphs are handicapped. They have the idea that earth has no sorrow that dough cannot heal; and they rely upon it solely. Al Raschid administered justice, rewarded the deserving, and punished whomsoever he disliked on the spot. He was the originator of the short-story contest. Whenever he succoured any chance pick-up in the bazaars he always made the succouree tell the sad story of his life. If the narrative lacked construction, style, and *esprit* he commanded his vizier to dole him out a couple of thousand ten-dollar notes of the First National Bank of the Bosphorus, or else gave him a soft job as Keeper of the Bird Seed for the Bulbuls in the Imperial Gardens. If the story was a cracker-jack, he had Mesrour, the executioner, whack off his head. The report that Haroun Al Raschid is yet alive and is editing the magazine that your grandmother used to subscribe for lacks confirmation.

And now follows the Story of the Millionaire, the Inefficacious Increment, and the Babes Drawn from the Wood.

Young Howard Pilkins, the millionaire, got his money ornithologically. He was a shrewd judge of storks, and got in on the ground floor at the residence of his immediate ancestors, the Pilkins Brewing Company. For his mother was a partner in the business. Finally old man Pilkins died from a torpid liver, and then Mrs. Pilkins died from worry on account of torpid delivery-waggons — and there you have young Howard Pilkins with 4,000,000; and a good fellow at that. He was an agreeable, modestly arrogant young man, who implicitly believed that money could buy anything that the world had to offer. And Bagdad-on-the-Subway for a long time did everything possible to encourage his belief.

But the Rat-trap caught him at last; he heard the spring snap, and found his heart in a wire cage regarding a piece of cheese whose other name was Alice von der Ruysling.

The Von der Ruyslings still live in that little square about which so much has been said, and in which so little has been done.   To-day you hear of Mr. Tilden's underground passage, and you hear Mr. Gould's elevated passage, and that about ends the noise in the world made by Gramercy Square.   But once it was different.   The Von der Ruyslings live there yet, and they received *the first key ever made to Gramercy Park*.

You shall have no description of Alice v. d. R.   Just call up in your mind the picture of your own Maggie or Vera or Beatrice, straighten her nose, soften her voice, tone her down and then tone her up, make her beautiful and unattainable — and you have a faint dry-point etching of Alice.   The family owned a crumbly brick house and a coachman named Joseph in a coat of many colours, and a horse so old that he claimed to belong to the order of the Perissodactyla, and had toes instead of hoofs.   In the year 1898 the family had to buy a new set of harness for the Perissodactyl.   Before using it they made Joseph smear it over with a mixture of ashes and soot.   It was the Von der Ruysling family that bought the territory between the Bowery and East River and Rivington Street and the Statue of Liberty, in the year 1649, from an Indian chief for a quart of passementerie and a pair of Turkey-red portières designed for a Harlem flat.   I have always admired that Indian's perspicacity and good taste.   All this is merely to convince you that the Von der Ruyslings were exactly the kind of poor aristocrats that turn down their noses at people who have money.   Oh, well, I don't mean that; I mean people who have *just* money.

One evening Pilkins went down to the red brick house in Gramercy Square, and made what he thought was a proposal to Alice v. d. R.   Alice, with her nose turned down, and thinking of his money, considered it a proposition, and refused it and him.   Pilkins, summoning all his resources as any good general would have done, made an indiscreet reference to the advantages that his money would provide.   That settled it.

The lady turned so cold that Walter Wellman himself would have waited until spring to make a dash for her in a dog-sled.

But Pilkins was something of a sport himself. You can't fool all the millionaires every time the ball drops on the Western Union Building.

"If, at any time," he said to A. v. d. R., "you feel that you would like to reconsider your answer, send me a rose like that."

Pilkins audaciously touched a Jacque rose that she wore loosely in her hair.

"Very well," said she. "And when I do, you will understand by it that either you or I have learned something new about the purchasing power of money. You've been spoiled, my friend. No, I don't think I could marry you. To-morrow I will send you back the presents you have given me."

"Presents!" said Pilkins in surprise. "I never gave you a present in my life. I would like to see a full-length portrait of the man that you would take a present from. Why, you never would let me send you flowers or candy or even art calendars."

"You've forgotten," said Alice v. d. R., with a little smile. "It was a long time ago when our families were neighbours. You were seven, and I was trundling my doll on the sidewalk. You gave me a little gray, hairy kitten, with shoe-buttony eyes. Its head came off and it was full of candy. You paid five cents for it — you told me so. I haven't the candy to return to you — I hadn't developed a conscience at three, so I ate it. But I have the kitten yet, and I will wrap it up neatly to-night and send it to you to-morrow."

Beneath the lightness of Alice v. d. R.'s talk the steadfastness of her rejection showed firm and plain. So there was nothing left for him but to leave the crumbly red brick house, and be off with his abhorred millions.

On his way back, Pilkins walked through Madison Square.

The hour hand of the clock hung about eight; the air was stingingly cool, but not at the freezing point. The dim little square seemed like a great, cold, unroofed room, with its four walls of houses, spangled with thousands of insufficient lights. Only a few loiterers were huddled here and there on the benches.

But suddenly Pilkins came upon a youth sitting brave and, as if conflicting with summer sultriness, coatless, his white shirt-sleeves conspicuous in the light from the globe of an electric. Close at his side was a girl, smiling, dreamy, happy. Around her shoulders was, palpably, the missing coat of the cold-defying youth. It appeared to be a modern panorama of the Babes in the Wood, revised and brought up to date, with the exception that the robins hadn't turned up yet with the protecting leaves.

With delight the money-caliphs view a situation that they think is relievable while you wait.

Pilkins sat on the bench, one seat removed from the youth. He glanced cautiously and saw (as men do see; and women — oh! never can) that they were of the same order.

Pilkins leaned over after a short time and spoke to the youth, who answered smilingly, and courteously. From general topics the conversation concentrated to the bed-rock of grim personalities. But Pilkins did it as delicately and heartily as any caliph could have done. And when it came to the point, the youth turned to him, soft-voiced and with his undiminished smile.

" I don't want to seem unappreciative, old man," he said, with a youth's somewhat too-early spontaneity of address, " but, you see, I can't accept anything from a stranger. I know you're all right, and I'm tremendously obliged, but I couldn't think of borrowing from anybody. You see, I'm Marcus Clayton — the Claytons of Roanoke County, Virginia, you know. The young lady is Miss Eva Bedford — I reckon you've heard of the Bedfords. She's seventeen and one of the Bedfords of Bedford County. We've eloped from home to get married, and we wanted to see New York. We got in this afternoon. Somebody got my pocketbook on the ferry-boat, and I had only three cents in change outside of it. I'll get some work somewhere to-morrow, and we'll get married."

"But, I say, old man," said Pilkins, in confidential low tones, "you can't keep the lady out here in the cold all night. Now, as for hotels —"

"I told you," said the youth, with a broader smile, "that I didn't have but three cents. Besides, if I had a thousand, we'd have to wait here until morning. You can understand that, of course. I'm much obliged, but I can't take any of your money. Miss Bedford and I have lived an outdoor life, and we don't mind a little cold. I'll get work of some kind to-morrow. We've got a paper bag of cakes and chocolates, and we'll get along all right."

"Listen," said the millionaire, impressively. "My name is Pilkins, and I'm worth several million dollars. I happen to have in my pockets about $800 or $900 in cash. Don't you think you are drawing it rather fine when you decline to accept as much of it as will make you and the young lady comfortable at least for the night?"

"I can't say, sir, that I do think so," said Clayton of Roanoke County. "I've been raised to look at such things differently. But I'm mightily obliged to you, just the same."

"Then you force me to say good night," said the millionaire.

Twice that day had his money been scorned by simple ones to whom his dollars had appeared as but tin tobacco-tags. He was no worshipper of the actual minted coin or stamped paper, but he had always believed in its almost unlimited power to purchase.

Pilkins walked away rapidly, and then turned abruptly

and returned to the bench where the young couple sat.   He
took off his hat and began to speak.   The girl looked at him
with the same sprightly, glowing interest that she had been
giving to the lights and statuary and sky-reaching buildings
that made the old square seem so far away from Bedford
County.

"Mr.— er — Roanoke," said Pilkins, "I admire your —
your indepen — your idiocy so much that I'm going to appeal
to your chivalry.   I believe that's what you Southerners call
it when you keep a lady sitting outdoors on a bench on a cold
night just to keep your old, out-of-date pride going.   Now,
I've a friend — a lady — whom I have known all my life —
who lives a few blocks from here — with her parents and sisters and aunts, and all that kind of endorsement, of course.
I am sure this lady would be happy and pleased to put up —
that is, to have Miss — er — Bedford give her the pleasure
of having her as a guest for the night.   Don't you think,
Mr. Roanoke, of — er — Virginia, that you could unbend your
prejudices that far?"

Clayton of Roanoke rose and held out his hand.

"Old man," he said, "Miss Bedford will be much pleased
to accept the hospitality of the lady you refer to."

He formally introduced Mr. Pilkins to Miss Bedford.   The
girl looked at him sweetly and comfortably.   "It's a lovely
evening, Mr. Pilkins — don't you think so?" she said slowly.

Pilkins conducted them to the crumbly red brick house of
the Von der Ruyslings.   His card brought Alice downstairs
wondering.   The runaways were sent into the drawing-room,
while Pilkins told Alice all about it in the hall.

"Of course, I will take her in," said Alice.   "Haven't
those Southern girls a thoroughbred air?   Of course, she will
stay here.   You will look after Mr. Clayton, of course."

"Will I?" said Pilkins, delightedly.   "Oh, yes, I'll look
after him!   As a citizen of New York, and therefore a part

owner of its public parks, I'm going to extend to him the hospitality of Madison Square to-night. He's going to sit there on a bench till morning. There's no use arguing with him. Isn't he wonderful? I'm glad you'll look after the little lady, Alice. I tell you those Babes in the Wood made my — that is, er — made Wall Street and the Bank of England look like penny arcades."

Miss von der Ruysling whisked Miss Bedford of Bedford County up to restful regions upstairs. When she came down, she put an oblong small pasteboard box into Pilkins' hands.

"Your present," she said, "that I am returning to you."

"Oh, yes, I remember," said Pilkins, with a sigh, "the woolly kitten."

He left Clayton on a park bench, and shook hands with him heartily.

"After I get work," said the youth, "I'll look you up. Your address is on your card, isn't it? Thanks. Well, good night. I'm awfully obliged to you for your kindness. No, thanks, I don't smoke. Good night."

In his room, Pilkins opened the box and took out the staring, funny kitten, long ago ravaged of his candy and minus one shoe-button eye. Pilkins looked at it sorrowfully.

"After all," he said, "I don't believe that just money alone will —"

And then he gave a shout and dug into the bottom of the box for something else that had been the kitten's resting-place — a crushed but red, red, fragrant, glorious, promising Jacqueminot rose.

IV

THE ENCHANTED PROFILE

THERE are few Caliphesses. Women are Scheherazades by birth, predilection, instinct, and arrangement of the vocal cords. The thousand and one stories are being told every day by hundreds of thousands of viziers' daughters to their respective sultans. But the bowstring will get some of 'em yet if they don't watch out.

I heard a story, though, of one lady Caliph. It isn't precisely an Arabian Nights story, because it brings in Cinderella, who flourished her dishrag in another epoch and country. So, if you don't mind the mixed dates (which seem to give it an Eastern flavour, after all), we'll get along.

In New York there is an old, old hotel. You have seen woodcuts of it in the magazines. It was built — let's see — at a time when there was nothing above Fourteenth Street except the old Indian trail to Boston and Hammerstein's office. Soon the old hostelry will be torn down. And, as the stout walls are riven apart and the bricks go roaring down the chutes, crowds of citizens will gather at the nearest corners and weep over the destruction of a dear old landmark. Civic pride is strong in New Bagdad; and the wettest weeper and the loudest howler against the iconoclasts will be the man (originally from Terre Haute) whose fond memories of the old hotel are limited to his having been kicked out from its free-lunch counter in 1873.

At this hotel always stopped Mrs. Maggie Brown. Mrs. Brown was a bony woman of sixty, dressed in the rustiest

black, and carrying a handbag made, apparently, from the
hide of the original animal that Adam decided to call an alligator. She always occupied a small parlour and bedroom at
the top of the hotel at a rental of two dollars per day. And
always, while she was there, each day came hurrying to see
her many men, sharp-faced, anxious-looking, with only seconds to spare. For Maggie Brown was said to be the third
richest woman in the world; and these solicitous gentlemen
were only the city's wealthiest brokers and business men seeking trifling loans of half a dozen millions or so from the
dingy old lady with the prehistoric handbag.

The stenographer and typewriter of the Acropolis Hotel
(there! I've let the name of it out!) was Miss Ida Bates.
She was a hold-over from the Greek classics. There wasn't
a flaw in her looks. Some old-timer in paying his regards to
a lady said: " To have loved her was a liberal education."
Well, even to have looked over the back hair and neat white
shirtwaist of Miss Bates was equal to a full course in any
correspondence school in the country. She sometimes did a
little typewriting for me and, as she refused to take the
money in advance, she came to look upon me as something of
a friend and protégé. She had unfailing kindliness and good
nature; and not even a white-lead drummer or a fur importer
had ever dared to cross the dead line of good behaviour in
her presence. The entire force of the Acropolis, from the
owner, who lived in Vienna, down to the head porter, who
had been bedridden for sixteen years, would have sprung to
her defence in a moment.

One day I walked past Miss Bates's little sanctum Rem-
ingtorium, and saw in her place a black-haired unit — un-
mistakably a person — pounding with each of her forefingers
upon the keys. Musing on the mutability of temporal affairs, I passed on. The next day I went on a two weeks'
vacation. Returning, I strolled through the lobby of the

'Acropolis, and saw, with a little warm glow of auld lang syne, Miss Bates, as Grecian and kind and flawless as ever, just putting the cover on her machine. The hour for closing had come; but she asked me in to sit for a few minutes in the dictation chair. Miss Bates explained her absence from and return to the Acropolis Hotel in words identical with or similar to these following:

"Well, Man, how are the stories coming?"

"Pretty regularly," said I. "About equal to their going."

"I'm sorry," said she. "Good typewriting is the main thing in a story. You've missed me, haven't you?"

"No one," said I, "whom I have ever known knows as well as you do how to space properly belt buckles, semi-colons, hotel guests, and hairpins. But you've been away, too. I saw a package of peppermint-pepsin in your place the other day."

"I was going to tell you about it," said Miss Bates, "if you hadn't interrupted me.

"Of course, you know about Maggie Brown, who stops here. Well, she's worth $40,000,000. She lives in Jersey in a ten-dollar flat. She's always got more cash on hand than half a dozen business candidates for vice-president. I don't know whether she carries it in her stocking or not, but I know she's mighty popular down in the part of the town where they worship the golden calf.

"Well, about two weeks ago, Mrs. Brown stops at the door and rubbers at me for ten minutes. I'm sitting with my side to her, striking off some manifold copies of a copper-mine proposition for a nice old man from Tonopah. But I always see everything all around me. When I'm hard at work I can see things through my side-combs; and I can leave one button unbuttoned in the back of my shirtwaist and see who's behind me. I didn't look around, because I make from eighteen to twenty dollars a week, and I didn't have to.

"That evening at knocking-off time she sends for me to come up to her apartment. I expected to have to typewrite about two thousand words of notes-of-hand, liens, and contracts, with a ten-cent tip in sight; but I went. Well, Man, I was certainly surprised. Old Maggie Brown had turned human.

"'Child,' says she, 'you're the most beautiful creature I ever saw in my life. I want you to quit your work and come and live with me. I've no kith or kin,' says she, 'except a husband and a son or two, and I hold no communication with any of 'em. They're extravagant burdens on a hard-working woman. I want you to be a daughter to me. They say I'm stingy and mean, and the papers print lies about my doing my own cooking and washing. It's a lie,' she goes on. 'I put my washing out, except the handkerchiefs and stockings and petticoats and collars, and light stuff like that. I've got forty million dollars in cash and stocks and bonds that are as negotiable as Standard Oil, preferred, at a church fair. I'm a lonely old woman and I need companionship. You're the most beautiful human being I ever saw,' says she. 'Will you come and live with me? I'll show 'em whether I can spend money or not,' she says.

"Well, Man, what would you have done? Of course, I fell to it. And, to tell you the truth, I began to like old Maggie. It wasn't all on account of the forty millions and what she could do for me. I was kind of lonesome in the world, too. Everybody's got to have somebody they can explain to about the pain in their left shoulder and how fast patent-leather shoes wear out when they begin to crack. And you can't talk about such things to men you meet in hotels — they're looking for just such openings.

"So I gave up my job in the hotel and went with Mrs. Brown. I certainly seemed to have a mash on her. She'd look at me for half an hour at a time when I was sitting, reading, or looking at the magazines.

"One time I says to her: 'Do I remind you of some deceased relative or friend of your childhood, Mrs. Brown? I've noticed you give me a pretty good optical inspection from time to time.'

"'You have a face,' she says, 'exactly like a dear friend of mine — the best friend I ever had. But I like you for yourself, child, too,' she says.

"And say, Man, what do you suppose she did? Loosened up like a Marcel wave in the surf at Coney. She took me to a swell dressmaker and gave her *a la carte* to fit me out — money no object. They were rush orders, and madame locked the front door and put the whole force to work.

"Then we moved to — where do you think? — no; guess again — that's right — the Hotel Bonton. We had a six-room apartment; and it cost $100 a day. I saw the bill. I began to love that old lady.

"And then, Man, when my dresses began to come in — oh, I won't tell you about 'em! you couldn't understand. And I began to call her Aunt Maggie. You've read about Cinderella, of course. Well, what Cinderella said when the prince fitted that 3½ A on her foot was a hard-luck story compared to the things I told myself.

"Then Aunt Maggie says she is going to give me a coming-out banquet in the Bonton that'll make moving Vans of all the old Dutch families on Fifth Avenue.

"'I've been out before, Aunt Maggie,' says I. 'But I'll come out again. But you know,' says I, 'that this is one of the swellest hotels in the city. And you know — pardon me — that it's hard to get a bunch of notables together unless you've trained for it.'

" ' Don't fret about that, child,' says Aunt Maggie. ' I don't send out invitations — I issue orders. I'll have fifty guests here that couldn't be brought together again at any reception unless it were given by King Edward or William Travers Jerome. They are men, of course, and all of 'em either owe me money or intend to. Some of their wives won't come, but a good many will.'

" Well, I wish you could have been at that banquet. The dinner service was all gold and cut glass. There were about forty men and eight ladies present besides Aunt Maggie and I. You'd never have known the third richest woman in the world. She had on a new black silk dress with so much passementerie on it that it sounded exactly like a hailstorm I heard once when I was staying all night with a girl that lived in a top-floor studio.

" And my dress! — say, Man, I can't waste the words on you. It was all hand-made lace — where there was any of it at all — and it cost $300. I saw the bill. The men were all bald-headed or white-side-whiskered, and they kept up a running fire of light repartee about 3-per cents. and Bryan and the cotton crop.

" On the left of me was something that talked like a banker, and on my right was a young fellow who said he was a newspaper artist. He was the only — well, I was going to tell you.

" After the dinner was over Mrs. Brown and I went up to the apartment. We had to squeeze our way through a mob of reporters all the way through the halls. That's one of the things money does for you. Say, do you happen to know a newspaper artist named Lathrop — a tall man with nice eyes and an easy way of talking? No, I don't remember what paper he works on. Well, all right.

" When we got upstairs Mrs. Brown telephones for the bill right away. It came, and it was $600. I saw the bill.

'Aunt Maggie fainted. I got her on a lounge and opened the bead-work.

"'Child,' says she, when she got back to the world, 'what was it? A raise of rent or an income-tax?'

"'Just a little dinner,' says I. 'Nothing to worry about — hardly a drop in the bucket-shop. Sit up and take notice — a dispossess notice, if there's no other kind.'

"But, say, Man, do you know what Aunt Maggie did? She got cold feet! She hustled me out of that Hotel Bonton at nine the next morning. We went to a rooming-house on the lower West Side. She rented one room that had water on the floor below and light on the floor above. After we got moved all you could see in the room was about $1,500 worth of new swell dresses and a one-burner gas-stove.

"Aunt Maggie had had a sudden attack of the hedges. I guess everybody has got to go on a spree once in their life. A man spends his on highballs, and a woman gets woozy on clothes. But with forty million dollars — say! I'd like to have a picture of — but, speaking of pictures, did you ever run across a newspaper artist named Lathrop — a tall — oh, I asked you that before, didn't I? He was mighty nice to me at the dinner. His voice just suited me. I guess he must have thought I was to inherit some of Aunt Maggie's money.

"Well, Mr. Man, three days of that light-housekeeping was plenty for me. Aunt Maggie was affectionate as ever. She'd hardly let me get out of her sight. But let me tell you. She was a hedger from Hedgersville, Hedger County. Seventy-five cents a day was the limit she set. We cooked our own meals in the room. There I was, with a thousand dollars' worth of the latest things in clothes, doing stunts over a one-burner gas-stove.

"As I say, on the third day I flew the coop. I couldn't stand for throwing together a fifteen-cent kidney stew while wearing, at the same time, a $150 house-dress, with Valenciennes lace insertion. So I goes into the closet and puts on the cheapest dress Mrs. Brown had bought for me — it's the one I've got on now — not so bad for $75, is it? I'd left all my own clothes in my sister's flat in Brooklyn.

"'Mrs. Brown, formerly "Aunt Maggie,"' says I to her, 'I am going to extend my feet alternately, one after the other, in such a manner and direction that this tenement will recede from me in the quickest possible time. I am no worshipper of money,' says I, 'but there are some things I can't stand. I can stand the fabulous monster that I've read about that blows hot birds and cold bottles with the same breath. But I can't stand a quitter,' says I. 'They say you've got forty million dollars — well, you'll never have any less. And I was beginning to like you, too,' says I.

"Well, the late Aunt Maggie kicks till the tears flow. She offers to move into a swell room with a two-burner stove and running water.

"'I've spent an awful lot of money, child,' says she. 'We'll have to economize for a while. You're the most beautiful creature I ever laid eyes on,' she says, 'and I don't want you to leave me.'

"Well, you see me, don't you? I walked straight to the Acropolis and asked for my job back, and I got it. How did you say your writings were getting along? I know you've lost out some by not having me to typewrite 'em. Do you ever have 'em illustrated? And, by the way, did you ever happen to know a newspaper artist — oh, shut up! I know I asked you before. I wonder what paper he works on? It's funny, but I couldn't help thinking that he wasn't thinking about the money he might have been thinking I was thinking I'd get from old Maggie Brown. If I only knew some of the newspaper editors I'd —"

The sound of an easy footstep came from the doorway. Ida

Bates saw who it was with her back-hair comb. I saw her turn pink, perfect statue that she was — a miracle that I share with Pygmalion only.

"Am I excusable?" she said to me — adorable petitioner that she became. "It's — it's Mr. Lathrop. I wonder if it really wasn't the money — I wonder, if after all, he —"

Of course, I was invited to the wedding. After the ceremony I dragged Lathrop aside.

"You an artist," said I, "and haven't figured out why Maggie Brown conceived such a strong liking for Miss Bates — that was? Let me show you."

The bride wore a simple white dress as beautifully draped as the costumes of the ancient Greeks. I took some leaves from one of the decorative wreaths in the little parlour, and made a chaplet of them, and placed them on née Bates shining chestnut hair, and made her turn her profile to her husband.

"By jingo!" said he. "Isn't Ida's a dead ringer for the lady's head on the silver dollar?"

V

"NEXT TO READING MATTER"

HE COMPELLED my interest as he stepped from the ferry at Desbrosses Street. He had the air of being familiar with hemispheres and worlds, and of entering New York as the lord of a demesne who revisited it in after years of absence. But I thought that, with all his air, he had never before set foot on the slippery cobblestones of the City of Too Many Caliphs.

He wore loose clothes of a strange bluish drab colour, and a conservative, round Panama hat without the cock-a-loop indentations and cants with which Northern fanciers disfigure the tropic head-gear. Moreover, he was the homeliest man I have ever seen. His ugliness was less repellent than startling — arising from a sort of Lincolnian ruggedness and irregularity of feature that spellbound you with wonder and dismay. So may have looked afrites or the shapes metamorphosed from the vapour of the fisherman's vase. As he afterward told me, his name was Judson Tate; and he may as well be called so at once. He wore his green silk tie through a topaz ring; and he carried a cane made of the vertebræ of a shark.

Judson Tate accosted me with some large and casual inquiries about the city's streets and hotels, in the manner of one who had but for the moment forgotten the trifling details. I could think of no reason for dispraising my own quiet hotel in the downtown district; so the mid-morning of the night found us already victualed and drinked (at my expense), and ready to be chaired and tobaccoed in a quiet corner of the lobby.

There was something on Judson Tate's mind, and, such as it was, he tried to convey it to me. Already he had accepted me as his friend; and when I looked at his great, snuff-brown first-mate's hand, with which he brought emphasis to his periods, within six inches of my nose, I wondered if, by any chance, he was as sudden in conceiving enmity against strangers.

When this man began to talk I perceived in him a certain power. His voice was a persuasive instrument, upon which he played with a somewhat specious but effective art. He did not try to make you forget his ugliness; he flaunted it in your face and made it part of the charm of his speech. Shutting your eyes, you would have trailed after this rat-catcher's pipes at least to the walls of Hamelin. Beyond that you would have had to be more childish to follow. But let him play his own tune to the words set down, so that if all is too dull, the art of music may bear the blame.

"Women," said Judson Tate, "are mysterious creatures."

My spirits sank. I was not there to listen to such a world-old hypothesis — to such a time-worn, long-ago-refuted, bald, feeble, illogical, vicious, patent sophistry — to an ancient, baseless, wearisome, ragged, unfounded, insidious, falsehood originated by women themselves, and by them insinuated, foisted, thrust, spread, and ingeniously promulgated into the ears of mankind by underhanded, secret and deceptive methods, for the purpose of argumenting, furthering, and reinforcing their own charms and designs.

"Oh, I don't know!" said I, vernacularly.

"Have you ever heard of Oratama?" he asked.

"Possibly," I answered. "I seem to recall a toe dancer — or a suburban addition — or was it a perfume? — of some such name."

"It is a town," said Judson Tate, "on the coast of a foreign country of which you know nothing and could understand less. It is a country governed by a dictator and controlled by revolutions and insubordination. It was there that a great life-drama was played, with Judson Tate, the homeliest man in America, and Fergus McMahan, the handsomest adventurer in history or fiction, and Señorita Anahela Zamora, the beautiful daughter of the alcalde of Oratama, as chief actors. And, another thing — nowhere else on the globe except in the department of Trienta y tres in Uruguay does the *chuchula* plant grow. The products of the country I speak of are valuable woods, dyestuffs, gold, rubber, ivory and cocoa."

"I was not aware," said I, "that South America produced any ivory."

"There you are twice mistaken," said Judson Tate, distributing the words over at least an octave of his wonderful voice. "I did not say that the country I spoke of was in South America — I must be careful, my dear man; I have been in politics there, you know. But, even so — I have played chess against its president with a set carved from the nasal bones of the tapir — one of our native specimens of the order of *perissodactyle ungulates* inhabiting the Cordilleras — which was as pretty ivory as you would care to see.

"But it was of romance and adventure and the ways of women that I was going to tell you, and not of zoölogical animals.

"For fifteen years I was the ruling power behind old Sancho Benavides, the Royal High Thumbscrew of the republic. You've seen his picture in the papers — a mushy black man with whiskers like the notes on a Swiss music-box cylinder, and a scroll in his right hand like the ones they write births on in the family Bible. Well, that chocolate potentate used to be the biggest item of interest anywhere between the colour line and the parallels of latitude. It was three throws, horses, whether he was to wind up in the Hall of Fame or the Bureau of Combustibles. He'd have been sure called the Roosevelt of the Southern Continent if it hadn't been that Grover Cleveland was President at the time. He'd hold office a couple of terms, then he'd sit out for a hand — always after appointing his own successor for the interims.

"But it was not Benavides, the Liberator, who was making all this fame for himself. Not him. It was Judson Tate. Benavides was only the chip over the bug. I gave him the tip when to declare war and increase import duties and wear his state trousers. But that wasn't what I wanted to tell you. How did I get to be It? I'll tell you. Because I'm the most gifted talker that ever made vocal sounds since Adam first opened his eyes, pushed aside the smelling-salts, and asked: 'Where am I?'

"As you observe, I am about the ugliest man you ever saw outside the gallery of photographs of the New England early Christian Scientists. So, at an early age, I perceived that what I lacked in looks I must make up in eloquence. That I've done. I get what I go after. As the back-stop and still small voice of old Benavides I made all the great historical powers-behind-the-throne, such as Talleyrand, Mrs. de Pompadour, and Loeb, look as small as the minority report of a Duma. I could talk nations into or out of debt, harangue armies to sleep on the battlefield, reduce insurrections, inflammations, taxes, appropriations or surpluses with a few words, and call up the dogs of war or the dove of peace with the same bird-like whistle. Beauty and epaulettes and curly moustaches and Grecian profiles in other men were never in my way. When people first look at me they shudder. Unless they are in the last stages of *angina pectoris* they are mine in ten minutes after I begin to talk. Women and men —

I win 'em as they come. Now, you wouldn't think women would fancy a man with a face like mine, would you?"

"Oh, yes, Mr. Tate," said I. "History is bright and fiction dull with homely men who have charmed women. There seems —"

"Pardon me," interrupted Judson Tate, "but you don't quite understand. You have yet to hear my story.

"Fergus McMahan was a friend of mine in the capital. For a handsome man I'll admit he was the duty-free merchandise. He had blond curls and laughing blue eyes and was featured regular. They said he was a ringer for the statue they call Herr Mees, the god of speech and eloquence resting in some museum at Rome. Some German anarchist, I suppose. They are always resting and talking.

"But Fergus was no talker. He was brought up with the idea that to be beautiful was to make good. His conversation was about as edifying as listening to a leak dropping in a tin dish-pan at the head of the bed when you want to go to sleep. But he and me got to be friends — maybe because we was so opposite, don't you think? Looking at the Hallowe'en mask that I call my face when I'm shaving seemed to give Fergus pleasure; and I'm sure that whenever I heard the feeble output of throat noises that he called conversation I felt contented to be a gargoyle with a silver tongue.

"One time I found it necessary to go down to this coast town of Oratama to straighten out a lot of political unrest and chop off a few heads in the customs and military departments. Fergus, who owned the ice and sulphur-match concessions of the republic, says he'll keep me company.

"So, in a jangle of mule-train bells, we gallops into Oratama, and the town belonged to us as much as Long Island Sound doesn't belong to Japan when T. R. is at Oyster Bay. I say us; but I mean me. Everybody for four nations, two oceans, one bay and isthmus, and five archipelagoes around had heard of Judson Tate. Gentleman adventurer, they called me. I had been written up in five columns of the yellow journals, 40,000 words (with marginal decorations) in a monthly magazine, and a stickful on the twelfth page of the New York *Times*. If the beauty of Fergus McMahan gained any part of our reception in Oratama, I'll eat the price-tag in my Panama. It was me that they hung out paper flowers and palm branches for. I am not a jealous man; I am stating facts. The people were Nebuchadnezzars; they bit the grass before me; there was no dust in the town for them to bite. They bowed down to Judson Tate. They knew that I was the power behind Sancho Benavides. A word from me was more to them than a whole deckle-edged library from East Aurora in sectional bookcases was from anybody else. And yet there are people who spend hours fixing their faces — rubbing in cold cream and massaging the muscles (always toward the eyes) and taking in the slack with tincture of benzoin and electrolyzing moles — to what end? Looking handsome. Oh, what a mistake! It's the larynx that the beauty doctors ought to work on. It's words more than warts, talk more than talcum, palaver more than powder, blarney more than bloom that counts — the phonograph instead of the photograph. But I was going to tell you.

"The local Astors put me and Fergus up at the Centipede Club, a frame building built on posts sunk in the surf. The tide's only nine inches. The Little Big High Low Jack-in-the-game of the town came around and kowtowed. Oh, it wasn't to Herr Mees. They had heard about Judson Tate.

"One afternoon me and Fergus McMahan was sitting on the seaward gallery of the Centipede, drinking iced rum and talking.

"'Judson,' says Fergus, 'there's an angel in Oratama.'

"'So long,' says I, 'as it ain't Gabriel, why talk as if you had heard a trump blow?'

"'It's the Señorita Anabela Zamora,' says Fergus. 'She's — she's — she's as lovely as — as hell!'

"'Bravo!' says I, laughing heartily. 'You have a true lover's eloquence to paint the beauties of your inamorata. You remind me,' says I, 'of Faust's wooing of Marguerite — that is, if he wooed her after he went down the trap-door of the stage.'

"'Judson,' says Fergus, 'you know you are as beautiless as a rhinoceros. You can't have any interest in women. I'm awfully gone on Miss Anabela. And that's why I'm telling you.'

"'Oh, *seguramente*,' says I. 'I know I have a front elevation like an Aztec god that guards a buried treasure that never did exist in Jefferson County, Yucatan. But there are compensations. For instance, I am It in this country as far as the eye can reach, and then a few perches and poles. And again,' says I, 'when I engage people in a set-to of oral, vocal, and laryngeal utterances, I do not usually confine my side of the argument to what may be likened to a cheap phonographic reproduction of the ravings of a jellyfish.'

"'Oh, I know,' says Fergus, amiable, 'that I'm not handy at small talk. Or large, either. That's why I'm telling you. I want you to help me.'

"'How can I do it?' I asked.

"'I have subsidized,' says Fergus, 'the services of Señorita Anabela's duenna, whose name is Francesca. You have a reputation in this country, Judson,' says Fergus, 'of being a great man and a hero.'

"'I have,' says I. 'And I deserve it.'

"'And I,' says Fergus, 'am the best-looking man between the arctic circle and antarctic ice pack.'

"'With limitations,' says I, 'as to physiognomy and geography, I freely concede you to be.'

"'Between the two of us,' says Fergus, 'we ought to land

the Señorita Anabela Zamora. The lady, as you know, is of
an old Spanish family, and further than looking at her driving
in the family *carruaje* of afternoons around the plaza, or
catching a glimpse of her through a barred window of evenings, she is as unapproachable as a star.'

" ' Land her for which one of us? ' says I.

" ' For me, of course,' says Fergus. ' You've never seen
her. Now, I've had Francesca point me out to her as being
you on several occasions. When she sees me on the plaza, she
thinks she's looking at Don Judson Tate, the greatest hero,
statesman, and romantic figure in the country. With your
reputation and my looks combined in one man, how can she re-
sist him? She's heard all about your thrilling history, of
course. And she's seen me. Can any woman want more? "
asks Fergus McMahan.

" ' Can she do with less? ' I ask. ' How can we separate
our mutual attractions, and how shall we apportion the pro-
ceeds? '

" Then Fergus tells me his scheme.

" The house of the alcalde, Don Luis Zamora, he says, has
a *patio*, of course — a kind of inner courtyard opening from
the street. In an angle of it is his daughter's window — as
dark a place as you could find. And what do you think he
wants me to do? Why, knowing my freedom, charm, and
skilfulness of tongue, he proposes that I go into the *patio* at
midnight, when the hobgoblin face of me cannot be seen, and
make love to her for him — for the pretty man that she has
seen on the plaza, thinking him to be Don Judson Tate.

" Why shouldn't I do it for him — for my friend, Fergus
McMahan? For him to ask me was a compliment — an ac-
knowledgment of his own shortcomings.

" ' You little, lily white, fine-haired, highly polished piece of
dumb sculpture,' says I, ' I'll help you. Make your arrangements and get me in the dark outside her window and my

stream of conversation opened up with the moonlight tremolo stop turned on, and she's yours.'

" ' Keep your face hid, Jud,' says Fergus. ' For heaven's sake, keep your face hid. I'm a friend of yours in all kinds of sentiment, but this is a business deal. If I could talk I wouldn't ask you. But seeing me and listening to you I don't see why she can't be landed.'

" ' By you? ' says I.

" ' By me,' says Fergus.

" Well, Fergus and the duenna, Francesca, attended to the details. And one night they fetched me a long black cloak with a high collar, and led me to the house at midnight. I stood by the window in the *patio* until I heard a voice as soft and sweet as an angel's whisper on the other side of the bars. I could see only a faint, white clad shape inside; and, true to Fergus, I pulled the collar of my cloak high up, for it was July in the wet season, and the nights were chilly. And, smothering a laugh as I thought of the tongue-tied Fergus, I began to talk.

" Well, sir, I talked an hour at the Señorita Anabela. I say ' at ' because it was not ' with.' Now and then she would say: ' Oh, Señor,' or ' Now, ain't you foolin'? ' or ' I know you don't mean that,' and such things as women will when they are being rightly courted. Both of us knew English and Spanish; so in two languages I tried to win the heart of the lady for my friend Fergus. But for the bars to the window I could have done it in one. At the end of the hour she dismissed me and gave me a big, red rose. I handed it over to Fergus when I got home.

" For three weeks every third or fourth night I impersonated my friend in the *patio* at the window of Señorita Anabela. At last she admitted that her heart was mine, and spoke of having seen me every afternoon when she drove in the plaza. It was Fergus she had seen, of course. But it was my talk that won her. Suppose Fergus had gone there and tried to make a hit in the dark with his beauty all invisible, and not a word to say for himself!

"On the last night she promised to be mine — that is, Fergus's. And she put her hand between the bars for me to kiss. I bestowed the kiss and took the news to Fergus.

"'You might have left that for me to do,' says he.

"'That'll be your job hereafter,' says I. 'Keep on doing that and don't try to talk. Maybe after she thinks she's in love she won't notice the difference between real conversation and the inarticulate sort of droning that you give forth.'

"Now, I had never seen Señorita Anabela. So, the next day Fergus asks me to walk with him through the plaza and view the daily promenade and exhibition of Oratama society, a sight that had no interest for me. But I went; and children and dogs took to the banana groves and mangrove swamps as soon as they had a look at my face.

"'Here she comes,' said Fergus, twirling his moustache — 'the one in white, in the open carriage with the black horse.'

"I looked and felt the ground rock under my feet. For Señorita Anabela Zamora was the most beautiful woman in the world, and the only one from that moment on, so far as Judson Tate was concerned. I saw at a glance that I must be hers and she mine forever. I thought of my face and nearly fainted; and then I thought of my other talents and stood upright again. And I had been wooing her for three weeks for another man!

"As Señorita Anabela's carriage rolled slowly past, she gave Fergus a long, soft glance from the corners of her night-black eyes, a glance that would have sent Judson Tate up into heaven in a rubber-tired chariot. But she never looked at me. And that handsome man only ruffles his curls and smirks and prances like a lady-killer at my side.

" ' What do you think of her, Judson? ' asks Fergus, with an air.

" ' This much,' says I. ' She is to be Mrs. Judson Tate. I am no man to play tricks on a friend. So take your warning.'

" I thought Fergus would die laughing.

" ' Well, well, well,' said he, ' you old doughface! Struck too, are you? That's great! But you're too late. Francesca tells me that Anabela talks of nothing but me, day and night. Of course, I'm awfully obliged to you for making that chin-music to her of evenings. But, do you know, I've an idea that I could have done it as well myself.'

" ' Mrs. Judson Tate,' says I. ' Don't forget the name. You've had the use of my tongue to go with your good looks, my boy. You can't lend me your looks; but hereafter my tongue is my own. Keep your mind on the name that's to be on the visiting cards two inches by three and a half —" Mrs. Judson Tate." That's all.'

" ' All right,' says Fergus, laughing again. ' I've talked with her father, the alcalde, and he's willing. He's to give a *baile* to-morrow evening in his new warehouse. If you were a dancing man, Jud, I'd expect you around to meet the future Mrs. McMahan.'

" But on the next evening, when the music was playing loudest at the Alcalde Zamora's *baile*, into the room steps Judson Tate in new white linen clothes as if he were the biggest man in the whole nation, which he was.

" Some of the musicians jumped off the key when they saw my face, and one or two of the timidest señoritas let out a screech or two. But up prances the alcalde and almost wipes the dust off my shoes with his forehead. No mere good looks could have won me that sensational entrance.

" ' I hear much, Señor Zamora,' says I, ' of the charm of your daughter. It would give me great pleasure to be presented to her.'

" There were about six dozen willow rocking-chairs, with pink tidies tied on to them, arranged against the walls. In one of them sat Señorita Anabela in white Swiss and red slippers, with pearls and fireflies in her hair. Fergus was at the other end of the room trying to break away from two maroons and a claybank girl.

" The alcalde leads me up to Anabela and presents me. When she took the first look at my face she dropped her fan and nearly turned her chair over from the shock. But I'm used to that.

" I sat down by her and began to talk. When she heard me speak she jumped, and her eyes got as big as alligator pears. She couldn't strike a balance between the tones of my voice and the face I carried. But I kept on talking in the key of C, which is the ladies' key; and presently she sat still in her chair and a dreamy look came into her eyes. She was coming my way. She knew of Judson Tate, and what a big man he was, and the big things he had done; and that was in my favour. But, of course, it was some shock to her to find out that I was not the pretty man that had been pointed out to her as the great Judson. And then I took the Spanish language, which is better than English for certain purposes, and played on it like a harp of a thousand strings. I ranged from the second G below the staff up to F-sharp above it. I set my voice to poetry, art, romance, flowers, and moonlight. I repeated some of the verses that I had murmured to her in the dark at her window; and I knew from a sudden soft sparkle in her eye that she recognized in my voice the tones of her midnight mysterious wooer.

" Anyhow, I had Fergus McMahan going. Oh, the vocal is the true art — no doubt about that. Handsome is as handsome palavers. That's the renovated proverb.

" I took Señorita Anabela for a walk in the lemon grove while Fergus, disfiguring himself with an ugly frown, was waltzing with the claybank girl. Before we returned I had permission to come to her window in the *patio* the next evening at midnight and talk some more.

" Oh, it was easy enough. In two weeks Anabela was engaged to me, and Fergus was out. He took it calm, for a handsome man, and told me he wasn't going to give in.

" ' Talk may be all right in its place, Judson,' he says to me, ' although I've never thought it worth cultivating. But,' says he, ' to expect mere words to back up successfully a face like yours in a lady's good graces is like expecting a man to make a square meal on the ringing of a dinner-bell.'

" But I haven't begun on the story I was going to tell you yet.

" One day I took a long ride in the hot sunshine, and then took a bath in the cold waters of a lagoon on the edge of the town before I'd cooled off.

" That evening after dark I called at the alcalde's to see Anabela. I was calling regular every evening then, and we were to be married in a month. She was looking like a bulbul, a gazelle, and a tea-rose, and her eyes were as soft and bright as two quarts of cream skimmed off from the Milky Way. She looked at my rugged features without any expression of fear or repugnance. Indeed, I fancied that I saw a look of deep admiration and affection, such as she had cast at Fergus on the plaza.

" I sat down, and opened my mouth to tell Anabela what she loved to hear — that she was a trust, monopolizing all the loveliness of earth. I opened my mouth, and instead of the usual vibrating words of love and compliment, there came forth a faint wheeze such as a baby with croup might emit. Not a word — not a syllable — not an intelligible sound. I had caught cold in my laryngeal regions when I took my injudicious bath.

" For two hours I sat trying to entertain Anabela. She

talked a certain amount, but it was perfunctory and diluted. The nearest approach I made to speech was to formulate a sound like a clam trying to sing 'A Life on the Ocean Wave' at low tide. It seemed that Anabela's eyes did not rest upon me as often as usual. I had nothing with which to charm her ears. We looked at pictures and she played the guitar occasionally, very badly. When I left, her parting manner seemed cool — or at least thoughtful.

"This happened for five evenings consecutively.

"On the sixth day she ran away with Fergus McMahan.

"It was known that they fled in a sailing yacht bound for Belize. I was only eight hours behind them in a small steam launch belonging to the Revenue Department.

"Before I sailed, I rushed into the *botica* of old Manuel Iquito, a half-breed Indian druggist. I could not speak, but I pointed to my throat and made a sound like escaping steam. He began to yawn. In an hour, according to the customs of the country, I would have been waited on. I reached across the counter, seized him by the throat, and pointed again to my own. He yawned once more, and thrust into my hand a small bottle containing a black liquid.

"'Take one small spoonful every two hours,' says he.

"I threw him a dollar and skinned for the steamer.

"I steamed into the harbour at Belize thirteen seconds behind the yacht that Anabela and Fergus were on. They started for the shore in a dory just as my skiff was lowered over the side. I tried to order my sailormen to row faster, but the sounds died in my larynx before they came to the light. Then I thought of old Iquito's medicine, and I got out his bottle and took a swallow of it.

"The two boats landed at the same moment. I walked straight up to Anabela and Fergus. Her eyes rested upon me for an instant; then she turned them, full of feeling and confidence, upon Fergus. I knew I could not speak, but I was desperate. In speech lay my only hope. I could not stand beside Fergus and challenge comparison in the way of beauty. Purely involuntarily, my larynx and epiglottis attempted to reproduce the sounds that my mind was calling upon my vocal organs to send forth.

"To my intense surprise and delight the words rolled forth beautifully clear, resonant, exquisitely modulated, full of power, expression, and long-repressed emotion.

"'Señorita Anabela,' says I, 'may I speak with you aside for a moment?'

"You don't want details about that, do you? Thanks. The old eloquence had come back all right. I led her under a cocoanut palm and put my old verbal spell on her again.

"'Judson,' says she, 'when you are talking to me I can hear nothing else — I can see nothing else — there is nothing and nobody else in the world for me.'

"Well, that's about all of the story. Anabela went back to Oratama in the steamer with me. I never heard what became of Fergus. I never saw him any more. Anabela is now Mrs. Judson Tate. Has my story bored you much?"

"No," said I. "I am always interested in psychological studies. A human heart — and especially a woman's — is a wonderful thing to contemplate."

"It is," said Judson Tate. "And so are the trachea and the bronchial tubes of man. And the larynx, too. Did you ever make a study of the windpipe?"

"Never," said I. "But I have taken much pleasure in your story. May I ask after Mrs. Tate, and inquire of her present health and whereabouts?"

"Oh, sure," said Judson Tate. "We are living in Bergen Avenue, Jersey City. The climate down in Oratama didn't suit Mrs. T. I don't suppose you ever dissected the arytenoid cartilages of the epiglottis, did you?"

"Why, no," said I, "I am no surgeon."

"Pardon me," said Judson Tate, "but every man should know enough of anatomy and therapeutics to safeguard his own health. A sudden cold may set up capillary bronchitis or inflammation of the pulmonary vesicles, which may result in a serious affection of the vocal organs."

"Perhaps so," said I, with some impatience; "but that is neither here nor there. Speaking of the strange manifestations of the affection of women, I —"

"Yes, yes," interrupted Judson Tate, "they have peculiar ways. But, as I was going to tell you: when I went back to Oratama I found out from Manuel Iquito what was in that mixture he gave me for my lost voice. I told you how quick it cured me. He made that stuff from the *chuchula* plant. Now, look here."

Judson Tate drew an oblong, white pasteboard box from his pocket.

"For any cough," he said, "or cold, or hoarseness, or bronchial affection whatsoever, I have here the greatest remedy in the world. You see the formula printed on the box. Each tablet contains licorice, 2 grains; balsam tolu, $\frac{1}{10}$ grain; oil of anise, $\frac{1}{20}$ minim; oil of tar, $\frac{1}{60}$ minim; oleo-resin of cubebs, $\frac{1}{60}$ minim; fluid extract of *chuchula*, $\frac{1}{10}$ minim.

"I am in New York," went on Judson Tate, "for the purpose of organizing a company to market the greatest remedy for throat affections ever discovered. At present I am introducing the lozenges in a small way. I have here a box containing four dozen, which I am selling for the small sum of fifty cents. If you are suffering —"

I got up and went away without a word. I walked slowly up to the little park near my hotel, leaving Judson Tate alone with his conscience. My feelings were lacerated. He had poured gently upon me a story that I might have used. There was a little of the breath of life in it, and some of the synthetic atmosphere that passes, when cunningly tinkered, in the marts. And, at the last it had proven to be a commercial pill, deftly coated with the sugar of fiction. The worst of it was that I·could not offer it for sale. Advertising departments and counting-rooms look down upon me. And it would never do for the literary. Therefore I sat upon a bench with other disappointed ones until my eyelids drooped.

I went to my room, and, as my custom is, read for an hour stories in my favourite magazines. This was to get my mind back to art again.

And as I read each story, I threw the magazines sadly and hopelessly, one by one, upon the floor. Each author, without one exception to bring balm to my heart, wrote liltingly and sprightly a story of some particular make of motor-car that seemed to control the sparking plug of his genius.

And when the last one was hurled from me I took heart.

" If readers can swallow so many proprietary automobiles," I said to myself, "they ought not to strain at one of Tate's Compound Magic Chuchula Bronchial Lozenges."

And so if you see this story in print you will understand that business is business, and that if Art gets very far ahead of Commerce, she will have to get up and hustle.

I may as well add, to make a clean job of it, that you can't buy the *chuchula* plant in the drug stores.

VI

ART AND THE BRONCO

OUT of the wilderness had come a painter. Genius, whose coronations alone are democratic, had woven a chaplet of chaparral for the brow of Lonny Briscoe. Art, whose divine expression flows impartially from the fingertips of a cowboy or a dilettante emperor, had chosen for a medium the Boy Artist of the San Saba. The outcome, seven feet by twelve of besmeared canvas, stood, gift-framed, in the lobby of the Capitol.

The legislature was in session; the capital city of that great Western state was enjoying the season of activity and profit that the congregation of the solons bestowed. The boarding-houses were corralling the easy dollars of the gamesome law-makers. The greatest state in the West, an empire in area and resources, had arisen and repudiated the old libel or barbarism, lawbreaking, and bloodshed. Order reigned within her borders. Life and property were as safe there, sir, as anywhere among the corrupt cities of the effete East. Pillow-shams, churches, strawberry feasts and *habeas corpus* flourished. With impunity might the tenderfoot ventilate his " stovepipe " or his theories of culture. The arts and sciences received nurture and subsidy. And, therefore, it behooved the legislature of this great state to make appropriation for the purchase of Lonny Briscoe's immortal painting.

Rarely has the San Saba country contributed to the spread of the fine arts. Its sons have excelled in the solider graces, in the throw of the lariat, the manipulation of the esteemed

.45, the intrepidity of the one-card draw, and the nocturnal stimulation of towns from undue lethargy; but, hitherto, it had not been famed as a stronghold of æsthetics. Lonny Briscoe's brush had removed that disability. Here, among the limestone rocks, the succulent cactus, and the drought-parched grass of that arid valley, had been born the Boy Artist. Why he came to woo art is beyond postulation. Beyond doubt, some spore of the afflatus must have sprung up within him in spite of the desert soil of San Saba. The tricksy spirit of creation must have incited him to attempted expression and then have sat hilarious among the white-hot sands of the valley, watching its mischievous work. For Lonny's picture, viewed as a thing of art, was something to have driven away dull care from the bosoms of the critics.

The painting — one might almost say panorama — was designed to portray a typical Western scene, interest culminating in a central animal figure, that of a stampeding steer, life-size, wild-eyed, fiery, breaking away in a mad rush from the herd that, close-ridden by a typical cowpuncher, occupied a position somewhat in the right background of the picture. The landscape presented fitting and faithful accessories. Chaparral, mesquit, and pear were distributed in just proportions. A Spanish dagger-plant, with its waxen blossoms in a creamy aggregation as large as a water-bucket, contributed floral beauty and variety. The distance was undulating prairie, bisected by stretches of the intermittent streams peculiar to the region lined with the rich green of live-oak and water-elm. A richly mottled rattlesnake lay coiled beneath a pale green clump of prickly pear in the foreground. A third of the canvas was ultramarine and lake white — the typical Western sky and the flying clouds, rainless and feathery.

Between two plastered pillars in the commodious hallway near the door of the chamber of representatives stood the painting. Citizens and lawmakers passed there by twos and groups and sometimes crowds to gaze upon it. Many — perhaps a majority of them — had lived the prairie life and recalled easily the familiar scene. Old cattlemen stood, reminiscent and candidly pleased, chatting with brothers of former camps and trails of the days it brought back to mind. Art critics were few in the town, and there was heard none of that jargon of colour, perspective, and feeling such as the East loves to use as a curb and a rod to the pretensions of the artist. 'Twas a great picture, most of them agreed, admiring the gilt frame — larger than any they had ever seen.

Senator Kinney was the picture's champion and sponsor. It was he who so often stepped forward and asserted, with the voice of a bronco-buster, that it would be a lasting blot, sir, upon the name of this great state if it should decline to recognize in a proper manner the genius that had so brilliantly transferred to imperishable canvas a scene so typical of the great sources of our state's wealth and prosperity, land — and — er — live-stock.

Senator Kinney represented a section of the state in the extreme West — 400 miles from the San Saba country — but the true lover of art is not limited by metes and bounds. Nor was Senator Mullens, representing the San Saba country, lukewarm in his belief that the state should purchase the painting of his constituent. He was advised that the San Saba country was unanimous in its admiration of the great painting by one of its own denizens. Hundreds of connoisseurs had straddled their broncos and ridden miles to view it before its removal to the capital. Senator Mullens desired reëlection, and he knew the importance of the San Saba vote. He also knew that with the help of Senator Kinney — who was a power in the legislature — the thing could be put through. Now, Senator Kinney had an irrigation bill that he wanted passed for the benefit of his own section, and he knew Senator Mullens could render him valuable aid and information the San Saba country already enjoying the benefits of similar legislation. With these interests happily dovetailed, wonder at the sudden interest in art at the state capital must, necessarily, be small. Few artists have uncovered their first picture to the world under happier auspices than did Lonny Briscoe.

Senators Kinney and Mullens came to an understanding in the matter of irrigation and art while partaking of long drinks in the café of the Empire Hotel.

" H'm! " said Senator Kinney, " I don't know. I'm no art critic, but it seems to me the thing won't work. It looks like the worst kind of a chromo to me. I don't want to cast any reflections upon the artistic talent of your constituent, Senator, but I, myself, wouldn't give six bits for the picture — without the frame. How are you going to cram a thing like that down the throat of a legislature that kicks about a little item in the expense bill of six hundred and eighty-one dollars for rubber erasers for only one term? It's wasting time. I'd like to help you, Mullens, but they'd laugh us out of the Senate chamber if we were to try it."

" But you don't get the point," said Senator Mullens, in his deliberate tones, tapping Kinney's glass with his long forefinger. " I have my own doubts as to what the picture is intended to represent, a bullfight or a Japanese allegory, but I want this legislature to make an appropriation to purchase. Of course, the subject of the picture should have been in the state historical line, but it's too late to have the paint scraped off and changed. The state won't miss the money and the picture can be stowed away in a lumber-room where it won't annoy any one. Now, here's the point to work on, leaving art to look after itself — the chap that painted the picture is the grandson of Lucien Briscoe."

" Say it again," said Kinney, leaning his head thoughtfully. " Of the old, original Lucien Briscoe? "

" Of him. 'The man who,' you know. The man who

carved the state out of the wilderness. The man who settled the Indians. The man who cleaned out the horse thieves. The man who refused the crown. The state's favourite son. Do you see the point now?"

"Wrap up the picture," said Kinney. "It's as good as sold. Why didn't you say that at first, instead of philandering along about art. I'll resign my seat in the Senate and go back to chain-carrying for the county surveyor the day I can't make this state buy a picture calcimined by a grandson of Lucien Briscoe. Did you ever hear of a special appropriation for the purchase of a home for the daughter of One-Eyed Smothers? Well, that went through like a motion to adjourn, and old One-Eyed never killed half as many Indians as Briscoe did. About what figure had you and the calciminer agreed upon to sandbag the treasury for?"

"I thought," said Mullens, "that maybe five hundred —"

"Five hundred!" interrupted Kinney, as he hammered on his glass for a lead pencil and looked around for a waiter. "Only five hundred for a red steer on the hoof delivered by a grandson of Lucien Briscoe! Where's your state pride, man? Two thousand is what it'll be. You'll introduce the bill and I'll get up on the floor of the Senate and wave the scalp of every Indian old Lucien ever murdered. Let's see, there was something else proud and foolish he did, wasn't there? Oh, yes; he declined all emoluments and benefits he was entitled to. Refused his head-right and veteran donation certificates. Could have been governor, but wouldn't. Declined a pension. Now's the state's chance to pay up. I'll have to take the picture, but then it deserves some punishment for keeping the Briscoe family waiting so long. We'll bring this thing up about the middle of the month, after the tax bill is settled. Now, Mullens, you send over, as soon as you can, and get me the figures on the cost of those irrigation ditches and the statistics about the increased production per acre. I'm going to need you when that bill of mine comes up. I reckon we'll be able to pull along pretty well together this session and maybe others to come, eh, Senator?"

Thus did fortune elect to smile upon the Boy Artist of the San Saba. Fate had already done her share when she arranged his atoms in the cosmogony of creation as the grandson of Lucien Briscoe.

The original Briscoe had been a pioneer both as to territorial occupation and in certain acts prompted by a great and simple heart. He had been one of the first settlers and crusaders against the wild forces of nature, the savage and the shallow politician. His name and memory were revered equally with any upon the list comprising Houston, Boone, Crockett, Clark, and Green. He had lived simply, independently, and unvexed by ambition. Even a less shrewd man than Senator Kinney could have prophesied that his state would hasten to honour and reward his grandson, come out of the chaparral at even so late a day.

And so, before the great picture by the door of the chamber of representatives at frequent times for many days could be found the breezy, robust form of Senator Kinney and be heard his clarion voice reciting the past deeds of Lucien Briscoe in connection with the handiwork of his grandson. Senator Mullens's work was more subdued in sight and sound, but directed along identical lines.

Then, as the day for the introduction of the bill for appropriation draws nigh, up from the San Saba country rides Lonny Briscoe and a loyal lobby of cowpunchers, broncoback, to boost the cause of art and glorify the name of friendship, for Lonny is one of them, a knight of stirrup and chaparreras, as handy with the lariat and .45 as he is with brush and palette.

On a March afternoon the lobby dashed, with a whoop, into town. The cowpunchers had adjusted their garb suitably from that prescribed for the range to the more conventional requirements of town. They had conceded their leather chaparreras and transferred their six-shooters and belts from their persons to the horns of their saddles. Among them rode Lonny, a youth of twenty-three, brown, solemn-faced, ingenuous, bowlegged, reticent, bestriding Hot Tamales, the most sagacious cow pony west of the Mississippi. Senator Mullens had informed him of the bright prospects of the situation; had even mentioned — so great was his confidence in the capable Kinney — the price that the state would, in all likelihood, pay. It seemed to Lonny that fame and fortune were in his hands. Certainly, a spark of the divine fire was in the little brown centaur's breast, for he was counting the two thousand dollars as but a means to future development of his talent. Some day he would paint a picture even greater than this — one, say, twelve feet by twenty, full of scope and atmosphere and action.

During the three days that yet intervened before the coming of the date fixed for the introduction of the bill, the centaur lobby did valiant service. Coatless, spurred, weather-tanned, full of enthusiasm expressed in bizarre terms, they loafed in front of the painting with tireless zeal. Reasoning not unshrewdly, they estimated that their comments upon its fidelity to nature would be received as expert evidence. Loudly they praised the skill of the painter whenever there were ears near to which such evidence might be profitably addressed. Lem Perry, the leader of the claque, had a somewhat set speech, being uninventive in the construction of new phrases.

" Look at that two-year-old, now," he would say, waving a cinnamon-brown hand toward the salient point of the picture. " Why, dang my hide, the critter's alive. I can jest hear him, ' lumpety-lump,' a-cuttin' away from the herd, pretendin' he's skeered. He's a mean scamp, that there steer. Look at his eyes a-wallin' and his tail a-wavin'. He's true and nat'ral to

life. He's jest hankerin' fur a cow pony to round him up
and send him scootin' back to the bunch. Dang my hide!
jest look at that tail of his'n a-wavin'. Never knowed a steer
to wave his tail any other way, dang my hide ef I did."

Jud Shelby, while admitting the excellence of the steer,
resolutely confined himself to open admiration of the landscape, to the end that the entire picture receive its meed of
praise.

" That piece of range," he declared, " is a dead ringer for
Dead Hoss Valley. Same grass, same lay of the land, same
old Whipperwill Creek skallyhootin' in and out of them motts
of timber. Them buzzards on the left is circlin' 'round over
Sam Kildrake's old paint hoss that killed hisself over-drinkin'
on a hot day. You can't see the hoss for that mott of ellums
on the creek, but he's thar. Anybody that was goin' to look
for Dead Hoss Valley and come across this picture, why, he'd
jest light off'n his bronco and hunt a place to camp."

Skinny Rogers, wedded to comedy, conceived a complimen-
tary little piece of acting that never failed to make an impression. Edging quite near to the picture, he would suddenly,
at favourable moments emit a piercing and awful " Yi-yi!"
leap high and away, coming down with a great stamp of
heels and whirring of rowels upon the stone-flagged floor.

" Jeeming Christopher!"— so ran his lines —" thought that
rattler was a gin-u-ine one. Ding baste my skin if I didn't.
Seemed to me I heard him rattle. Look at the blamed, unconverted insect a-layin' under that pear. Little more, and
somebody would a-been snake-bit."

With these artful dodges, contributed by Lonny's faithful
coterie, with the sonorous Kinney perpetually sounding the picture's merits, and with the solvent prestige of the pioneer
Briscoe covering it like a precious varnish, it seemed that the
San Saba country could not fail to add a reputation as an art
centre to its well-known superiority in steer-roping contests

and achievements with the precarious busted flush. Thus was created for the picture an atmosphere, due rather to externals than to the artist's brush, but through it the people seemed to gaze with more of admiration. There was a magic in the name of Briscoe that counted high against faulty technique and crude colouring. The old Indian fighter and wolf slayer would have smiled grimly in his happy hunting grounds had he known that his dilettante ghost was thus figuring as an art patron two generations after his uninspired existence.

Came the day when the Senate was expected to pass the bill of Senator Mullens appropriating two thousand dollars for the purchase of the picture. The gallery of the Senate chamber was early preëmpted by Lonny and the San Saba lobby. In the front row of chairs they sat, wild-haired, self-conscious, jingling, creaking, and rattling, subdued by the majesty of the council hall.

The bill was introduced, went to the second reading, and then Senator Mullens spoke for it dryly, tediously, and at length. Senator Kinney then arose, and the welkin seized the bellrope preparatory to ringing. Oratory was at that time a living thing; the world had not quite come to measure its questions by geometry and the multiplication table. It was the day of the silver tongue, the sweeping gesture, the decorative apostrophe, the moving peroration.

The Senator spoke. The San Saba contingent sat, breathing hard, in the gallery, its disordered hair hanging down to its eyes, its sixteen-ounce hats shifted restlessly from knee to knee. Below, the distinguished Senators either lounged at their desks with the abandon of proven statesmanship or maintained correct attitudes indicative of a first term.

Senator Kinney spoke for an hour. History was his theme — history mitigated by patriotism and sentiment. He referred casually to the picture in the outer hall — it was unnecessary, he said, to dilate upon its merits — the Senators had seen for

themselves. The painter of the picture was the grandson
of Lucien Briscoe. Then came the word-pictures of Briscoe's
life set forth in thrilling colours. His rude and venturesome
life, his simple-minded love for the commonwealth he helped
to upbuild, his contempt for rewards and praise, his extreme
and sturdy independence, and the great services he had ren-
dered the state. The subject of the oration was Lucien Briscoe; the painting stood in the background serving simply as
a means, now happily brought forward, through which the
state might bestow a tardy recompense upon the descendant
of its favourite son. Frequent enthusiastic applause from the
Senators testified to the well reception of the sentiment.

The bill passed without an opposing vote. To-morrow it
would be taken up by the House. Already was it fixed to
glide through that body on rubber tires. Blandford, Gray-
son, and Plummer, all wheel-horses and orators, and provided
with plentiful memoranda concerning the deeds of pioneer
Briscoe, had agreed to furnish the motive power.

The San Saba lobby and its *protégé* stumbled awkwardly
down the stairs and out into the Capitol yard. Then they
herded closely and gave one yell of triumph. But one of
them — Buck-Kneed Summers it was — hit the key with the
thoughtful remark:

"She cut the mustard," he said, "all right. I reckon
they're goin' to buy Lon's steer. I ain't right much on the
parlyment'ry, but I gather that's what the signs added up.
But she seems to me, Lonny, the argyment ran principal to
grandfather, instead of paint. It's reasonable calculatin' that
you want to be glad you got the Briscoe brand on you, my
son."

That remark clinched in Lonny's mind an unpleasant, vague
suspicion to the same effect. His reticence increased, and he
gathered grass from the ground, chewing it pensively. The
picture as a picture had been humiliatingly absent from the

Senator's arguments. The painter had been held up as a grandson, pure and simple. While this was gratifying on certain lines, it made art look little and slab-sided. The Boy Artist was thinking.

The hotel Lonny stopped at was near the Capitol. It was near to the one o'clock dinner hour when the appropriation had been passed by the Senate. The hotel clerk told Lonny that a famous artist from New York had arrived in town that day and was in the hotel. He was on his way westward to New Mexico to study the effect of sunlight upon the ancient walls of the Zuñis. Modern stone reflects light. Those ancient building materials absorb it. The artist wanted this effect in a picture he was painting and was traveling two thousand miles to get it.

Lonny sought this man out after dinner and told his story. The artist was an unhealthy man, kept alive by genius and indifference to life. He went with Lonny to the Capitol and stood there before the picture. The artist pulled his beard and looked unhappy.

" Should like to have your sentiments," said Lonny, " just as they run out of the pen."

" It's the way they'll come," said the painter man. " I took three different kinds of medicine before dinner — by the tablespoonful. The taste still lingers. I am primed for telling the truth. You want to know if the picture is, or if it isn't? "

" Right," said Lonny. " Is it wool or cotton? Should I paint some more or cut it out and ride herd a-plenty? "

" I heard a rumour during pie," said the artist, " that the state is about to pay you two thousand dollars for this picture."

" It's passed the Senate," said Lonny, " and the House rounds it up to-morrow."

" That's lucky," said the pale man. " Do you carry a rabbit's foot? "

" No," said Lonny, " but it seems I had a grandfather. He's considerable mixed up in the colour scheme. It took me a year to paint that picture. Is she entirely awful or not? Some says, now, that that steer's tail ain't badly drawed. They think it's proportioned nice. Tell me."

The artist glanced at Lonny's wiry figure and nut-brown skin. Something stirred him to a passing irritation.

" For Art's sake, son," he said, fractiously, " don't spend any more money for paint. It isn't a picture at all. It's a gun. You hold up the state with it, if you like, and get your two thousand, but don't get in front of any more canvas. Live under it. Buy a couple of hundred ponies with the money — I'm told they're that cheap — and ride, ride, ride. Fill your lungs and eat and sleep and be happy. No more pictures. You look healthy. That's genius. Cultivate it." He looked at his watch. " Twenty minutes to three. Four capsules and one tablet at three. That's all you wanted to know, isn't it? "

At three o'clock the cowpunchers rode up for Lonny, bringing Hot Tamales, saddled. Traditions must be observed. To celebrate the passage of the bill by the Senate the gang must ride wildly through the town, creating uproar and excitement. Liquor must be partaken of, the suburbs shot up, and the glory of the San Saba country vociferously proclaimed. A part of the programme had been carried out in the saloons on the way up.

Lonny mounted Hot Tamales, the accomplished little beast prancing with fire and intelligence. He was glad to feel Lonny's bowlegged grip against his ribs again. Lonny was his friend, and he was willing to do things for him.

" Come on, boys," said Lonny, urging Hot Tamales into a gallop with his knees. With a whoop, the inspired lobby tore after him through the dust. Lonny led his cohorts straight for the Capitol. With a wild yell, the gang indorsed

his now evident intention of riding into it. Hooray for San
Saba!

Up the six broad, limestone steps clattered the broncos of
the cowpunchers. Into the resounding hallway they pattered,
scattering in dismay those passing on foot. Lonny, in the
lead, shoved Hot Tamales direct for the great picture. At that
hour a downpouring, soft light from the second-story windows
bathed the big canvas. Against the darker background of the
hall the painting stood out with valuable effect. In spite of
the defects of the art you could almost fancy that you gazed
out upon a landscape. You might well flinch a step from the
convincing figure of the life-sized steer stampeding across the
grass. Perhaps it thus seemed to Hot Tamales. The scene
was in his line. Perhaps he only obeyed the will of his rider.
His ears pricked up; he snorted. Lonny leaned forward in
the saddle and elevated his elbows, wing-like. Thus signals
the cowpuncher to his steed to launch himself full speed ahead.
Did Hot Tamales fancy he saw a steer, red and cavorting, that
should be headed off and driven back to herd? There was
a fierce clatter of hoofs, a rush, a gathering of steely flank
muscles, a leap to the jerk of the bridle rein, and Tot Tamales,
with Lonny bending low in the saddle to dodge the top of the
frame, ripped through the great canvas like a shell from a
mortar, leaving the cloth hanging in ragged shreds about a
monstrous hole.

Quickly Lonny pulled up his pony, and rounded the pillars.
Spectators came running, too astounded to add speech to the
commotion. The sergeant-at-arms of the House came forth,
frowned, looked ominous, and then grinned. Many of the
legislators crowded out to observe the tumult. Lonny's cowpunchers were stricken to silent horror by his mad deed.

Senator Kinney, happened to be among the earliest to
emerge. Before he could speak Lonny leaned in his saddle

as Hot Tamales pranced, pointed his quirt at the Senator, and said, calmly:

"That was a fine speech you made to-day, mister, but you might as well let up on that 'propriation business. I ain't askin' the state to give me nothin'. I thought I had a picture to sell to it, but it wasn't one. You said a heap of things about Grandfather Briscoe that makes me kind of proud I'm his grandson. Well, the Briscoes ain't takin' presents from the state yet. Anybody can have the frame that wants it. Hit her up, boys."

Away scuttled the San Saba delegation out of the hall, down the steps, along the dusty street.

Halfway to the San Saba country they camped that night. At bedtime Lonny stole away from the campfire and sought Hot Tamales, placidly eating grass at the end of his stake rope. Lonny hung upon his neck, and his art aspirations went forth forever in one long, regretful sigh. But as he thus made renunciation his breath formed a word or two.

"You was the only one, Tamales, what seen anything in it. It *did* look like a steer, didn't it, old hoss?"

VII

PHŒBE

"**Y**OU are a man of many novel adventures and varied enter-prises," I said to Captain Patricio Maloné. "Do you believe that the possible element of good luck or bad luck — if there is such a thing as luck — has influenced your career or per-sisted for or against you to such an extent that you were forced to attribute results to the operation of the aforesaid good luck or bad luck?"

This question (of almost the dull insolence of legal phrase-ology) was put while we sat in Rousselin's little red-tiled café near Congo Square in New Orleans.

Brown-faced, white-hatted, finger-ringed captains of adven-ture came often to Rousselin's for the cognac. They came from sea and land, and were chary of relating the things they had seen — not because they were more wonderful than the fantasies of the Ananiases of print, but because they were so different. And I was a perpetual wedding-guest, always striv-ing to cast my buttonhole over the finger of one of these mariners of fortune. This Captain Maloné was a Hiberno-Iberian creole who had gone to and fro in the earth and walked up and down in it. He looked like any other well-dressed man of thirty-five whom you might meet, except that he was hopelessly weather-tanned, and wore on his chain an ancient ivory-and-gold Peruvian charm against evil, which has nothing at all to do with his story.

"My answer to your question," said the captain, smiling,

" will be to tell you the story of Bad-Luck Kearny. That is, if you don't mind hearing it."

My reply was to pound on the table for Rousselin.

" Strolling along Tchoupitoulas Street one night," began Captain Maloné, " I noticed, without especially taxing my interest, a small man walking rapidly toward me. He stepped upon a wooden cellar door, crashed through it, and disappeared. I rescued him from a heap of soft coal below. He dusted himself briskly, swearing fluently in a mechanical tone, as an underpaid actor recites the gipsy's curse. Gratitude and the dust in his throat seemed to call for fluids to clear them away. His desire for liquidation was expressed so heartily that I went with him to a café down the street where we had some vile vermouth and bitters.

" Looking across that little table I had my first clear sight of Francis Kearny. He was about five feet seven, but as tough as a cypress knee. His hair was darkest red, his mouth such a mere slit that you wondered how the flood of his words came rushing from it. His eyes were the brightest and lightest blue and the hopefulest that I ever saw. He gave the double impression that he was at bay and that you had better not crowd him further.

" ' Just in from a gold-hunting expedition on the coast of Costa Rica,' he explained. ' Second mate of a banana steamer told me the natives were panning out enough from the beach sands to buy all the rum, red calico, and parlour melodeons in the world. The day I got there a syndicate named Incorporated Jones gets a government concession to all minerals from a given point. For a next choice I take coast fever and count green and blue lizards for six weeks in a grass hut. I had to be notified when I was well, for the reptiles were actually there. Then I shipped back as third cook on a Norwegian tramp that blew up her boiler two miles below

Quarantine. I was due to bust through that cellar door here
to-night, so I hurried the rest of the way up the river, rousta-
bouting on a lower coast packet that made a landing for every
fisherman that wanted a plug of tobacco. And now I'm here
for what comes next. And it'll be along, it'll be along,' said
this queer Mr. Kearny; 'it'll be along on the beams of my
bright but not very particular star.'

"From the first the personality of Kearny charmed me.
I saw in him the bold heart, the restless nature, and the valiant
front against the buffets of fate that make his countrymen
such valuable comrades in risk and adventure. And just then
I was wanting such men. Moored at a fruit company's pier
I had a 500-ton steamer ready to sail the next day with a
cargo of sugar, lumber, and corrugated iron for a port in —
well, let us call the country Esperando — it has not been long
ago, and the name of Patricio Maloné is still spoken there when
its unsettled politics are discussed. Beneath the sugar and
iron were packed a thousand Winchester rifles. In Aguas
Frias, the capital, Don Rafael Valdevia, Minister of War, Esperando's greatest-hearted and most able patriot, awaited my
coming. No doubt you have heard, with a smile, of the insig-
nificant wars and uprisings in those little tropic republics.
They make but a faint clamour against the din of great nations' battles; but down there, under all the ridiculous uniforms and petty diplomacy and senseless countermarching and
intrigue, are to be found statesmen and patriots. Don Rafael
Valdevia was one. His great ambition was to raise Esperando
into peace and honest prosperity and the respect of the serious
nations. So he waited for my rifles in Aguas Frias. But
one would think I am trying to win a recruit in you! No;
it was Francis Kearny I wanted. And so I told him, speaking long over our execrable vermouth, breathing the stifling
odour from garlic and tarpaulins, which, as you know, is the
distinctive flavour of cafés in the lower slant of our city. I

spoke of the tyrant President Cruz and the burdens that his greed and insolent cruelty laid upon the people. And at that Kearny's tears flowed. And then I dried them with a picture of the fat rewards that would be ours when the oppressor should be overthrown and the wise and generous Valdevia in his seat. Then Kearny leaped to his feet and wrung my hand with the strength of a roustabout. He was mine, he said, till the last minion of the hated despot was hurled from the highest peaks of the Cordilleras into the sea.

"I paid the score and we went out. Near the door Kearny's elbow overturned an upright glass showcase, smashing it into little bits. I paid the storekeeper the price he asked.

"'Come to my hotel for the night,' I said to Kearny. 'We sail to-morrow at noon.'

"He agreed; but on the sidewalk he fell to cursing again in the dull, monotonous, glib way that he had done when I pulled him out of the coal cellar.

"'Captain,' said he, 'before we go any further, it's no more than fair to tell you that I'm known from Baffin's Bay to Terra del Fuego as "Bad-Luck" Kearny. And I'm It. Everything I get into goes up in the air except a balloon. Every bet I ever made I lost except when I coppered it. Every boat I ever sailed on sank except the submarines. Everything I was ever interested in went to pieces except a patent bombshell that I invented. Everything I ever took hold of and tried to run I ran into the ground except when I tried to plough. And that's why they call me Bad-Luck Kearny. I thought I'd tell you.'

"'Bad luck,' said I, 'or what goes by the name, may now and then tangle the affairs of any man. But if it persist beyond the estimate of what we may call the "averages" there must be a cause for it.'

"'There is,' said Kearny emphatically, 'and when we walk another square I will show it to you.'

" Surprised, I kept by his side until we came to Canal Street and out into the middle of its great width.

" Kearny seized me by an arm and pointed a tragic forefinger at a rather brilliant star that shone steadily about thirty degrees above the horizon.

" ' That's Saturn,' said he, ' the star that presides over bad luck and evil and disappointment and nothing doing and trouble. I was born under that star. Every move I make, up bobs Saturn and blocks it. He's the hoodoo planet of the heavens. They say he's 73,000 miles in diameter and no solider of body than split-pea soup, and he's got as many disreputable and malignant rings as Chicago. Now, what kind of a star is that to be born under? '

" I asked Kearny where he had obtained all this astonishing knowledge.

" ' From Azrath, the great astrologer of Cleveland, Ohio,' said he. ' That man looked at a glass ball and told me my name before I'd taken a chair. He prophesied the date of my birth and death before I'd said a word. And then he cast my horoscope, and the sidereal system socked me in the solar plexus. It was bad luck for Francis Kearny from A to Izard and for his friends that were implicated with him. For that I gave up ten dollars. This Azrath was sorry, but he respected his profession too much to read the heavens wrong for any man. It was night time, and he took me out on a balcony and gave me a free view of the sky. And he showed me which Saturn was, and how to find it in different balconies and longitudes.

" ' But Saturn wasn't all. He was only the man higher up. He furnishes so much bad luck that they allow him a gang of deputy sparklers to help hand it out. They're circulating and revolving and hanging around the main supply all the time, each one throwing the hoodoo on his own particular district.

"'You see that ugly little red star about eight inches above and to the right of Saturn?' Kearny asked me. 'Well, that's her. That's Phœbe. She's got me in charge. "By the day of your birth," says Azrath to me, "your life is subjected to the influence of Saturn. By the hour and minute of it you must dwell under the sway and direct authority of Phœbe, the ninth satellite." So said this Azrath.' Kearny shook his fist viciously skyward. 'Curse her, she's done her work well,' said he. 'Ever since I was astrologized, bad luck has followed me like my shadow, as I told you. And for many years before. Now, Captain, I've told you my handicap as a man should. If you're afraid this evil star of mine might cripple your scheme, leave me out of it.'

"I reassured Kearny as well as I could. I told him that for the time we would banish both astrology and astronomy from our heads. The manifest valour and enthusiasm of the man drew me. 'Let us see what a little courage and diligence will do against bad luck,' I said. 'We will sail to-morrow for Esperando.'

"Fifty miles down the Mississippi our steamer broke her rudder. We sent for a tug to tow us back and lost three days. When we struck the blue waters of the Gulf, all the storm clouds of the Atlantic seemed to have concentrated above us. We thought surely to sweeten those leaping waves with our sugar, and to stack our arms and lumber on the floor of the Mexican Gulf.

"Kearny did not seek to cast off one iota of the burden of our danger from the shoulders of his fatal horoscope. He weathered every storm on deck, smoking a black pipe, to keep which alight rain and sea-water seemed but as oil. And he shook his fist at the black clouds behind which his baleful star winked its unseen eye. When the skies cleared one evening, he reviled his malignant guardian with grim humour.

"'On watch, aren't you, you red-headed vixen? Out making it hot for little Francis Kearny and his friends, according to Hoyle. Twinkle, twinkle, little devil! You're a lady, aren't you? — dogging a man with bad luck just because he happened to be born while your boss was floorwalker. Get busy and sink the ship, you one-eyed banshee. Phœbe! H'm! Sounds as mild as a milkmaid. You can't judge a woman by her name. Why couldn't I have had a man star? I can't make the remarks to Phœbe that I could to a man. Oh, Phœbe, you be — blasted!'

"For eight days gales and squalls and waterspouts beat us from our course. Five days only should have landed us in Esperando. Our Jonah swallowed the bad credit of it with appealing frankness; but that scarcely lessened the hardships our cause was made to suffer.

"At last one afternoon we steamed into the calm estuary of the little Rio Escondido. Three miles up this we crept, feeling for the shallow channel between the low banks that were crowded to the edge with gigantic trees and riotous vegetation. Then our whistle gave a little toot, and in five minutes we heard a shout, and Carlos — my brave Carlos Quintana — crashed through the tangled vines waving his cap madly for joy.

"A hundred yards away was his camp, where three hundred chosen patriots of Esperando were awaiting our coming. For a month Carlos had been drilling them there in the tactics of war, and filling them with the spirit of revolution and liberty.

"'My Captain — *compadre mio!*' shouted Carlos, while yet my boat was being lowered. 'You should see them in the drill by *companies* — in the column wheel — in the march by fours — they are superb! Also in the manual of arms — but, alas! performed only with sticks of bamboo. The guns, *capitan* — say that you have brought the guns!'"

"'A thousand Winchesters, Carlos,' I called to him. 'And two Gatlings.'

"'*Valgame Dios!*' he cried, throwing his cap in the air. 'We shall sweep the world!'

"At that moment Kearny tumbled from the steamer's side into the river. He could not swim, so the crew threw him a rope and drew him back aboard. I caught his eye and his look of pathetic but still bright and undaunted consciousness of his guilty luck. I told myself that although he might be a man to shun, he was also one to be admired.

"I gave orders to the sailing-master that the arms, ammunition, and provisions were to be landed at once. That was easy in the steamer's boats, except for the two Gatling guns. For their transportation ashore we carried a stout flatboat, brought for the purpose in the steamer's hold.

"In the meantime I walked with Carlos to the camp and made the soldiers a little speech in Spanish, which they received with enthusiasm; and then I had some wine and a cigarette in Carlos's tent. Later we walked back to the river to see how the unloading was being conducted.

"The small arms and provisions were already ashore, and the petty officers had squads of men conveying them to camp. One Gatling had been safely landed; the other was just being hoisted over the side of the vessel as we arrived. I noticed Kearny darting about on board, seeming to have the ambition of ten men, and to be doing the work of five. I think his zeal bubbled over when he saw Carlos and me. A rope's end was swinging loose from some part of the tackle. Kearny leaped impetuously and caught it. There was a crackle and a hiss and a smoke of scorching hemp, and the Gatling dropped straight as a plummet through the bottom of the flatboat and buried itself in twenty feet of water and five feet of river mud.

"I turned my back on the scene. I heard Carlos's loud cries as if from some extreme grief too poignant for words. I heard the complaining murmur of the crew and the maledictions of Torres, the sailing-master — I could not bear to look.

" By night some degree of order had been restored in camp. Military rules were not drawn strictly, and the men were grouped about the fires of their several messes, playing games of chance, singing their native songs, or discussing with voluble animation the contingencies of our march upon the capital.

" To my tent, which had been pitched for me close to that of my chief lieutenant, came Kearny, indomitable, smiling, bright-eyed, bearing no traces of the buffets of his evil star. Rather was his aspect that of a heroic martyr whose tribulations were so high-sourced and glorious that he even took a splendour and a prestige from them.

" ' Well, Captain,' said he, ' I guess you realize that Bad-Luck Kearny is still on deck. It was a shame, now, about that gun. She only needed to be slewed two inches to clear the rail; and that's why I grabbed that rope's end. Who'd have thought that a sailor — even a Sicilian lubber on a banana coaster — would have fastened a line in a bow-knot? Don't think I'm trying to dodge the responsibility, Captain. It's my luck.'

" ' There are men, Kearny,' said I gravely, ' who pass through life blaming upon luck and chance the mistakes that result from their own faults and incompetency. I do not say that you are such a man. But if all your mishaps are traceable to that tiny star, the sooner we endow our colleges with chairs of moral astronomy, the better.'

" ' It isn't the size of the star that counts,' said Kearny; ' it's the quality. Just the way it is with women. That's why they gave the biggest planets masculine names, and the little stars feminine ones — to even things up when it comes to getting their work in. Suppose they had called my star Agamemnon or Bill McCarty or something like that instead of Phœbe. Every time one of those old boys touched their calamity button and sent me down one of their wireless pieces of bad luck, I could talk back and tell 'em what I thought of 'em in suitable terms. But you can't address such remarks to a Phœbe.'

"'It pleases you to make a joke of it, Kearny,' said I, without smiling. 'But it is no joke to me to think of my Gatling mired in the river ooze.'

"'As to that,' said Kearny, abandoning his light mood at once, 'I have already done what I could. I have had some experience in hoisting stone in quarries. Torres and I have already spliced three hawsers and stretched them from the steamer's stern to a tree on shore. We will rig a tackle and have the gun on terra firma before noon to-morrow.'

"One could not remain long at outs with Bad-Luck Kearny.

"'Once more,' said I to him, 'we will waive this question of luck. Have you ever had experience in drilling raw troops?'

"'I was first sergeant and drill-master,' said Kearny, 'in the Chilean army for one year. And captain of artillery for another.'

"'What became of your command?' I asked.

"'Shot down to a man,' said Kearny, 'during the revolutions against Balmaceda.'

"Somehow the misfortunes of the evil-starred one seemed to turn to me their comedy side. I lay back upon my goat's-hide cot and laughed until the woods echoed. Kearny grinned. 'I told you how it was," he said.

"'To-morrow,' I said, 'I shall detail one hundred men under your command for manual-of-arms drill and company evolutions. You will rank as lieutenant. Now, for God's sake, Kearny,' I urged him, 'try to combat this superstition if it is one. Bad luck may be like any other visitor — preferring to stop where it is expected. Get your mind off stars. Look upon Esperando as your planet of good fortune.'

"'I thank you, Captain,' said Kearny quietly. 'I will try to make it the best handicap I ever ran.'

" By noon the next day the submerged Gatling was rescued, as Kearny had promised. Then Carlos and Manuel Ortiz and Kearny (my lieutenants) distributed Winchesters among the troops and put them through an incessant rifle drill. We fired no shots, blank or solid, for of all coasts Esperando is the stillest; and we had no desire to sound any warnings in the ear of that corrupt government until they should carry with them the message of Liberty and the downfall of Oppression.

" In the afternoon came a mule-rider bearing a written message to me from Don Rafael Valdevia in the capital, Aguas Frias.

" Whenever that man's name comes to my lips, words of tribute to his greatness, his noble simplicity, and his conspicuous genuis follow irrepressibly. He was a traveller, a student of peoples and governments, a master of sciences, a poet, an orator, a leader, a soldier, a critic of the world's campaigns and the idol of the people of Esperando. I had been honoured by his friendship for years. It was I who first turned his mind to the thought that he should leave for his monument a new Esperando — a country freed from the rule of unscrupulous tyrants, and a people made happy and prosperous by wise and impartial legislation. When he had consented he threw himself into the cause with the undivided zeal with which he endowed all of his acts. The coffers of his great fortune were opened to those of us to whom were entrusted the secret moves of the game. His popularity was already so great that he had practically forced President Cruz to offer him the portfolio of Minister of War.

" The time, Don Rafael said in his letter, was ripe. Success, he prophesied, was certain. The people were beginning to clamour publicly against Cruz's misrule. Bands of citizens in the capital were even going about of nights hurling stones at public buildings and expressing their dissatisfaction. A bronze statue of President Cruz in the Botanical Gardens had been lassoed about the neck and overthrown. It only remained for me to arrive with my force and my thousand rifles, and for himself to come forward and proclaim himself the people's saviour, to overthrow Cruz in a single day. There would be but a half-hearted resistance from the six hundred government troops stationed in the capital. The country was ours. He presumed that by this time my steamer had arrived at Quintana's camp. He proposed the eighteenth of July for the attack. That would give us six days in which to strike camp and march to Aguas Frias. In the meantime Don Rafael remained my good friend and *compadre en la causa de la libertad.*

"On the morning of the 14th we began our march toward the sea-following range of mountains, over the sixty-mile trail to the capital. Our small arms and provisions were laden on pack mules. Twenty men harnessed to each Gatling gun rolled them smoothly along the flat, alluvial lowlands. Our troops, well-shod and well-fed, moved with alacrity and heartiness. I and my three lieutenants were mounted on the tough mountain ponies of the country.

"A mile out of camp one of the pack mules, becoming stubborn, broke away from the train and plunged from the path into the thicket. The alert Kearny spurred quickly after it and intercepted its flight. Rising in his stirrups, he released one foot and bestowed upon the mutinous animal a hearty kick. The mule tottered and fell with a crash broadside upon the ground. As we gathered around it, it walled its great eyes almost humanly toward Kearny and expired. That was bad; but worse, to our minds, was the concomitant disaster. Part of the mule's burden had been one hundred pounds of the finest coffee to be had in the tropics. The bag burst and spilled the priceless brown mass of the ground berries among the dense vines and weeds of the swampy land. *Mala suerte!*

When you take away from an Esperandan his coffee, you abstract his patriotism and 50 per cent. of his value as a soldier. The men began to rake up the precious stuff; but I beckoned Kearny back along the trail where they would not hear. The limit had been reached.

"I took from my pocket a wallet of money and drew out some bills.

"'Mr. Kearny,' said I, 'here are some funds belonging to Don Rafael Valdevia, which I am expending in his cause. I know of no better service it can buy for him than this. Here is one hundred dollars. Luck or no luck, we part company here. Star or no star, calamity seems to travel by your side. You will return to the steamer. She touches at Amotapa to discharge her lumber and iron, and then puts back to New Orleans. Hand this note to the sailing-master, who will give you passage.' I wrote on a leaf torn from my book, and placed it and the money in Kearny's hand.

"'Good-bye,' I said, extending my own. 'It is not that I am displeased with you; but there is no place in this expedition for — let us say, the Señorita Phœbe.' I said this with a smile, trying to smooth the thing for him. 'May you have better luck, *companero*.'

"Kearny took the money and the paper.

"'It was just a little touch,' said he, 'just a little lift with the toe of my boot — but what's the odds? — that blamed mule would have died if I had only dusted his ribs with a powder puff. It was my luck. Well, Captain, I would have liked to be in that little fight with you over in Aguas Frias. Success to the cause. *Adios!*'

"He turned around and set off down the trail without looking back. The unfortunate mule's pack-saddle was transferred to Kearny's pony, and we again took up the march.

"Four days we journeyed over the foot-hills and mountains, fording icy torrents, winding around the crumbling brows of ragged peaks, creeping along rocky flanges that overlooked awful precipices, crawling breathlessly over tottering bridges that crossed bottomless chasms.

"On the evening of the seventeenth we camped by a little stream on the bare hills five miles from Aguas Frias. At daybreak we were to take up the march again.

"At midnight I was standing outside my tent inhaling the fresh cold air. The stars were shining bright in the cloudless sky, giving the heavens their proper aspect of illimitable depth and distance when viewed from the vague darkness of the blotted earth. Almost at its zenith was the planet Saturn; and with a half-smile I observed the sinister red sparkle of his malignant attendant — the demon star of Kearny's ill luck. And then my thoughts strayed across the hills to the scene of our coming triumph where the heroic and noble Don Rafael awaited our coming to set a new and shining star in the firmament of nations.

"I heard a slight rustling in the deep grass to my right. I turned and saw Kearny coming toward me. He was ragged and dew-drenched and limping. His hat and one boot were gone. About one foot he had tied some makeshift of cloth and grass. But his manner as he approached was that of a man who knows his own virtues well enough to be superior to rebuffs.

"'Well, sir,' I said, staring at him coldly, 'if there is anything in persistence, I see no reason why you should not succeed in wrecking and ruining us yet.'

"'I kept half a day's journey behind,' said Kearny, fishing out a stone from the covering of his lame foot 'so the bad luck wouldn't touch you. I couldn't help it, Captain; I wanted to be in on this game. It was a pretty tough trip, especially in the department of the commissary. In the low grounds there were always bananas and oranges. Higher up it was worse; but your men left a good deal of goat meat hanging on the bushes in the camps. Here's your hundred dollars. You're nearly there now, captain. Let me in on the scrapping to-morrow.'

" ' Not for a hundred times a hundred would I have the tiniest thing go wrong with my plans now,' I said, ' whether caused by evil planets or the blunders of mere man. But yonder is Aguas Frias, five miles away, and a clear road. I am of the mind to defy Saturn and all his satellites to spoil our success now. At any rate, I will not turn away to-night as weary a traveller and as good a soldier as you are, Lieutenant Kearny. Manuel Ortiz's tent is there by the brightest fire. Rout him out and tell him to supply you with food and blankets and clothes. We march again at daybreak.'

" Kearny thanked me briefly but feelingly and moved away.

" He had gone scarcely a dozen steps when a sudden flash of bright light illumined the surrounding hills; a sinister, growing, hissing sound like escaping steam filled my ears. Then followed a roar as of distant thunder, which grew louder every instant. This terrifying noise culminated in a tremendous explosion, which seemed to rock the hills as an earthquake would; the illumination waxed to a glare so fierce that I clapped my hands to my eyes to save them. I thought the end of the world had come. I could think of no natural phenomenon that would explain it. My wits were staggering. The deafening explosion trailed off into the rumbling roar that had preceded it; and through this I heard the frightened shouts of my troops as they stumbled from their resting-places and rushed wildly about. Also I heard the harsh tones of Kearny's voice crying: ' They'll blame it on me, of course, and what the devil it is, it's not Francis Kearny that can give you an answer.'

" I opened my eyes. The hills were still there, dark and solid. It had not been, then, a volcano or an earthquake. I looked up at the sky and saw a comet-like trail crossing the zenith and extending westward — a fiery trail waning fainter and narrower each moment.

"'A meteor!' I called aloud. 'A meteor has fallen. There is no danger.'

"And then all other sounds were drowned by a great shout from Kearny's throat. He had raised both hands above his head and was standing tiptoe.

"'PHŒBE'S GONE!' he cried, with all his lungs. 'She's busted and gone to hell. Look, Captain, the little red-headed hoodoo has blown herself to smithereens. She found Kearny too tough to handle, and she puffed up with spite and meanness till her boiler blew up. It'll be Bad-Luck Kearny no more. Oh, let us be joyful!

> "'Humpty Dumpty sat on a wall;
> Humpty busted, and that'll be all!'

"I looked up, wondering, and picked out Saturn in his place. But the small red twinkling luminary in his vicinity, which Kearny had pointed out to me as his evil star, had vanished. I had seen it there but half an hour before; there was no doubt that one of those awful and mysterious spasms of nature had hurled it from the heavens.

"I clapped Kearny on the shoulder.

"'Little man,' said I, 'let this clear the way for you. It appears that astrology has failed to subdue you. Your horoscope must be cast anew with pluck and loyalty for controlling stars. I play you to win. Now, get to your tent, and sleep. Daybreak is the word.'

"At nine o'clock on the morning of the eighteenth of July I rode into Aguas Frias with Kearny at my side. In his clean linen suit and with his military poise and keen eye he was a model of a fighting adventurer. I had visions of him riding as commander of President Valdevia's body-guard when the plums of the new republic should begin to fall.

" Carlos followed with the troops and supplies. He was to halt in a wood outside the town and remain concealed there until he received the word to advance.

" Kearny and I rode down the Calle Ancha toward the *residencia* of Don Rafael at the other side of the town. As we passed the superb white buildings of the University of Esperando, I saw at an open window the gleaming spectacles and bald head of Herr Bergowitz, professor of the natural sciences and friend of Don Rafael and of me and of the cause. He waved his hand to me, with his broad, bland smile.

" There was no excitement apparent in Aguas Frias. The people went about leisurely as at all times; the market was thronged with bareheaded women buying fruit and *carne;* we heard the twang and tinkle of string bands in the patios of the *cantinas.* We could see that it was a waiting game that Don Rafael was playing.

" His *residencia* was a large but low building around a great courtyard in grounds crowded with ornamental trees and tropic shrubs. At his door an old woman who came informed us that Don Rafael had not yet arisen.

" ' Tell him,' said I, ' that Captain Maloné and a friend wish to see him at once. Perhaps he has overslept.'

" She came back looking frightened.

" ' I have called,' she said, ' and rung his bell many times, but he does not answer.'

" I knew where his sleeping-room was. Kearny and I pushed by her and went to it. I put my shoulder against the thin door and forced it open.

" In an armchair by a great table covered with maps and books sat Don Rafael with his eyes closed. I touched his hand. He had been dead many hours. On his head above one ear was a wound caused by a heavy blow. It had ceased to bleed long before.

"I made the old woman call a *mozo*, and dispatched him in haste to fetch Herr Bergowitz.

"He came, and we stood about as if we were half stunned by the awful shock. Thus can the letting of a few drops of blood from one man's veins drain the life of a nation.

"Presently Herr Bergowitz stooped and picked up a darkish stone the size of an orange which he saw under the table. He examined it closely through his great glasses with the eye of science.

"'A fragment,' said he, 'of a detonating meteor. The most remarkable one in twenty years exploded above this city a little after midnight this morning.'

"The professor looked quickly up at the ceiling. We saw the blue sky through a hole the size of an orange nearly above Don Rafael's chair.

"I heard a familiar sound, and turned. Kearny had thrown himself on the floor and was babbling his compendium of bitter, blood-freezing curses against the star of his evil luck.

"Undoubtedly Phœbe had been feminine. Even when hurtling on her way to fiery dissolution and everlasting doom, the last word had been hers."

Captain Maloné was not unskilled in narrative. He knew the point where a story should end. I sat reveling in his effective conclusion when he aroused me by continuing:

"Of course," said he, "our schemes were at an end. There was no one to take Don Rafael's place. Our little army melted away like dew before the sun.

"One day after I had returned to New Orleans I related this story to a friend who holds a professorship in Tulane University.

"When I had finished he laughed and asked whether I had

any knowledge of Kearny's luck afterward. I told him no, that I had seen him no more; but that when he left me, he had expressed confidence that his future would be successful now that his unlucky star had been overthrown.

"'No doubt,' said the professor, 'he is happier not to know one fact. If he derives his bad luck from Phœbe, the ninth satellite of Saturn, that malicious lady is still engaged in overlooking his career. The star close to Saturn that he imagined to be her was near that planet simply by the chance of its orbit — probably at different times he has regarded many other stars that happened to be in Saturn's neighbourhood as his evil one. The real Phœbe is visible only through a very good telescope.'

"About a year afterward," continued Captain Maloné, "I was walking down a street that crossed the Poydras Market. An immensely stout, pink-faced lady in black satin crowded me from the narrow sidewalk with a frown. Behind her trailed a little man laden to the gunwales with bundles and bags of goods and vegetables.

"It was Kearny — but changed. I stopped and shook one of his hands, which still clung to a bag of garlic and red peppers.

"'How is the luck, old *companero?*' I asked him. I had not the heart to tell him the truth about his star.

"'Well,' said he, 'I am married, as you may guess.'

"'Francis!' called the big lady, in deep tones, 'are you going to stop in the street talking all day?'

"'I am coming, Phœbe dear,' said Kearny, hastening after her."

Captain Maloné ceased again.

"After all, do you believe in luck?" I asked.

"'Do you?'" answered the captain, with his ambiguous smile shaded by the brim of his soft straw hat.

VIII

A DOUBLE-DYED DECEIVER

THE trouble began in Laredo. It was the Llano Kid's fault, for he should have confined his habit of manslaughter to Mexicans. But the Kid was past twenty; and to have only Mexicans to one's credit at twenty is to blush unseen on the Rio Grande border.

It happened in old Justo Valdos's gambling house. There was a poker game at which sat players who were not all friends, as happens often where men ride in from afar to shoot Folly as she gallops. There was a row over so small a matter as a pair of queens; and when the smoke had cleared away it was found that the Kid had committed an indiscretion, and his adversary had been guilty of a blunder. For, the unfortunate combatant, instead of being a Greaser, was a high-blooded youth from the cow ranches, of about the Kid's own age and possessed of friends and champions. His blunder in missing the Kid's right ear only a sixteenth of an inch when he pulled his gun did not lessen the indiscretion of the better marksman.

The Kid, not being equipped with a retinue, nor bountifully supplied with personal admirers and supporters — on account of a rather umbrageous reputation, even for the border — considered it not incompatible with his indisputable gameness to perform that judicious tractional act known as " pulling his freight."

Quickly the avengers gathered and sought him. Three of them overtook him within a rod of the station. The Kid turned and showed his teeth in that brilliant but mirthless smile that usually preceded his deeds of insolence and violence, and his pursuers fell back without making it necessary for him even to reach for his weapon.

But in this affair the Kid had not felt the grim thirst for encounter that usually urged him on to battle. It had been a purely chance row, born of the cards and certain epithets impossible for a gentleman to brook that had passed between the two. The Kid had rather liked the slim, haughty, brown-faced young chap whom his bullet had cut off in the first pride of manhood. And now he wanted no more blood. He wanted to get away and have a good long sleep somewhere in the sun on the mesquit grass with his handkerchief over his face. Even a Mexican might have crossed his path in safety while he was in this mood.

The Kid openly boarded the north-bound passenger train that departed five minutes later. But at Webb, a few miles out, where it was flagged to take on a traveller, he abandoned that manner of escape. There were telegraph stations ahead; and the Kid looked askance at electricity and steam. Saddle and spur were his rocks of safety.

The man whom he had shot was a stranger to him. But the Kid knew that he was of the Coralitos outfit from Hidalgo; and that the punchers from that ranch were more relentless and vengeful than Kentucky feudists when wrong or harm was done to one of them. So, with the wisdom that has characterized many great fighters, the Kid decided to pile up as many leagues as possible of chaparral and pear between himself and the retaliation of the Coralitos bunch.

Near the station was a store; and near the store, scattered among the mesquits and elms, stood the saddled horses of the customers. Most of them waited, half asleep, with sagging limbs and drooping heads. But one, a long-legged roan with a curved neck, snorted and pawed the turf. Him the Kid mounted, gripped with his knees, and slapped gently with the owner's own quirt.

If the slaying of the temerarious card-player had cast a cloud over the Kid's standing as a good and true citizen, this last act of his veiled his figure in the darkest shadows of disrepute. On the Rio Grande border if you take a man's life you sometimes take trash; but if you take his horse, you take a thing the loss of which renders him poor, indeed, and which enriches you not — if you are caught. For the Kid there was no turning back now.

With the springing roan under him he felt little care or uneasiness. After a five-mile gallop he drew in to the plainsman's jogging trot, and rode northeastward toward the Nueces River bottoms. He knew the country well — its most tortuous and obscure trails through the great wilderness of brush and pear, and its camps and lonesome ranches where one might find safe entertainment. Always he bore to the east; for the Kid had never seen the ocean, and he had a fancy to lay his hand upon the mane of the great Gulf, the gamesome colt of the greater waters.

So after three days he stood on the shore at Corpus Christi, and looked out across the gentle ripples of a quiet sea.

Captain Boone, of the schooner *Flyaway,* stood near his skiff, which one of his crew was guarding in the surf. When ready to sail he had discovered that one of the necessaries of life, in the parallelogrammatic shape of plug tobacco, had been forgotten. A sailor had been dispatched for the missing cargo. Meanwhile the captain paced the sands, chewing profanely at his pocket store.

A slim, wiry youth in high-heeled boots came down to the water's edge. His face was boyish, but with a premature severity that hinted at a man's experience. His complexion was naturally dark; and the sun and wind of an outdoor life had burned it to a coffee brown. His hair was as black and straight as an Indian's; his face had not yet been upturned to the humiliation of a razor; his eyes were a cold and steady blue. He carried his left arm somewhat away from his body, for pearl-handled .45s are frowned upon by town marshals, and are a little bulky when packed in the left armhole of one's vest. He looked beyond Captain Boone at the gulf with the impersonal and expressionless dignity of a Chinese emperor.

"Thinkin' of buyin' that'ar gulf, buddy?" asked the captain, made sarcastic by his narrow escape from a tobaccoless voyage.

"Why, no," said the Kid gently, "I reckon not. I never saw it before. I was just looking at it. Not thinking of selling it, are you?"

"Not this trip," said the captain. "I'll send it to you C. O. D. when I get back to Buenas Tierras. Here comes that capstanfooted lubber with the chewin'. I ought to've weighed anchor an hour ago."

"Is that your ship out there?" asked the Kid.

"Why, yes," answered the captain, "if you want to call a schooner a ship, and I don't mind lyin'. But you better say Miller and Gonzales, owners, and ordinary plain, Billy-be-damned old Samuel K. Boone, skipper."

"Where are you going to?" asked the refugee.

"Buenas Tierras, coast of South America — I forgot what they called the country the last time I was there. Cargo — lumber, corrugated iron, and machetes."

"What kind of a country is it?" asked the Kid —"hot or cold?"

"Warmish, buddy," said the captain. "But a regular Paradise Lost for elegance of scenery and be-yooty of geography. Ye're wakened every morning by the sweet singin' of red birds with seven purple tails, and the sighin' of breezes in the posies and roses. And the inhabitants never work, for they can reach out and pick steamer baskets of the choicest hothouse fruit without gettin' out of bed. And there's no Sunday and no ice and no rent and no troubles and no use and no nothin'. It's a great country for a man to go to sleep with, and wait for somethin' to turn up. The bananys and oranges and hurricanes and pineapples that ye eat comes from there."

"That sounds to me!" said the Kid, at last betraying interest. "What'll the expressage be to take me out there with you?"

"Twenty-four dollars," said Captain Boone; "grub and transportation. Second cabin. I haven't got a first cabin."

"You've got my company," said the Kid, pulling out a buckskin bag.

With three hundred dollars he had gone to Laredo for his regular "blowout." The duel in Valdos's had cut short his season of hilarity, but it had left him with nearly $200 for aid in the fight that it had made necessary.

"All right, buddy," said the captain. "I hope your ma won't blame me for this little childish escapade of yours." He beckoned to one of the boat's crew. "Let Sanchez lift you out to the skiff so you won't get your feet wet."

Thacker, the United States consul at Buenas Tierras, was not yet drunk. It was only eleven o'clock; and he never arrived at his desired state of beatitude — a state wherein he sang ancient maudlin vaudeville songs and pelted his screaming parrot with banana peels — until the middle of the afternoon. So, when he looked up from his hammock at the sound of a slight cough, and saw the Kid standing in the door of the consulate, he was still in a condition to extend the hospitality and courtesy due from the representative of a great nation. "Don't disturb yourself," said the Kid easily. "I just dropped in. They told me it was customary to light at your camp before starting in to round up the town. I just came in on a ship from Texas."

"Glad to see you, Mr.——," said the consul.

The Kid laughed.

"Sprague Dalton," he said. "It sounds funny to me to hear it. I'm called the Llano Kid in the Rio Grande country."

"I'm Thacker," said the consul. "Take that cane-bottom chair. Now if you've come to invest, you want somebody to advise you. These dingies will cheat you out of the gold in your teeth if you don't understand their ways. Try a cigar?"

"Much obliged," said the Kid, "but if it wasn't for my corn shucks and the little bag in my back pocket I couldn't live a minute." He took out his "makings," and rolled a cigarette.

"They speak Spanish here," said the consul. "You'll need an interpreter. If there's anything I can do, why, I'd be delighted. If you're buying fruit lands or looking for a concession of any sort, you'll want somebody who knows the ropes to look out for you."

"I speak Spanish," said the Kid, "about nine times better than I do English. Everybody speaks it on the range where I come from. And I'm not in the market for anything."

"You speak Spanish?" said Thacker thoughtfully. He regarded the Kid absorbedly.

"You look like a Spaniard, too," he continued. "And you're from Texas. And you can't be more than twenty or twenty-one. I wonder if you've got any nerve."

"You got a deal of some kind to put through?" asked the Texan, with unexpected shrewdness.

"Are you open to a proposition?" said Thacker.

"What's the use to deny it?" said the Kid. "I got into a little gun frolic down in Laredo and plugged a white man. There wasn't any Mexican handy. And I come down to your parrot-and-monkey range just for to smell the morning-glories and marigolds. Now, do you *sabe?* "

Thacker got up and closed the door.

" Let me see your hand," he said.

He took the Kid's left hand, and examined the back of it closely.

" I can do it," he said excitedly. " Your flesh is as hard as wood and as healthy as a baby's. It will heal in a week."

" If it's a fist fight you want to back me for," said the Kid, " don't put your money up yet. Make it gun work, and I'll keep you company. But no barehanded scrapping, like ladies at a tea-party, for me."

" It's easier than that," said Thacker. " Just step here, will you? "

Through the window he pointed to a two-story white-stuccoed house with wide galleries rising amid the deep-green tropical foliage on a wooded hill that sloped gently from the sea.

" In that house," said Thacker, " a fine old Castilian gentleman and his wife are yearning to gather you into their arms and fill your pockets with money. Old Santos Urique lives there. He owns half the gold-mines in the country."

" You haven't been eating loco weed, have you? " asked the Kid.

" Sit down again," said Thacker, " and I'll tell you. Twelve years ago they lost a kid. No, he didn't die — although most of 'em here do from drinking the surface water. He was a wild little devil, even if he wasn't but eight years old. Everybody knows about it. Some Americans who were through here prospecting for gold had letters to Señor Urique, and the boy was a favourite with them. They filled his head with big stories about the States; and about a month after they left, the kid disappeared, too. He was supposed to have stowed himself away among the banana bunches on a fruit

steamer, and gone to New Orleans. He was seen once afterward in Texas, it was thought, but they never heard anything
more of him. Old Urique has spent thousands of dollars having him looked for. The madam was broken up worst of all.
The kid was her life. She wears mourning yet. But they say
she believes he'll come back to her some day, and never gives
up hope. On the back of the boy's left hand was tattooed
a flying eagle carrying a spear in his claws. That's old
Urique's coat of arms or something that he inherited in Spain."

The Kid raised his left hand slowly and gazed at it
curiously.

"That's it," said Thacker, reaching behind the official desk
for his bottle of smuggled brandy. "You're not so slow. I
can do it. What was I consul at Sandakan for? I never
knew till now. In a week I'll have the eagle bird with the
frog-sticker blended in so you'd think you were born with it.
I brought a set of the needles and ink just because I was sure
you'd drop in some day, Mr. Dalton."

"Oh, hell," said the Kid. "I thought I told you my
name!"

"All right, ' Kid,' then. It won't be that long. How does
Señorito Urique sound, for a change?"

"I never played son any that I remember of," said the
Kid. "If I had any parents to mention they went over the
divide about the time I gave my first bleat. What is the plan
of your round-up?"

Thacker leaned back against the wall and held his glass
up to the light.

"We've come now," said he, "to the question of how far
you're willing to go in a little matter of the sort."

"I told you why I came down here," said the Kid simply.

"A good answer," said the consul. "But you won't have
to go that far. Here's the scheme. After I get the trade-
mark tattooed on your hand I'll notify old Urique. In the

meantime I'll furnish you with all of the family history I can find out, so you can be studying up points to talk about. You've got the looks, you speak the Spanish, you know the facts, you can tell about Texas, you've got the tattoo mark. When I notify them that the rightful heir has returned and is waiting to know whether he will be received and pardoned, what will happen? They'll simply rush down here and fall on your neck, and the curtain goes down for refreshments and a stroll in the lobby."

" I'm waiting," said the Kid. " I haven't had my saddle off in your camp long, pardner, and I never met you before; but if you intend to let it go at a parental blessing, why, I'm mistaken in my man, that's all."

" Thanks," said the consul. " I haven't met anybody in a long time that keeps up with an argument as well as you do. The rest of it is simple. If they take you in only for a while it's long enough. Don't give 'em time to hunt up the strawberry mark on your left shoulder. Old Urique keeps anywhere from $50,000 to $100,000 in his house all the time in a little safe that you could open with a shoe buttoner. Get it. My skill as a tattooer is worth half the boodle. We go halves and catch a tramp steamer for Rio Janeiro. Let the United States go to pieces if it can't get along without my services. *Que dice, senor?* "

" It sounds to me! " said the Kid, nodding his head. " I'm out for the dust."

" All right, then," said Thacker. " You'll have to keep close until we get the bird on you. You can live in the back room here. I do my own cooking, and I'll make you as comfortable as a parsimonious Government will allow me."

Thacker had set the time at a week, but it was two weeks before the design that he patiently tattooed upon the Kid's hand was to his notion. And then Thacker called a *muchacho,* and dispatched this note to the intended victim:

EL SEÑOR DON SANTOS URIQUE,

    La Casa Blanca,

MY DEAR SIR:

I beg permission to inform you that there is in my house as a temporary guest a young man who arrived in Buenas Tierras from the United States some days ago. Without wishing to excite any hopes that may not be realized, I think there is a possibility of his being your long-absent son. It might be well for you to call and see him. If he is, it is my opinion that his intention was to return to his home, but upon arriving here, his courage failed him from doubts as to how he would be received.   Your true servant,

THOMPSON THACKER.

Half an hour afterward — quick time for Buenas Tierras — Señor Urique's ancient landau drove to the consul's door, with the barefooted coachman beating and shouting at the team of fat, awkward horses.

A tall man with a white moustache alighted, and assisted to the ground a lady who was dressed and veiled in unrelieved black.

The two hastened inside, and were met by Thacker with his best diplomatic bow. By his desk stood a slender young man with clear-cut, sun-browned features and smoothly brushed black hair.

Señora Urique threw back her heavy veil with a quick gesture. She was past middle age, and her hair was beginning to silver, but her full, proud figure and clear olive skin retained traces of the beauty peculiar to the Basque province. But, once you had seen her eyes, and comprehended the great sadness that was revealed in their deep shadows and hopeless expression, you saw that the woman lived only in some memory.

She bent upon the young man a long look of the most agonized questioning. Then her great black eyes turned, and her gaze rested upon his left hand. And then with a sob, not loud, but seeming to shake the room, she cried " *Hijo mio!* " and caught the Llano Kid to her heart.

A month afterward the Kid came to the consulate in response to a message sent by Thacker.

He looked the young Spanish *caballero*. His clothes were imported, and the wiles of the jewellers had not been spent upon him in vain. A more than respectable diamond shone on his finger as he rolled a shuck cigarette.

" What's doing? " asked Thacker.

" Nothing much," said the Kid calmly. " I eat my first iguana steak to-day. They're them big lizards, you *sabe?* I reckon, though, that frijoles and side bacon would do me about as well. Do you care for iguanas, Thacker? "

" No, nor for some other kinds of reptiles," said Thacker.

It was three in the afternoon, and in another hour he would be in his state of beatitude.

" It's time you were making good, sonny," he went on, with an ugly look on his reddened face. " You're not playing up to me square. You've been the prodigal son for four weeks now, and you could have had veal for every meal on a gold dish if you'd wanted it. Now, Mr. Kid, do you think it's right to leave me out so long on a husk diet? What's the trouble? Don't you get your filial eyes on anything that looks like cash in the Casa Blanca? Don't tell me you don't. Everybody knows where old Urique keeps his stuff. It's U. S. currency, too; he don't accept anything else. What's doing? Don't say ' nothing ' this time."

" Why, sure," said the Kid, admiring his diamond, " there's plenty of money up there. I'm no judge of collateral in bunches, but I will undertake for to say that I've seen the rise of $50,000 at a time in that tin grub box that my adopted father calls his safe. And he lets me carry the key sometimes just to show me that he knows I'm the real little Francisco that strayed from the herd a long time ago."

" Well, what are you waiting for? " asked Thacker angrily. " Don't you forget that I can upset your apple-cart any day

I want to. If old Urique knew you were an impostor, what sort of things would happen to you? Oh, you don't know this country, Mr. Texas Kid. The laws here have got mustard spread between 'em. These people here'd stretch you out like a frog that had been stepped on, and give you about fifty sticks at every corner of the plaza. And they'd wear every stick out, too. What was left of you they'd feed to alligators."

"I might as well tell you now, pardner," said the Kid, sliding down low on his steamer chair, "that things are going to stay just as they are. They're about right now."

"What do you mean?" asked Thacker, rattling the bottom of his glass on his desk.

"The scheme's off," said the Kid. "And whenever you have the pleasure of speaking to me address me as Don Francisco Urique. I'll guarantee I'll answer to it. We'll let Colonel Urique keep his money. His little tin safe is as good as the time-locker in the First National Bank of Laredo as far as you and me are concerned."

"You're going to throw me down, then, are you?" said the consul.

"Sure," said the Kid cheerfully. "Throw you down. That's it. And now I'll tell you why. The first night I was up at the colonel's house they introduced me to a bedroom. No blankets on the floor — a real room, with a bed and things in it. And before I was asleep, in comes this artificial mother of mine and tucks in the covers. 'Panchito,' she says, 'my little lost one, God has brought you back to me. I bless His name forever.' It was that, or some truck like that, she said. And down comes a drop or two of rain and hits me on the nose. And all that stuck by me, Mr. Thacker. And it's been that way ever since. And it's got to stay that way. Don't you think that it's for what's in it for me, either, that I say so. If you have any such ideas, keep 'em to yourself. I haven't had much truck with women in my life, and no mothers to speak of, but here's a lady that we've got to keep fooled. Once she stood it; twice she won't. I'm a low-down wolf, and the devil may have sent me on this trail instead of God, but I'll travel it to the end. And now, don't forget that I'm Don Francisco Urique whenever you happen to mention my name."

"I'll expose you to-day, you — you double-dyed traitor," stammered Thacker.

The Kid arose and, without violence, took Thacker by the throat with a hand of steel, and shoved him slowly into a corner. Then he drew from under his left arm his pearl-handled .45 and poked the cold muzzle of it against the consul's mouth.

"I told you why I come here," he said, with his old freezing smile. "If I leave here, you'll be the reason. Never forget it, pardner. Now, what is my name?"

"Er — Don Francisco Urique," gasped Thacker.

From outside came a sound of wheels, and the shouting of some one, and the sharp thwacks of a wooden whipstock upon the backs of fat horses.

The Kid put up his gun, and walked toward the door. But he turned again and came back to the trembling Thacker, and held up his left hand with its back toward the consul.

"There's one more reason," he said slowly, "why things have got to stand as they are. The fellow I killed in Laredo had one of them same pictures on his left hand."

Outside, the ancient landau of Don Santos Urique rattled to the door. The coachman ceased his bellowing. Señora Urique, in a voluminous gay gown of white lace and flying ribbons, leaned forward with a happy look in her great soft eyes.

"Are you within, dear son?" she called, in the rippling Castilian.

"*Madre mia, yo vengo* [mother, I come]," answered the young Don Francisco Urique.

IX

THE PASSING OF BLACK EAGLE

FOR some months of a certain year a grim bandit infested the Texas border along the Rio Grande. Peculiarly striking to the optic nerve was this notorious marauder. His personality secured him the title of " Black Eagle, the Terror of the Border." Many fearsome tales are of record concerning the doings of him and his followers. Suddenly, in the space of a single minute, Black Eagle vanished from earth. He was never heard of again. His own band never even guessed the mystery of his disappearance. The border ranches and settlements feared he would come again to ride and ravage the mesquite flats. He never will. It is to disclose the fate of Black Eagle that this narrative is written.

The initial movement of the story is furnished by the foot of a bartender in St. Louis. His discerning eye fell upon the form of Chicken Ruggles as he pecked with avidity at the free lunch. Chicken was a " hobo." He had a long nose like the bill of a fowl, an inordinate appetite for poultry, and a habit of gratifying it without expense, which accounts for the name given him by his fellow vagrants.

Physicians agree that the partaking of liquids at meal times is not a healthy practice. The hygiene of the saloon promulgates the opposite. Chicken had neglected to purchase a drink to accompany his meal. The bartender rounded the counter, caught the injudicious diner by the ear with a lemon squeezer, led him to the door and kicked him into the street.

Thus the mind of Chicken was brought to realize the signs

of coming winter. The night was cold; the stars shone with unkindly brilliancy; people were hurrying along the streets in two egotistic, jostling streams. Men had donned their overcoats, and Chicken knew to an exact percentage the increased difficulty of coaxing dimes from those buttoned-in vest pockets. The time had come for his annual exodus to the south.

A little boy, five or six years old, stood looking with covetous eyes in a confectioner's window. In one small hand he held an empty two-ounce vial; in the other he grasped tightly something flat and round, with a shining milled edge. The scene presented a field of operations commensurate to Chicken's talents and daring. After sweeping the horizon to make sure that no official tug was cruising near, he insidiously accosted his prey. The boy, having been early taught by his household to regard altruistic advances with extreme suspicion, received the overtures coldly.

Then Chicken knew that he must make one of those desperate, nerve-shattering plunges into speculation that fortune sometimes requires of those who would win her favour. Five cents was his capital, and this he must risk against the chance of winning what lay within the close grasp of the youngster's chubby hand. It was a fearful lottery, Chicken knew. But he must accomplish his end by strategy, since he had a wholesome terror of plundering infants by force. Once, in a park, driven by hunger, he had committed an onslaught upon a bottle of peptonized infant's food in the possession of an occupant of a baby carriage. The outraged infant had so promptly opened its mouth and pressed the button that communicated with the welkin that help arrived, and Chicken did his thirty days in a snug coop. Wherefore he was, as he said, " leary of kids."

Beginning artfully to question the boy concerning his choice of sweets, he gradually drew out the information he wanted. Mamma said he was to ask the drug store man for ten cents' worth of paregoric in the bottle; he was to keep his hand shut tight over the dollar; he must not stop to talk to anyone in the street; he must ask the drug-store man to wrap up the change and put it in the pocket of his trousers. Indeed, they had pockets — two of them! And he liked chocolate creams best.

Chicken went into the store and turned plunger. He invested his entire capital in C. A. N. D. Y. stocks, simply to pave the way to the greater risk following.

He gave the sweets to the youngster, and had the satisfaction of perceiving that confidence was established. After that it was easy to obtain leadership of the expedition; to take the investment by the hand and lead it to a nice drug store he knew of in the same block. There Chicken, with a parental air, passed over the dollar and called for the medicine, while the boy crunched his candy, glad to be relieved of the responsibility of the purchase. And then the successful investor, searching his pockets, found an overcoat button — the extent of his winter trousseau — and, wrapping it carefully, placed the ostensible change in the pocket of confiding juvenility. Setting the youngster's face homeward, and patting him benevolently on the back — for Chicken's heart was as soft as those of his feathered namesakes — the speculator quit the market with a profit of 1,700 per cent. on his invested capital.

Two hours later an Iron Mountain freight engine pulled out of the railroad yards, Texas bound, with a string of empties. In one of the cattle cars, half buried in excelsior, Chicken lay at ease. Beside him in his nest was a quart bottle of very poor whisky and a paper bag of bread and cheese. Mr. Ruggles, in his private car, was on his trip south for the winter season.

For a week that car was trundled southward, shifted, laid

over, and manipulated after the manner of rolling stock, but Chicken stuck to it, leaving it only at necessary times to satisfy his hunger and thirst. He knew it must go down to the cattle country, and San Antonio, in the heart of it, was his goal. There the air was salubrious and mild; the people indulgent and long-suffering. The bartenders there would not kick him. If he should eat too long or too often at one place they would swear at him as if by rote and without heat. They swore so drawlingly, and they rarely paused short of their full vocabulary, which was copious, so that Chicken had often gulped a good meal during the process of the vituperative prohibition. The season there was always spring-like; the plazas were pleasant at night, with music and gayety; except during the slight and infrequent cold snaps one could sleep comfortably out of doors in case the interiors should develop inhospitality.

At Texarkana his car was switched to the I. and G. N. Then still southward it trailed until, at length, it crawled across the Colorado bridge at Austin, and lined out, straight as an arrow, for the run to San Antonio.

When the freight halted at that town Chicken was fast asleep. In ten minutes the train was off again for Laredo, the end of the road. Those empty cattle cars were for distribution along the line at points from which the ranches shipped their stock.

When Chicken awoke his car was stationary. Looking out between the slats he saw it was a bright, moonlit night. Scrambling out, he saw his car with three others abandoned on a little siding in a wild and lonesome country. A cattle pen and chute stood on one side of the track. The railroad bisected a vast, dim ocean of prairie, in the midst of which Chicken, with his futile rolling stock, was as completely stranded as was Robinson with his land-locked boat.

A white post stood near the rails. Going up to it, Chicken

read the letters at the top, S. A. 90. Laredo was nearly as far to the south. He was almost a hundred miles from any town. Coyotes began to yelp in the mysterious sea around him. Chicken felt lonesome. He had lived in Boston without an education, in Chicago without nerve, in Philadelphia without a sleeping place, in New York without a pull, and in Pittsburg sober, and yet he had never felt so lonely as now.

Suddenly through the intense silence, he heard the whicker of a horse. The sound came from the side of the track toward the east, and Chicken began to explore timorously in that direction. He stepped high along the mat of curly mesquit grass, for he was afraid of everything there might be in this wilderness — snakes, rats, brigands, centipedes, mirages, cowboys, fandangoes, tarantulas, tamales — he had read of them in the story papers. Rounding a clump of prickly pear that reared high its fantastic and menacing array of rounded heads, he was struck to shivering terror by a snort and a thunderous plunge, as the horse, himself startled, bounded away some fifty yards, and then resumed his grazing. But here was the one thing in the desert that Chicken did not fear. He had been reared on a farm; he had handled horses, understood them, and could ride.

Approaching slowly and speaking soothingly, he followed the animal, which, after its first flight, seemed gentle enough, and secured the end of the twenty-foot lariat that dragged after him in the grass. It required him but a few moments to contrive the rope into an ingenious nose-bridle, after the style of the Mexican *borsal*. In another he was upon the horse's back and off at a splendid lope, giving the animal free choice of direction. "He will take me somewhere," said Chicken to himself.

It would have been a thing of joy, that untrammelled gallop over the moonlit prairie, even to Chicken, who loathed exertion, but that his mood was not for it. His head ached;

a growing thirst was upon him; the "somewhere" whither his lucky mount might convey him was full of dismal peradventure.

And now he noted that the horse moved to a definite goal. Where the prairie lay smooth he kept his course straight as an arrow's toward the east. Deflected by hill or arroyo or impracticable spinous brakes, he quickly flowed again into the current, charted by his unerring instinct. At last, upon the side of a gentle rise, he suddenly subsided to a complacent walk. A stone's cast away stood a little mott of coma trees; beneath it a *jacal* such as the Mexicans erect — a one-room house of upright poles daubed with clay and roofed with grass or tule reeds. An experienced eye would have estimated the spot as the headquarters of a small sheep ranch. In the moonlight the ground in the nearby corral showed pulverized to a level smoothness by the hoofs of the sheep. Everywhere was carelessly distributed the paraphernalia of the place — ropes, bridles, saddles, sheep pelts, wool sacks, feed troughs, and camp litter. The barrel of drinking water stood in the end of the two-horse wagon near the door. The harness was piled, promiscuous, upon the wagon tongue, soaking up the dew.

Chicken slipped to earth, and tied the horse to a tree. He halloed again and again, but the house remained quiet. The door stood open, and he entered cautiously. The light was sufficient for him to see that no one was at home. He struck a match and lighted a lamp that stood on a table. The room was that of a bachelor ranchman who was content with the necessaries of life. Chicken rummaged intelligently until he found what he had hardly dared hope for — a small, brown jug that still contained something near a quart of his desire.

Half an hour later, Chicken — now a gamecock of hostile aspect — emerged from the house with unsteady steps. He had drawn upon the absent ranchman's equipment to replace his own ragged attire. He wore a suit of coarse brown ducking, the coat being a sort of rakish bolero, jaunty to a degree. Boots he had donned, and spurs that whirred with every lurching step. Buckled around him was a belt full of cartridges with a big six-shooter in each of its two holsters.

Prowling about, he found blankets, a saddle and bridle with which he caparisoned his steed. Again mounting, he rode swiftly away, singing a loud and tuneless song.

Bud King's band of desperadoes, outlaws and horse and cattle thieves were in camp at a secluded spot on the bank of the Frio. Their depredations in the Rio Grande country, while no bolder than usual, had been advertised more extensively, and Captain Kinney's company of rangers had been ordered down to look after them. Consequently, Bud King, who was a wise general, instead of cutting out a hot trail for the upholders of the law, as his men wished to do, retired for the time to the prickly fastnesses of the Frio valley.

Though the move was a prudent one, and not incompatible with Bud's well-known courage, it raised dissension among the members of the band. In fact, while they thus lay ingloriously *perdu* in the brush, the question of Bud King's fitness for the leadership was argued, with closed doors, as it were, by his followers. Never before had Bud's skill or efficiency been brought to criticism; but his glory was waning (and such is glory's fate) in the light of a newer star. The sentiment of the band was crystallizing into the opinion that Black Eagle could lead them with more lustre, profit, and distinction.

This Black Eagle — sub-titled the "Terror of the Border" — had been a member of the gang about three months.

One night while they were in camp on the San Miguel water-hole a solitary horseman on the regulation fiery steed dashed in among them. The newcomer was of a portentous and devastating aspect. A beak-like nose with a predatory curve projected above a mass of bristling, blue-black whiskers. His eye was cavernous and fierce. He was spurred, sombreroed, booted, garnished with revolvers, abundantly drunk, and very much unafraid. Few people in the country drained by the Rio Bravo would have cared thus to invade alone the camp of Bud King. But this fell bird swooped fearlessly upon them and demanded to be fed.

Hospitality in the prairie country is not limited. Even if your enemy pass your way you must feed him before you shoot him. You must empty your larder into him before you empty your lead. So the stranger of undeclared intentions was set down to a mighty feast.

A talkative bird he was, full of most marvellous loud tales and exploits, and speaking a language at times obscure but never colourless. He was a new sensation to Bud King's men, who rarely encountered new types. They hung, delighted, upon his vainglorious boasting, the spicy strangeness of his lingo, his contemptuous familiarity with life, the world, and remote places, and the extravagant frankness with which he conveyed his sentiments.

To their guest the band of outlaws seemed to be nothing more than a congregation of country bumpkins whom he was " stringing for grub " just as he would have told his stories at the back door of a farmhouse to wheedle a meal. And, indeed, his ignorance was not without excuse, for the "bad man " of the Southwest does not run to extremes. Those brigands might justly have been taken for a little party of peaceable rustics assembled for a fish-fry or pecan gathering. Gentle of manner, slouching of gait, soft-voiced, unpicturesquely clothed; not one of them presented to the eye any witness of the desperate records they had earned.

For two days the glittering stranger within the camp was feasted. Then, by common consent, he was invited to become

a member of the band. He consented, presenting for en-
rollment the prodigious name of " Captain Montressor." This
name was immediately overruled by the band, and " Piggy "
substituted as a compliment to the awful and insatiate appetite of its owner.

Thus did the Texas border receive the most spectacular
brigand that ever rode its chaparral.

For the next three months Bud King conducted business
as usual, escaping encounters with law officers and being content with reasonable profits. The band ran off some very
good companies of horses from the ranges, and a few bunches
of fine cattle which they got safely across the Rio Grande
and disposed of to fair advantage. Often the band would
ride into the little villages and Mexican settlements, terror-
izing the inhabitants and plundering for the provisions and
ammunition they needed. It was during these bloodless raids
that Piggy's ferocious aspect and frightful voice gained him
a renown more widespread and glorious than those other gen-
tle-voiced and sad-faced desperadoes could have acquired in
a lifetime.

The Mexicans, most apt in nomenclature, first called him
The Black Eagle, and used to frighten the babes by threatening them with tales of the dreadful robber who carried off
little children in his great beak. Soon the name extended,
and Black Eagle, the Terror of the Border, became a recognized factor in exaggerated newspaper reports and ranch
gossip.

The country from the Nueces to the Rio Grande was a
wild but fertile stretch, given over to the sheep and cattle
ranches. Range was free; the inhabitants were few; the law
was mainly a letter, and the pirates met with little opposition
until the flaunting and garish Piggy gave the band undue
advertisement. Then McKinney's ranger company headed
for those precincts, and Bud King knew that it meant grim

and sudden war or else temporary retirement. Regarding the risk to be unnecessary, he drew off his band to an almost inaccessible spot on the bank of the Frio. Wherefore, as has been said, dissatisfaction arose among the members, and impeachment proceedings against Bud were premeditated, with Black Eagle in high favour for the succession. Bud King was not unaware of the sentiment, and he called aside Cactus Taylor, his trusted lieutenant, to discuss it.

"If the boys," said Bud, "ain't satisfied with me, I'm willin' to step out. They're buckin' against my way of handlin' 'em. And 'specially because I concludes to hit the brush while Sam Kinney is ridin' the line. I saves 'em from bein' shot or sent up on a state contract, and they up and says I'm no good."

"It ain't so much that," explained Cactus, "as it is they're plum locoed about Piggy. They want them whiskers and that nose of his to split the wind at the head of the column."

"There's somethin' mighty seldom about Piggy," declared Bud, musingly. "I never yet see anything on the hoof that he exactly grades up with. He can shore holler a plenty, and he straddles a hoss from where you laid the chunk. But he ain't never been smoked yet. You know, Cactus, we ain't had a row since he's been with us. Piggy's all right for skearin' the greaser kids and layin' waste a cross-roads store. I reckon he's the finest canned oyster buccaneer and cheese pirate that ever was, but how's his appetite for fightin'? I've knowed some citizens you'd think was starvin' for trouble get a bad case of dyspepsy the first dose of lead they had to take."

"He talks all spraddled out," said Cactus, "'bout the rookuses he's been in. He claims to have saw the elephant and hearn the owl."

"I know," replied Bud, using the cowpuncher's expressive phrase of skepticism, "but it sounds to me!"

This conversation was held one night in camp while the other members of the band — eight in number — were sprawling around the fire, lingering over their supper. When Bud and Cactus ceased talking they heard Piggy's formidable voice holding forth to the others as usual while he was engaged in checking, though never satisfying, his ravening appetite.

"Wat's de use," he was saying, "of chasin' little red cowses and hosses 'round for t'ousands of miles? Dere ain't nuttin' in it. Gallopin' t'rough dese bushes and briers, and gettin' a t'irst dat a brewery couldn't put out, and missin' meals! Say! You know what I'd do if I was main finger of dis bunch? I'd stick up a train. I'd blow de express car and make hard dollars where you guys gets wind. Youse makes me tired. Dis sook-cow kind of cheap sport gives me a pain."

Later on, a deputation waited on Bud. They stood on one leg, chewed mesquit twigs and circumlocuted, for they hated to hurt his feelings. Bud foresaw their business, and made it easy for them. Bigger risks and larger profits was what they wanted.

The suggestion of Piggy's about holding up a train had fired their imagination and increased their admiration for the dash and boldness of the instigator. They were such simple, artless, and custom-bound bush-rangers that they had never before thought of extending their habits beyond the running off of live-stock and the shooting of such of their acquaintances as ventured to interfere.

Bud acted "on the level," agreeing to take a subordinate place in the gang until Black Eagle should have been given a trial as leader.

After a great deal of consultation, studying of time-tables, and discussion of the country's topography, the time and place for carrying out their new enterprise was decided upon. At that time there was a feedstuff famine in Mexico and a cattle famine in certain parts of the United States, and there was a brisk international trade. Much money was being shipped along the railroads that connected the two republics. It was agreed that the most promising place for the contemplated robbery was at Espina, a little station on the I. and G. N., about forty miles north of Laredo. The train stopped there one minute; the country around was wild and unsettled; the station consisted of but one house in which the agent lived.

Black Eagle's band set out, riding by night. Arriving in the vicinity of Espina they rested their horses all day in a thicket a few miles distant.

The train was due at Espina at 10.30 P.M. They could rob the train and be well over the Mexican border with their booty by daylight the next morning.

To do Black Eagle justice, he exhibited no signs of flinching from the responsible honours that had been conferred upon him.

He assigned his men to their respective posts with discretion, and coached them carefully as to their duties. On each side of the track four of the band were to lie concealed in the chaparral. Gotch-Ear Rodgers was to stick up the station agent. Bronco Charlie was to remain with the horses, holding them in readiness. At a spot where it was calculated the engine would be when the train stopped, Bud King was to lie hidden on one side, and Black Eagle himself on the other. The two would get the drop on the engineer and fireman, force them to descend and proceed to the rear. Then the express car would be looted, and the escape made. No one was to move until Black Eagle gave the signal by firing his revolver. The plan was perfect.

At ten minutes to train time every man was at his post, effectually concealed by the thick chaparral that grew almost to the rails. The night was dark and lowering, with a fine drizzle falling from the flying gulf clouds. Black Eagle crouched behind a bush within five yards of the track. Two six-shooters were belted around him. Occasionally he drew a large black bottle from his pocket and raised it to his mouth.

A star appeared far down the track which soon waxed into the headlight of the approaching train. It came on with an increasing roar; the engine bore down upon the ambushing desperadoes with a glare and a shriek like some avenging monster come to deliver them to justice. Black Eagle flattened himself upon the ground. The engine, contrary to their calculations, instead of stopping between him and Bud King's place of concealment, passed fully forty yards farther before it came to a stand.

The bandit leader rose to his feet and peered around the bush. His men all lay quiet, awaiting the signal. Immediately opposite Black Eagle was a thing that drew his attention. Instead of being a regular passenger train it was a mixed one. Before him stood a box car, the door of which, by some means, had been left slightly open. Black Eagle went up to it and pushed the door farther open. An odour came forth — a damp, rancid, familiar, musty, intoxicating, beloved odour stirring strongly at old memories of happy days and travels. Black Eagle sniffed at the witching smell as the returned wanderer smells of the rose that twines his boyhood's cottage home. Nostalgia seized him. He put his hand inside. Excelsior — dry, springy, curly, soft, enticing, covered the floor. Outside the drizzle had turned to a chilling rain.

The train bell clanged. The bandit chief unbuckled his belt and cast it, with its revolvers, upon the ground. His spurs followed quickly, and his broad sombrero. Black Eagle was moulting. The train started with a rattling jerk. The ex-Terror of the Border scrambled into the box car and closed the door. Stretched luxuriously upon the excelsior, with the black bottle clasped closely to his breast, his eyes closed, and a foolish, happy smile upon his terrible features Chicken Ruggles started upon his return trip.

Undisturbed, with the band of desperate bandits lying motionless, awaiting the signal to attack, the train pulled out from Espina. As its speed increased, and the black masses of chaparral went whizzing past on either side, the express messenger, lighting his pipe, looked through his window and remarked, feelingly:

"What a jim-dandy place for a hold-up!"

X

A RETRIEVED REFORMATION

A GUARD came to the prison shoe-shop, where Jimmy Valentine was assiduously stitching uppers, and escorted him to the front office. There the warden handed Jimmy his pardon, which had been signed that morning by the governor. Jimmy took it in a tired kind of way. He had served nearly ten months of a four-year sentence. He had expected to stay only about three months, at the longest. When a man with as many friends on the outside as Jimmy Valentine had is received in the " stir " it is hardly worth while to cut his hair.

" Now, Valentine," said the warden, " you'll go out in the morning. Brace up, and make a man of yourself. You're not a bad fellow at heart. Stop cracking safes, and live straight."

" Me? " said Jimmy, in surprise. " Why, I never cracked a safe in my life."

" Oh, no," laughed the warden. " Of course not. Let's see, now. How was it you happened to get sent up on that Springfield job? Was it because you wouldn't prove an alibi for fear of compromising somebody in extremely high-toned society? Or was it simply a case of a mean old jury that had it in for you? It's always one or the other with you innocent victims."

" Me? " said Jimmy, still blankly virtuous. " Why, warden, I never was in Springfield in my life!"

" Take him back, Cronin," smiled the warden, " and fix

him up with outgoing clothes. Unlock him at seven in the morning, and let him come to the bull-pen. Better think over my advice, Valentine."

At a quarter past seven on the next morning Jimmy stood in the warden's outer office. He had on a suit of the villainously fitting, ready-made clothes and a pair of the stiff, squeaky shoes that the state furnishes to its discharged compulsory guests.

The clerk handed him a railroad ticket and the five-dollar bill with which the law expected him to rehabilitate himself into good citizenship and prosperity. The warden gave him a cigar, and shook hands. Valentine, 9762, was chronicled on the books "Pardoned by Governor," and Mr. James Valentine walked out into the sunshine.

Disregarding the song of the birds, the waving green trees, and the smell of the flowers, Jimmy headed straight for a restaurant. There he tasted the first sweet joys of liberty in the shape of a broiled chicken and a bottle of white wine — followed by a cigar a grade better than the one the warden had given him. From there he proceeded leisurely to the depot. He tossed a quarter into the hat of a blind man sitting by the door, and boarded his train. Three hours set him down in a little town near the state line. He went to the café of one Mike Dolan and shook hands with Mike, who was alone behind the bar.

"Sorry we couldn't make it sooner, Jimmy, me boy," said Mike. "But we had that protest from Springfield to buck against, and the governor nearly balked. Feeling all right?"

"Fine," said Jimmy. "Got my key?"

He got his key and went up-stairs, unlocking the door of a room at the rear. Everything was just as he had left it. There on the floor was still Ben Price's collar-button that had been torn from that eminent detective's shirt-band when they had overpowered Jimmy to arrest him.

Pulling out from the wall a folding-bed, Jimmy slid back a panel in the wall and dragged out a dust-covered suit-case. He opened this and gazed fondly at the finest set of burglar's tools in the East. It was a complete set, made of specially tempered steel, the latest designs in drills, punches, braces and bits, jimmies, clamps, and augers, with two or three novelties, invented by Jimmy himself, in which he took pride. Over nine hundred dollars they had cost him to have made at ——, a place where they make such things for the profession.

In half an hour Jimmy went down stairs and through the café. He was now dressed in tasteful and well-fitting clothes, and carried his dusted and cleaned suit-case in his hand.

" Got anything on? " asked Mike Dolan, genially.

" Me? " said Jimmy, in a puzzled tone. " I don't understand. I'm representing the New York Amalgamated Short Snap Biscuit Cracker and Frazzled Wheat Company."

This statement delighted Mike to such an extent that Jimmy had to take a seltzer-and-milk on the spot. He never touched " hard " drinks.

A week after the release of Valentine, 9762, there was a neat job of safe-burglary done in Richmond, Indiana, with no clue to the author. A scant eight hundred dollars was all that was secured. Two weeks after that a patented, improved, burglar-proof safe in Logansport was opened like a cheese to the tune of fifteen hundred dollars, currency; securities and silver untouched. That began to interest the rogue-catchers. Then an old-fashioned bank-safe in Jefferson City became active and threw out of its crater an eruption of bank-notes amounting to five thousand dollars. The losses were now high enough to bring the matter up into Ben Price's class of work. By comparing notes, a remarkable similarity in the methods of the burglaries was noticed.

Ben Price investigated the scenes of the robberies, and was heard to remark:

"That's Dandy Jim Valentine's autograph. He's resumed business. Look at that combination knob — jerked out as easy as pulling up a radish in wet weather. He's got the only clamps that can do it. And look how clean those tumblers were punched out! Jimmy never has to drill but one hole. Yes, I guess I want Mr. Valentine. He'll do his bit next time without any short-time or clemency foolishness."

Ben Price knew Jimmy's habits. He had learned them while working up the Springfield case. Long jumps, quick get-aways, no confederates, and a taste for good society — these ways had helped Mr. Valentine to become noted as a successful dodger of retribution. It was given out that Ben Price had taken up the trail of the elusive cracksman, and other people with burglar-proof safes felt more at ease.

One afternoon Jimmy Valentine and his suit-case climbed out of the mail-hack in Elmore, a little town five miles off the railroad down in the black-jack country of Arkansas. Jimmy, looking like an athletic young senior just home from college, went down the board side-walk toward the hotel.

A young lady crossed the street, passed him at the corner and entered a door over which was the sign "The Elmore Bank." Jimmy Valentine looked into her eyes, forgot what he was, and became another man. She lowered her eyes and coloured slightly. Young men of Jimmy's style and looks were scarce in Elmore.

Jimmy collared a boy that was loafing on the steps of the bank as if he were one of the stockholders, and began to ask him questions about the town, feeding him dimes at intervals. By and by the young lady came out, looking royally unconscious of the young man with the suit-case, and went her way.

"Isn't that young lady Miss Polly Simpson?" asked Jimmy, with specious guile.

"Naw," said the boy. "She's Annabel Adams. Her pa owns this bank. What'd you come to Elmore for? Is that a gold watch-chain? I'm going to get a bulldog. Got any more dimes?"

Jimmy went to the Planters' Hotel, registered as Ralph D. Spencer, and engaged a room. He leaned on the desk and declared his platform to the clerk. He said he had come to Elmore to look for a location to go into business. How was the shoe business, now, in the town? He had thought of the shoe business. Was there an opening?

The clerk was impressed by the clothes and manner of Jimmy. He, himself, was something of a pattern of fashion to the thinly gilded youth of Elmore, but he now perceived his shortcomings. While trying to figure out Jimmy's manner of tying his four-in-hand he cordially gave information.

Yes, there ought to be a good opening in the shoe line. There wasn't an exclusive shoe-store in the place. The dry-goods and general stores handled them. Business in all lines was fairly good. Hoped Mr. Spencer would decide to locate in Elmore. He would find it a pleasant town to live in, and the people very sociable.

Mr. Spencer thought he would stop over in the town a few days and look over the situation. No, the clerk needn't call the boy. He would carry up his suit-case, himself; it was rather heavy.

Mr. Ralph Spencer, the phœnix that arose from Jimmy Valentine's ashes — ashes left by the flame of a sudden and alterative attack of love — remained in Elmore, and prospered. He opened a shoe-store and secured a good run of trade.

Socially he was also a success, and made many friends.

'And he accomplished the wish of his heart. He met Miss
'Annabel Adams, and became more and more captivated by
her charms.

At the end of a year the situation of Mr. Ralph Spencer
was this: he had won the respect of the community, his shoe-
store was flourishing, and he and Annabel were engaged to
be married in two weeks. Mr. Adams, the typical, plod-
ding, country banker, approved of Spencer. Annabel's pride
in him almost equalled her affection. He was as much at
home in the family of Mr. Adams and that of Annabel's married sister as if he were already a member.

One day Jimmy sat down in his room and wrote this letter, which he mailed to the safe address of one of his old
friends in St. Louis:

DEAR OLD PAL:

I want you to be at Sullivan's place, in Little Rock, next Wednes-
day night, at nine o'clock. I want you to wind up some little matters for me. And, also, I want to make you a present of my kit of
tools. I know you'll be glad to get them — you couldn't duplicate
the lot for a thousand dollars. Say, Billy, I've quit the old business — a year ago. I've got a nice store. I'm making an honest living, and I'm going to marry the finest girl on earth two weeks from
now. It's the only life, Billy — the straight one. I wouldn't touch
a dollar of another man's money now for a million. After I get
married I'm going to sell out and go West, where there won't be so
much danger of having old scores brought up against me. I tell
you, Billy, she's an angel. She believes in me; and I wouldn't
do another crooked thing for the whole world. Be sure to be at
Sully's, for I must see you. I'll bring along the tools with me.

Your old friend,
JIMMY.

On the Monday night after Jimmy wrote this letter, Ben
Price jogged unobtrusively into Elmore in a livery buggy.
He lounged about town in his quiet way until he found out
what he wanted to know. From the drug-store across the

street from Spencer's shoe-store he got a good look at Ralph D. Spencer.

"Going to marry the banker's daughter are you, Jimmy?" said Ben to himself, softly. "Well, I don't know!"

The next morning Jimmy took breakfast at the Adamses. He was going to Little Rock that day to order his wedding-suit and buy something nice for Annabel. That would be the first time he had left town since he came to Elmore. It had been more than a year now since those last professional "jobs," and he thought he could safely venture out.

After breakfast quite a family party went downtown together — Mr. Adams, Annabel, Jimmy, and Annabel's married sister with her two little girls, aged five and nine. They came by the hotel where Jimmy still boarded, and he ran up to his room and brought along his suit-case. Then they went on to the bank. There stood Jimmy's horse and buggy and Dolph Gibson, who was going to drive him over to the railroad station.

All went inside the high, carved oak railings into the banking-room — Jimmy included, for Mr. Adams's future son-in-law was welcome anywhere. The clerks were pleased to be greeted by the good-looking, agreeable young man who was going to marry Miss Annabel. Jimmy set his suit-case down. Annabel, whose heart was bubbling with happiness and lively youth, put on Jimmy's hat, and picked up the suit-case. "Wouldn't I make a nice drummer?" said Annabel. "My! Ralph, how heavy it is? Feels like it was full of gold bricks."

"Lot of nickel-plated shoe-horns in there," said Jimmy, coolly, "that I'm going to return. Thought I'd save express charges by taking them up. I'm getting awfully economical."

The Elmore Bank had just put in a new safe and vault. Mr. Adams was very proud of it, and insisted on an inspec-

tion by every one. The vault was a small one, but it had a
new, patented door. It fastened with three solid steel bolts
thrown simultaneously with a single handle, and had a time-
lock. Mr. Adams beamingly explained its workings to Mr.
Spencer, who showed a courteous but not too intelligent interest. The two children, May and Agatha, were delighted
by the shining metal and funny clock and knobs.

While they were thus engaged Ben Price sauntered in and
leaned on his elbow, looking casually inside between the railings. He told the teller that he didn't want anything; he
was just waiting for a man he knew.

Suddenly there was a scream or two from the women, and
a commotion. Unperceived by the elders, May, the nine-
year-old girl, in a spirit of play, had shut Agatha in the vault.
She had then shot the bolts and turned the knob of the combination as she had seen Mr. Adams do.

The old banker sprang to the handle and tugged at it for
a moment. "The door can't be opened," he groaned. "The
clock hasn't been wound nor the combination set."

Agatha's mother screamed again, hysterically.

"Hush!" said Mr. Adams, raising his trembling hand.
"All be quiet for a moment. Agatha!" he called as loudly
as he could. "Listen to me." During the following silence
they could just hear the faint sound of the child wildly shrieking in the dark vault in a panic of terror.

"My precious darling!" wailed the mother. "She will die
of fright! Open the door! Oh, break it open! Can't you
men do something?"

"There isn't a man nearer than Little Rock who can open
that door," said Mr. Adams, in a shaky voice. "My God!
Spencer, what shall we do? That child — she can't stand
it long in there. There isn't enough air, and, besides, she'll
go into convulsions from fright."

Agatha's mother, frantic now, beat the door of the vault

with her hands. Somebody wildly suggested dynamite. Annabel turned to Jimmy, her large eyes full of anguish, but not yet despairing. To a woman nothing seems quite impossible to the powers of the man she worships.

" Can't you do something, Ralph — *try*, won't you? "

He looked at her with a queer, soft smile on his lips and in his keen eyes.

" Annabel," he said, " give me that rose you are wearing, will you? "

Hardly believing that she heard him aright, she unpinned the bud from the bosom of her dress, and placed it in his hand. Jimmy stuffed it into his vest-pocket, threw off his coat and pulled up his shirt-sleeves. With that act Ralph D. Spencer passed away and Jimmy Valentine took his place.

" Get away from the door, all of you," he commanded, shortly.

He set his suit-case on the table, and opened it out flat. From that time on he seemed to be unconscious of the presence of any one else. He laid out the shining, queer implements swiftly and orderly, whistling softly to himself as he always did when at work. In a deep silence and immovable, the others watched him as if under a spell.

In a minute Jimmy's pet drill was biting smoothly into the steel door. In ten minutes — breaking his own burglarious record — he threw back the bolts and opened the door.

Agatha, almost collapsed, but safe, was gathered into her mother's arms.

Jimmy Valentine put on his coat, and walked outside the railings toward the front door. As he went he thought he heard a far-away voice that he once knew call " Ralph! " But he never hesitated.

At the door a big man stood somewhat in his way.

" Hello, Ben! " said Jimmy, still with his strange smile.

"Got around at last, have you? Well, let's go. I don't know that it makes much difference, now."

And then Ben Price acted rather strangely.

"Guess you're mistaken, Mr. Spencer," he said. "Don't believe I recognize you. Your buggy's waiting for you, ain't it?"

And Ben Price turned and strolled down the street.

XI

CHERCHEZ LA FEMME

Robbins, reporter for the *Picayune*, and Dumars, of *L'Abeille* — the old French newspaper that has buzzed for nearly a century — were good friends, well proven by years of ups and down together. They were seated where they had a habit of meeting — in the little, Creole-haunted café of Madame Tibault, in Dumaine Street. If you know the place, you will experience a thrill of pleasure in recalling it to mind. It is small and dark, with six little polished tables, at which you may sit and drink the best coffee in New Orleans, and concoctions of absinthe equal to Sazerac's best. Madame Tibault, fat and indulgent, presides at the desk, and takes your money. Nicolette and Mémé, madame's nieces, in charming bib aprons, bring the desirable beverages.

Dumars, with true Creole luxury, was sipping his absinthe, with half-closed eyes, in a swirl of cigarette smoke. Robbins was looking over the morning *Pic.*, detecting, as young reporters will, the gross blunders in the make-up, and the envious blue-pencilling his own stuff had received. This item, in the advertising colums, caught his eye, and with an exclamation of sudden interest he read it aloud to his friend.

Public Auction.— At three o'clock this afternoon there will be sold to the highest bidder all the common property of the Little Sisters of Samaria, at the home of the Sisterhood, in Bonhomme Street. The sale will dispose of the building, ground, and the complete furnishings of the house and chapel, without reserve.

This notice stirred the two friends to a reminiscent talk concerning an episode in their journalistic career that had occurred about two years before. They recalled the incidents, went over the old theories, and discussed it anew from the different perspective time had brought.

There were no other customers in the café. Madame's fine ear had caught the line of their talk, and she came over to their table — for had it not been her lost money — her vanished twenty thousand dollars — that had set the whole matter going?

The three took up the long-abandoned mystery, threshing over the old, dry chaff of it. It was in the chapel of this house of the Little Sisters of Samaria that Robbins and Dumars had stood during that eager, fruitless news search of theirs, and looked upon the gilded statue of the Virgin.

" Thass so, boys," said madame, summing up. " Thass ver' wicked man, M'sieur Morin. Everybody shall be cert' he steal those money I plaze in his hand for keep safe. Yes. He's boun' spend that money, somehow." Madame turned a broad and comprehensive smile upon Dumars. " I ond'stand you, M'sieur Dumars, those day you come ask me fo' tell ev'ything I know 'bout M'sieur Morin. Ah! yes, I know most time when those men lose money you say ' *Cherchez la femme* '— there is somewhere the woman. But not for M'sieur Morin. No, boys. Before he shall die, he is like one saint. You might's well, M'sieur Dumars, go try find those money in those statue of Virgin Mary that M'sieur Morin present at those *p'tite sœurs*, as try find one *femme*."

At Madame Tibault's last words, Robbins started slightly and cast a keen, sidelong glance at Dumars. The Creole sat, unmoved, dreamily watching the spirals of his cigarette smoke.

It was then nine o'clock in the morning and, a few minutes later, the two friends separated, going different ways to their

day's duties. And now follows the brief story of Madame
Tibault's vanished thousands:

New Orleans will readily recall to mind the circumstances
attendant upon the death of Mr. Gaspard Morin, in that
city. Mr. Morin was an artistic goldsmith and jeweller in
the old French Quarter, and a man held in the highest esteem.
He belonged to one of the oldest French families, and was
of some distinction as an antiquary and historian. He was
a bachelor, about fifty years of age. He lived in quiet comfort, at one of those rare old hostelries in Royal Street. He
was found in his rooms, one morning, dead from unknown
causes.

When his affairs came to be looked into, it was found that
he was practically insolvent, his stock of goods and personal
property barely — but nearly enough to free him from cen-
sure — covering his liabilities. Following came the disclosure that he had been intrusted with the sum of twenty thousand dollars by a former upper servant in the Morin family,
one Madame Tibault, which she had received as a legacy from
relatives in France.

The most searching scrutiny by friends and the legal au-
thorities failed to reveal the disposition of the money. It
had vanished, and left no trace. Some weeks before his
death, Mr. Morin had drawn the entire amount, in gold coin,
from the bank where it had been placed while he looked about
(he told Madame Tibault) for a safe investment. Therefore, Mr. Morin's memory seemed doomed to bear the cloud
of dishonesty, while madame was, of course, disconsolate.

Then it was that Robbins and Dumars, representing their
respective journals, began one of those pertinacious private investigations which, of late years, the press has adopted as a
means to glory and the satisfaction of public curiosity.

" *Cherchez la femme,*" said Dumars.

" That's the ticket! " agreed Robbins. " All roads lead to the eternal feminine. We will find the woman."

They exhausted the knowledge of the staff of Mr. Morin's hotel, from the bell-boy down to the proprietor. They gently, but inflexibly, pumped the family of the deceased as far as his cousins twice removed. They artfully sounded the employees of the late jeweller, and dogged his customers for information concerning his habits. Like bloodhounds they traced every step of the supposed defaulter, as nearly as might be, for years along the limited and monotonous paths he had trodden.

At the end of their labours, Mr. Morin stood, an immaculate man. Not one weakness that might be served up as a criminal tendency, not one deviation from the path of rectitude, not even a hint of a predilection for the opposite sex, was found to be placed to his debit. His life had been as regular and austere as a monk's; his habits, simple and unconcealed. Generous, charitable, and a model in propriety, was the verdict of all who knew him.

" What, now? " asked Robbins, fingering his empty notebook.

" *Cherchez la femme*," said Dumars, lighting a cigarette. " Try Lady Bellairs."

This piece of femininity was the race-track favourite of the season. Being feminine, she was erratic in her gaits, and there were a few heavy losers about town who had believed she could be true. The reporters applied for information.

Mr. Morin? Certainly not. He was never even a spectator at the races. Not that kind of a man. Surprised the gentlemen should ask.

" Shall we throw it up? " suggested Robbins, " and let the puzzle department have a try? "

" *Cherchez la femme*," hummed Dumars, reaching for a match. " Try the Little Sisters of What-d'-you-call-'em."

It had developed, during the investigation, that Mr. Morin had held this benevolent order in particular favour. He had .contributed liberally toward its support and had chosen its chapel as his favourite place of private worship. It was said that he went there daily to make his devotions at the altar. Indeed, toward the last of his life his whole mind seemed to have fixed itself upon religious matters, perhaps to the detriment of his worldly affairs.

Thither went Robbins and Dumars, and were admitted through the narrow doorway in the blank stone wall that frowned upon Bonhomme Street. An old woman was sweeping the chapel. She told them that Sister Félicité, the head of the order, was then at prayer at the altar in the alcove. In a few moments she would emerge. Heavy, black curtains screened the alcove. They waited.

Soon the curtains were disturbed, and Sister Félicité came forth. She was tall, tragic, bony, and plain-featured, dressed in the black gown and severe bonnet of the sisterhood.

Robbins, a good rough-and-tumble reporter, but lacking the delicate touch, began to speak.

They represented the press. The lady had, no doubt, heard of the Morin affair. It was necessary, in justice to that gentleman's memory, to probe the mystery of the lost money. It was known that he had come often to this chapel. Any information, now, concerning Mr. Morin's habits, tastes, the friends he had, and so on, would be of value in doing him posthumous justice.

Sister Félicité had heard. Whatever she knew would be willingly told, but it was very little. Monsieur Morin had been a good friend to the order, sometimes contributing as much as a hundred dollars. The sisterhood was an independent one, depending entirely upon private contributions for the means to carry on its charitable work. Mr. Morin had presented the chapel with silver candlesticks and an altar cloth.

He came every day to worship in the chapel, sometimes remaining for an hour. He was a devout Catholic, consecrated to holiness. Yes, and also in the alcove was a statue of the Virgin that he had himself modeled, cast, and presented to the order. Oh, it was cruel to cast a doubt upon so good a man!

Robbins was also profoundly grieved at the imputation. But, until it was found what Mr. Morin had done with Madame Tibault's money, he feared the tongue of slander would not be stilled. Sometimes — in fact, very often — in affairs of the kind there was — er — as the saying goes — er — a lady in the case. In absolute confidence, now — if — perhaps —

Sister Félicité's large eyes regarded him solemnly.

"There was one woman," she said, slowly, "to whom he bowed — to whom he gave his heart."

Robbins fumbled rapturously for his pencil.

"Behold the woman!" said Sister Félicité, suddenly, in deep tones.

She reached a long arm and swept aside the curtain of the alcove. In there was a shrine, lit to a glow of soft colour by the light pouring through a stained-glass window. Within a deep niche in the bare stone wall stood an image of the Virgin Mary, the colour of pure gold.

Dumars, a conventional Catholic, succumbed to the dramatic in the act. He bowed his head for an instant and made the sign of the cross. The somewhat abashed Robbins, murmuring an indistinct apology, backed awkwardly away. Sister Félicité drew back the curtain, and the reporters departed.

On the narrow stone sidewalk of Bonhomme Street, Robbins turned to Dumars, with unworthy sarcasm.

"Well, what next? Churchy law fem?"

"Absinthe," said Dumars.

With the history of the missing money thus partially related, some conjecture may be formed of the sudden idea
that Madame Tibault's words seemed to have suggested to
Robbins's brain.

Was it so wild a surmise — that the religious fanatic had
offered up his wealth — or, rather, Madame Tibault's — in
the shape of a material symbol of his consuming devotion?
· Stranger things have been done in the name of worship. Was
it not possible that the lost thousands were molded into that
lustrous image? That the goldsmith had formed it of the
pure and precious metal, and set it there, through some hope
of a perhaps disordered brain to propitiate the saints and
pave the way to his own selfish glory?

That afternoon, at five minutes to three, Robbins entered
the chapel door of the Little Sisters of Samaria. He saw,
in the dim light, a crowd of perhaps a hundred people gathered to attend the sale. Most of them were members of various religious orders, priests and churchmen, come to purchase the paraphernalia of the chapel, lest they fall into dese-
crating hands. Others were business men and agents come
to bid upon the realty. A clerical-looking brother had volunteered to wield the hammer, bringing to the office of auc-
tioneer the anomaly of choice diction and dignity of manner.

A few of the minor articles were sold, and then two assistants brought forward the image of the Virgin.

Robbins started the bidding at ten dollars. A stout man,
in an ecclesiastical garb, went to fifteen. A voice from another part of the crowd raised to twenty. The three bid
alternately, raising by bids of five, until the offer was fifty
dollars. Then the stout man dropped out, and Robbins, as a
sort of *coup de main*, went to a hundred.

"One hundred and fifty," said the other voice.

"Two hundred," bid Robbins, boldly.

"Two-fifty," called his competitor, promptly.

The reporter hesitated for the space of a lightning flash, estimating how much he could borrow from the boys in the office, and screw from the business manager from his next month's salary.

" Three hundred," he offered.

" Three-fifty," spoke up the other, in a louder voice — a voice that sent Robbins diving suddenly through the crowd in its direction, to catch Dumars, its owner, ferociously by the collar.

" You unconverted idiot!" hissed Robbins, close to his ear —" pool!"

" Agreed!" said Dumars, coolly. " I couldn't raise three hundred and fifty dollars with a search-warrant, but I can stand half. What you come bidding against me for?"

" I thought I was the only fool in the crowd," explained Robbins.

No one else bidding, the statue was knocked down to the syndicate at their last offer. Dumars remained with the prize, while Robbins hurried forth to wring from the resources and credit of both the price. He soon returned with the money, and the two musketeers loaded their precious package into a carriage and drove with it to Dumars's room, in old Chartres Street, nearby. They lugged it, covered with a cloth, up the stairs, and deposited it on a table. A hundred pounds it weighed, if an ounce, and at that estimate, according to their calculation, if their daring theory were correct, it stood there, worth twenty thousand golden dollars.

Robbins removed the covering, and opened his pocket-knife.

" *Sacré!* " muttered Dumars, shuddering. " It is the Mother of Christ. What would you do?"

" Shut up, Judas!" said Robbins, coldly. " It's too late for you to be saved now."

With a firm hand, he chipped a slice from the shoulder of

the image. The cut showed a dull, grayish metal, with a thin coating of gold leaf.

"Lead!" announced Robbins, hurling his knife to the floor —"gilded!"

"To the devil with it!" said Dumars, forgetting his scruples. "I must have a drink."

Together they walked moodily to the café of Madame Tibault, two squares away.

It seemed that madame's mind had been stirred that day to fresh recollections of the past services of the two young men in her behalf.

"You mustn't sit by those table," she interposed, as they were about to drop into their accustomed seats. "Thass so, boys. But no. I mek you come at this room, like my *trés bons amis.* Yes. I goin' mek for you myself one *anisette* and one *café royale* ver' fine. Ah! I lak treat my fren' nize. Yes. Plis come in this way."

Madame led them into the little back room, into which she sometimes invited the especially favoured of her customers. In two comfortable armchairs, by a big window that opened upon the courtyard, she placed them, with a low table between. Bustling hospitably about, she began to prepare the promised refreshments.

It was the first time the reporters had been honoured with admission to the sacred precincts. The room was in dusky twilight, flecked with gleams of the polished, fine woods and burnished glass and metal that the Creoles love. From the little courtyard a tiny fountain sent in an insinuating sound of trickling waters, to which a banana plant by the window kept time with its tremulous leaves.

Robbins, an investigator by nature, sent a curious glance roving about the room. From some barbaric ancestor, madame had inherited a *penchant* for the crude in decoration.

The walls were adorned with cheap lithographs — florid libels upon nature, addressed to the taste of the *bourgeoisie* — birthday cards, garish newspaper supplements, and specimens of art-advertising calculated to reduce the optic nerve to stunned submission. A patch of something unintelligible in the midst of the more candid display puzzled Robbins, and he rose and took a step nearer, to interrogate it at closer range. Then he leaned weakly against the wall, and called out:

"Madame Tibault! Oh, madame! Since when — oh! since when have you been in the habit of papering your walls with five thousand dollar United States four per cent. gold bonds? Tell me — is this a Grimm's fairy tale, or should I consult an oculist?"

At his words, Madame Tibault and Dumars approached.

"H'what you say?" said madame, cheerily. "H'what you say, M'sieur Robbin'? *Bon!* Ah! those nize li'l peezes papier! One tam I think those w'at you call calendair, wiz ze li'l day of mont' below. But, no. Those wall is broke in those plaze, M'sieur Robbin', and I plaze those li'l peezes papier to conceal ze crack. I did think the couleur harm'nize so well with the wall papier. Where I get them from? Ah, yes, I remem' ver' well. One day M'sieur Morin, he come at my houze — thass 'bout one mont' before he shall die — thass 'long 'bout tam he promise fo' inves' those money fo' me. M'sieur Morin, he leave thoze li'l peezes papier in those table, and say ver' much 'bout money thass hard for me to ond'stan. *Mais* I never see those money again. Thass ver' wicked man, M'sieur Morin. H'what you call those peezes papier, M'sieur Robbin'— *bon!*"

Robbins explained.

"There's your twenty thousand dollars, with coupons attached," he said, running his thumb around the edge of the four bonds. " Better get an expert to peel them off for you. Mister Morin was all right. I'm going out to get my ears trimmed."

He dragged Dumars by the arm into the outer room. Madame was screaming for Nicolette and Mémé to come and observe the fortune returned to her by M'sieur Morin, that best of men, that saint in glory.

" Marsy," said Robbins, " I'm going on a jamboree. For three days the esteemed *Pic.* will have to get along without my valuable services. I advise you to join me. Now, that green stuff you drink is no good. It stimulates thought. What we want to do is to forget to remember. I'll introduce you to the only lady in this case that is guaranteed to produce the desired results. Her name is Belle of Kentucky, twelve-year-old Bourbon. In quarts. How does the idea strike you? "

" *Allons!* " said Dumars. *Cherchez la femme.*"

XII

FRIENDS IN SAN ROSARIO

THE west-bound stopped at San Rosario on time at 8.20 A. M. A man with a thick black-leather wallet under his arm left the train and walked rapidly up the main street of the town. There were other passengers who also got off at San Rosario, but they either slouched limberly over to the railroad eating-house or the Silver Dollar saloon, or joined the groups of idlers about the station.

Indecision had no part in the movements of the man with the wallet. He was short in stature, but strongly built, with very light, closely-trimmed hair, smooth, determined face, and aggressive, gold-rimmed nose glasses. He was well dressed in the prevailing Eastern style. His air denoted a quiet but conscious reserve force, if not actual authority.

After walking a distance of three squares he came to the centre of the town's business area. Here another street of importance crossed the main one, forming the hub of San Rosario's life and commerce. Upon one corner stood the post-office. Upon another Rubensky's Clothing Emporium. The other two diagonally opposing corners were occupied by the town's two banks, the First National and the Stockmen's National. Into the First National Bank of San Rosario the newcomer walked, never slowing his brisk step until he stood at the cashier's window. The bank opened for business at nine, and the working force was already assembled, each member preparing his department for the day's business. The cashier was examining the mail when he noticed the stranger standing at his window.

" Bank doesn't open 'til nine," he remarked, curtly, but without feeling. He had had to make that statement so often to early birds since San Rosario adopted city banking hours.

" I am well aware of that," said the other man, in cool, brittle tones. " Will you kindly receive my card? "

The cashier drew the small, spotless parallelogram inside the bars of his wicket, and read:

```
J. F. C. NETTLEWICK

National Bank Examiner
```

" Oh — er — will you walk around inside, Mr.— er — Nettlewick. Your first visit — didn't know your business, of course. Walk right around, please."

The examiner was quickly inside the sacred precincts of the bank, where he was ponderously introduced to each employee in turn by Mr. Edlinger, the cashier — a middle-aged gentleman of deliberation, discretion, and method.

" I was kind of expecting Sam Turner round again, pretty soon," said Mr. Edlinger. " Sam's been examining us now, for about four years. I guess you'll find us all right, though, considering the tightness in business. Not overly much money on hand, but able to stand the storms, sir, stand the storms."

" Mr. Turner and I have been ordered by the Comptroller to exchange districts," said the examiner, in his decisive, formal tones. " He is covering my old territory in Southern Illinois and Indiana. I will take the cash first, please."

Perry Dorsey, the teller, was already arranging his cash on the counter for the examiner's inspection. He knew it was right to a cent, and he had nothing to fear, but he was nervous and flustered. So was every man in the bank. There was something so icy and swift, so impersonal and uncompromising about this man that his very presence seemed an accusation. He looked to be a man who would never make nor overlook an error.

Mr. Nettlewick first seized the currency, and with a rapid, almost juggling motion, counted it by packages. Then he spun the sponge cup toward him and verified the count by bills. His thin, white fingers flew like some expert musician's upon the keys of a piano. He dumped the gold upon the counter with a crash, and the coins whined and sang as they skimmed across the marble slab from the tips of his nimble digits. The air was full of fractional currency when he came to the halves and quarters. He counted the last nickle and dime. He had the scales brought, and he weighed every sack of silver in the vault. He questioned Dorsey concerning each of the cash memoranda — certain checks, charge slips, etc., carried over from the previous day's work — with unimpeachable courtesy, yet with something so mysteriously momentous in his frigid manner, that the teller was reduced to pink cheeks and a stammering tongue.

This newly-imported examiner was so different from Sam Turner. It had been Sam's way to enter the bank with a shout, pass the cigars, and tell the latest stories he had picked up on his rounds. His customary greeting to Dorsey had been, " Hello, Perry! Haven't skipped out with the boodle yet, I see." Turner's way of counting the cash had been different, too. He would finger the packages of bills in a tired kind of way, and then go into the vault and kick over a few sacks of silver, and the thing was done. Halves and quarters and dimes? Not for Sam Turner. " No chicken feed for me," he would say when they were set before him. " I'm not in the agricultural department." But, then, Turner was a Texan, an old friend of the bank's president, and had known Dorsey since he was a baby.

While the examiner was counting the cash, Major Thomas B. Kingman — known to every one as " Major Tom "— the president of the First National, drove up to the side door with his old dun horse and buggy, and came inside. He saw the examiner busy with the money, and, going into the little " pony corral," as he called it, in which his desk was railed off, he began to look over his letters.

Earlier, a little incident had occurred that even the sharp eyes of the examiner had failed to notice. When he had begun his work at the cash counter, Mr. Edlinger had winked significantly at Roy Wilson, the youthful bank messenger, and nodded his head slightly toward the front door. Roy understood, got his hat and walked leisurely out, with his collector's book under his arm. Once outside, he made a bee-line for the Stockmen's National. That bank was also getting ready to open. No customers had, as yet, presented themselves.

" Say, you people! " cried Roy, with the familiarity of youth and long acquaintance, " you want to get a move on you. There's a new bank examiner over at the First, and he's a stem-winder. He's counting nickles on Perry, and he's got the whole outfit bluffed. Mr. Edlinger gave me the tip to let you know."

Mr. Buckley, president of the Stockmen's National — a stout, elderly man, looking like a farmer dressed for Sunday — heard Roy from his private office at the rear and called him.

" Has Major Kingman come down to the bank yet? " he asked of the boy.

" Yes, sir, he was just driving up as I left," said Roy.

" I want you to take him a note. Put it into his own hands as soon as you get back."

Mr. Buckley sat down and began to write.

Roy returned and handed to Major Kingman the envelope

containing the note. The major read it, folded it, and slipped it into his vest pocket. He leaned back in his chair for a few moments as if he were meditating deeply, and then rose and went into the vault. He came out with the bulky, old-fashioned leather note case stamped on the back in gilt letters, " Bills Discounted." In this were the notes due the bank with their attached securities, and the major, in his rough way, dumped the lot upon his desk and began to sort them over.

By this time Nettlewick had finished his count of the cash. His pencil fluttered like a swallow over the sheet of paper on which he had set his figures. He opened his black wallet, which seemed to be also a kind of secret memorandum book, made a few rapid figures in it, wheeled and transfixed Dorsey with the glare of his spectacles. That look seemed to say: " You're safe this time, but —"

" Cash all correct," snapped the examiner. He made a dash for the individual bookkeeper, and, for a few minutes there was a fluttering of ledger leaves and a sailing of balance sheets through the air.

" How often do you balance your pass-books? " he demanded, suddenly.

" Er — once a month," faltered the individual bookkeeper, wondering how many years they would give him.

" All right," said the examiner, turning and charging upon the general bookkeeper, who had the statements of his foreign banks and their reconcilement memoranda ready. Everything there was found to be all right. Then the stub book of the certificates of deposit. Flutter — flutter — zip — zip — check! All right. List of over-drafts, please. Thanks. H'm-m. Unsigned bills of the bank, next. All right.

Then came the cashier's turn, and easy-going Mr. Edlinger rubbed his nose and polished his glasses nervously under the quick fire of questions concerning the circulation, undivided profits, bank real estate, and stock ownership.

Presently Nettlewick was aware of a big man towering above him at his elbow — a man sixty years of age, rugged and hale, with a rough, grizzled beard, a mass of gray hair, and a pair of penetrating blue eyes that confronted the formidable glasses of the examiner without a flicker.

" Er — Major Kingman, our president — er — Mr. Nettlewick," said the cashier.

Two men of very different types shook hands. One was a finished product of the world of straight lines, conventional methods, and formal affairs. The other was something freer, wider and nearer to nature. Tom Kingman had not been cut to any pattern. He had been mule-driver, cowboy, ranger, soldier, sheriff, prospector, and cattleman. Now, when he was bank president. his old comrades from the prairies, of the saddle, tent, and trail found no change in him. He had made his fortune when Texas cattle were at the high tide of value, and had organized the First National Bank of San Rosario. In spite of his largeness of heart and sometimes unwise generosity toward his old friends, the bank had prospered, for Major Tom Kingman knew men as well as he knew cattle. Of late years the cattle business had known a depression, and the major's bank was one of the few whose losses had not been great.

" And now," said the examiner, briskly, pulling out his watch, " the last thing is the loans. We will take them up now, if you please."

He had gone through the First National at almost record-breaking speed — but thoroughly, as he did everything. The running order of the bank was smooth and clean, and that had facilitated his work. There was but one other bank in the town. He received from the Government a fee of twenty-five dollars for each bank that he examined. He should be able to go over those loans and discounts in half an hour. If so, he could examine the other bank immediately afterward, and catch the 11.45, the only other train that day in the direction he was working. Otherwise, he would have to spend the night and Sunday in this uninteresting Western town. That was why Mr. Nettlewick was rushing matters.

"Come with me, sir," said Major Kingman, in his deep voice, that united the Southern drawl with the rhythmic twang of the West; "We will go over them together. Nobody in the bank knows those notes as I do. Some of 'em are a little wobbly on their legs, and some are mavericks without extra many brands on their backs, but they'll most all pay out at the round-up."

The two sat down at the president's desk. First, the examiner went through the notes at lightning speed, and added up their total, finding it to agree with the amount of loans carried on the book of daily balances. Next, he took up the larger loans, inquiring scrupulously into the condition of their indorsers or securities. The new examiner's mind seemed to course and turn and make unexpected dashes hither and thither like a bloodhound seeking a trail. Finally he pushed aside all the notes except a few, which he arranged in a neat pile before him, and began a dry, formal little speech.

"I find, sir, the condition of your bank to be very good, considering the poor crops and the depression in the cattle interests of your state. The clerical work seems to be done accurately and punctually. Your past-due paper is moderate in amount, and promises only a small loss. I would recommend the calling in of your large loans, and the making of only sixty and ninety day or call loans until general business revives. And now, there is one thing more, and I will have finished with the bank. Here are six notes aggregating something like $40,000. They are secured, according to their faces, by various stocks, bonds, shares, etc. to the value of $70,000. Those securities are missing from the notes to which they should be attached. I suppose you have them in the safe or vault. You will permit me to examine them."

Major Tom's light-blue eyes turned unflinchingly toward the examiner.

" No, sir," he said, in a low but steady tone; " those securities are neither in the safe nor the vault. I have taken them. You may hold me personally responsible for their absence."

Nettlewick felt a slight thrill. He had not expected this. He had struck a momentous trail when the hunt was drawing to a close.

" Ah! " said the examiner. He waited a moment, and then continued: " May I ask you to explain more definitely? "

" The securities were taken by me," repeated the major. " It was not for my own use, but to save an old friend in trouble. Come in here, sir, and we'll talk it over."

He led the examiner into the bank's private office at the rear, and closed the door. There was a desk, and a table, and half-a-dozen leather-covered chairs. On the wall was the mounted head of a Texas steer with horns five feet from tip to tip. Opposite hung the major's old cavalry saber that he had carried at Shiloh and Fort Pillow.

Placing a chair for Nettlewick, the major seated himself by the window, from which he could see the post-office and the carved limestone front of the Stockman's National. He did not speak at once, and Nettlewick felt, perhaps, that the ice should be broken by something so near its own temperature as the voice of official warning.

" Your statement," he began, " since you have failed to modify it, amounts, as you must know, to a very serious thing. You are aware, also, of what my duty must compel me to do. I shall have to go before the United States Commissioner and make —"

" I know, I know," said Major Tom, with a wave of his

hand. "You don't suppose I'd run a bank without being posted on national banking laws and the revised statutes! Do your duty. I'm not asking any favours. But, I spoke of my friend. I did want you to hear me tell you about Bob."

Nettlewick settled himself in his chair. There would be no leaving San Rosario for him that day. He would have to telegraph to the Comptroller of the Currency; he would have to swear out a warrant before the United States Commissioner for the arrest of Major Kingman; perhaps he would be ordered to close the bank on account of the loss of the securities. It was not the first crime the examiner had unearthed. Once or twice the terrible upheaval of human emotions that his investigations had loosed had almost caused a ripple in his official calm. He had seen bank men kneel and plead and cry like women for a chance — an hour's time — the overlooking of a single error. One cashier had shot himself at his desk before him. None of them had taken it with the dignity and coolness of this stern old Westerner. Nettlewick felt that he owed it to him at least to listen if he wished to talk. With his elbow on the arm of his chair, and his square chin resting upon the fingers of his right hand, the bank examiner waited to hear the confession of the president of the First National Bank of San Rosario.

"When a man's your friend," began Major Tom, somewhat didactically, "for forty years, and tried by water, fire, earth, and cyclones, when you can do him a little favour you feel like doing it."

("Embezzle for him $70,000 worth of securities," thought the examiner.)

"We were cowboys together, Bob and I," continued the major, speaking slowly, and deliberately, and musingly, as if his thoughts were rather with the past than the critical present, "and we prospected together for gold and silver over Arizona, New Mexico, and a good part of California.

We were both in the war of 'sixty-one, but in different com-
mands. We've fought Indians and horse thieves side by side;
we've starved for weeks in a cabin in the Arizona mountains,
buried twenty feet deep in snow; we've ridden herd together
when the wind blew so hard the lightning couldn't strike —
well, Bob and I have been through some rough spells since
the first time we met in the branding camp of the old Anchor-
Bar ranch. And during that time we've found it necessary
more than once to help each other out of tight places. In
those days it was expected of a man to stick to his friend,
and he didn't ask any credit for it. Probably next day you'd
need him to get at your back and help stand off a band of
Apaches, or put a tourniquet on your leg above a rattlesnake
bite and ride for whisky. So, after all, it was give and take,
and if you didn't stand square with your pardner, why, you
might be shy one when you needed him. But Bob was a man who
was willing to go further than that. He never played a limit.

"Twenty years ago I was sheriff of this county, and I
made Bob my chief deputy. That was before the boom in
cattle when we both made our stake. I was sheriff and collector, and it was a big thing for me then. I was married,
and we had a boy and a girl — a four and a six year old.
There was a comfortable house next to the courthouse,
furnished by the county, rent free, and I was saving some
money. Bob did most of the office work. Both of us had seen
rough times and plenty of rustling and danger, and I tell you
it was great to hear the rain and the sleet dashing against
the windows of nights, and be warm and safe and comfortable, and know you could get up in the morning and be
shaved and have folks call you 'mister.' And then, I had
the finest wife and kids that ever struck the range, and my
old friend with me enjoying the first fruits of prosperity and
white shirts, and I guess I was happy. Yes, I was happy
about that time."

The major sighed and glanced casually out of the window. The bank examiner changed his position, and leaned his chin upon his other hand.

"One winter," continued the major, "the money for the county taxes came pouring in so fast that I didn't have time to take the stuff to the bank for a week. I just shoved the checks into a cigar box and the money into a sack, and locked them in the big safe that belonged in the sheriff's office.

"I had been overworked that week, and was about sick, anyway. My nerves were out of order, and my sleep at night didn't seem to rest me. The doctor had some scientific name for it, and I was taking medicine. And so, added to the rest, I went to bed at night with that money on my mind. Not that there was much need of being worried, for the safe was a good one, and nobody but Bob and I knew the combination. On Friday night there was about $6,500 in cash in the bag. On Saturday morning I went to the office as usual. The safe was locked, and Bob was writing at his desk. I opened the safe, and the money was gone. I called Bob, and roused everybody in the court-house to announce the robbery. It struck me that Bob took it pretty quiet, considering how much it reflected upon both him and me.

"Two days went by and we never got a clew. It couldn't have been burglars, for the safe had been opened by the combination in the proper way. People must have begun to talk, for one afternoon in comes Alice — that's my wife — and the boy and girl, and Alice stamps her foot, and her eyes flash, and she cries out, 'The lying wretches — Tom, Tom!' and I catch her in a faint, and bring her 'round little by little, and she lays her head down and cries and cries for the first time since she took Tom Kingman's name and fortunes. And Jack and Zilla — the youngsters — they were always wild as tiger cubs to rush at Bob and climb all over him whenever they were allowed to come to the court-house — they stood and kicked their little shoes, and herded together like scared partridges. They were having their first trip down into the shadows of life. Bob was working at his desk, and he got up and went out without a word. The grand jury was in session then, and the next morning Bob went before them and confessed that he stole the money. He said he lost it in a poker game. In fifteen minutes they had found a true bill and sent me the warrant to arrest the man with whom I'd been closer than a thousand brothers for many a year.

"I did it, and then I said to Bob, pointing: 'There's my house, and here's my office, and up there's Maine, and out that way is California, and over there is Florida — and that's your range 'til court meets. You're in my charge, and I take the responsibility. You be here when you're wanted.'

"'Thanks, Tom,' he said, kind of carelessly; 'I was sort of hoping you wouldn't lock me up. Court meets next Monday, so, if you don't object, I'll just loaf around the office until then. I've got one favour to ask, if it isn't too much. If you'd let the kids come out in the yard once in a while and have a romp I'd like it.'

"'Why not?' I answered him. 'They're welcome, and so are you. And come to my house, the same as ever.' You see, Mr. Nettlewick, you can't make a friend of a thief, but neither can you make a thief of a friend, all at once."

The examiner made no answer. At that moment was heard the shrill whistle of a locomotive pulling into the depot. That was the train on the little, narrow-gauge road that struck into San Rosario from the south. The major cocked his ear and listened for a moment, and looked at his watch. The narrow-gauge was in on time — 10.35. The major continued:

"So Bob hung around the office, reading the papers and smoking. I put another deputy to work in his place, and, after a while, the first excitement of the case wore off.

"One day when we were alone in the office Bob came over

to where I was sitting. He was looking sort of grim and blue — the same look he used to get when he'd been up watching for Indians all night or herd-riding.

"'Tom,' says he, 'it's harder than standing off redskins; it's harder than lying in the lava desert forty miles from water; but I'm going to stick it out to the end. You know that's been my style. But if you'd tip me the smallest kind of a sign — if you'd just say, "Bob I understand," why, it would make it lots easier.'

"I was surprised. 'I don't know what you mean, Bob,' I said. 'Of course, you know that I'd do anything under the sun to help you that I could. But you've got me guessing.'

"'All right, Tom,' was all he said, and he went back to his newspaper and lit another cigar.

"It was the night before court met when I found out what he meant. I went to bed that night with that same old, light-headed, nervous feeling come back upon me. I dropped off to sleep about midnight. When I awoke I was standing half dressed in one of the court-house corridors. Bob was holding one of my arms, our family doctor the other, and Alice was shaking me and half crying. She had sent for the doctor without my knowing it, and when he came they had found me out of bed and missing, and had begun a search.

"'Sleep-walking,' said the doctor.

"All of us went back to the house, and the doctor told us some remarkable stories about the strange things people had done while in that condition. I was feeling rather chilly after my trip out, and, as my wife was out of the room at the time, I pulled open the door of an old wardrobe that stood in the room and dragged out a big quilt I had seen in there. With it tumbled out the bag of money for stealing which Bob was to be tried — and convicted — in the morning.

"'How the jumping rattlesnakes did that get there?' I

yelled, and all hands must have seen how surprised I was. Bob knew in a flash.

"'You darned old snoozer,' he said, with the old-time look on his face, 'I saw you put it there. I watched you open the safe and take it out, and I followed you. I looked through the window and saw you hide it in that wardrobe.'

"'Then, you blankety-blank, flop-eared, sheep-headed coyote, what did you say you took it, for?'

"'Because,' said Bob, simply, 'I didn't know you were asleep.'

"I saw him glance toward the door of the room where Jack and Zilla were, and I knew then what it meant to be a man's friend from Bob's point of view."

Major Tom paused, and again directed his glance out of the window. He saw some one in the Stockmen's National Bank reach and draw a yellow shade down the whole length of its plate-glass, big front window, although the position of the sun did not seem to warrant such a defensive movement against its rays.

Nettlewick sat up straight in his chair. He had listened patiently, but without consuming interest, to the major's story. It had impressed him as irrelevant to the situation, and it could certainly have no effect upon the consequences. Those Western people, he thought, had an exaggerated sentimentality. They were not business-like. They needed to be protected from their friends. Evidently the major had concluded. And what he had said amounted to nothing.

"May I ask," said the examiner, "if you have anything further to say that bears directly upon the question of those abstracted securities?"

"Abstracted securities, sir!" Major Tom turned suddenly in his chair, his blue eyes flashing upon the examiner. "What do you mean, sir?"

He drew from his coat pocket a batch of folded papers

held together by a rubber band, tossed them into Nettlewick's hands, and rose to his feet.

" You'll find those securities there, sir, every stock, bond, and share of 'em. I took them from the notes while you were counting the cash. Examine and compare them for yourself."

The major led the way back into the banking room. The examiner, astounded, perplexed, nettled, at sea, followed. He felt that he had been made the victim of something that was not exactly a hoax, but that left him in the shoes of one who had been played upon, used, and then discarded, without even an inkling of the game. Perhaps, also, his official position had been irreverently juggled with. But there was nothing he could take hold of. An official report of the matter would be an absurdity. And, somehow, he felt that he would never know anything more about the matter than he did then.

Frigidly, mechanically, Nettlewick examined the securities, found them to tally with the notes, gathered his black wallet, and rose to depart.

" I will say," he protested, turning the indignant glare of his glasses upon Major Kingman, " that your statements — your misleading statements, which you have not condescended to explain — do not appear to be quite the thing, regarded either as business or humour. I do not understand such motives or actions."

Major Tom looked down at him serenely and not unkindly.

" Son," he said, " there are plenty of things in the chaparral, and on the prairies, and up the cañons that you don't understand. But I want to thank you for listening to a garrulous old man's prosy story. We old Texans love to talk about our adventures and our old comrades, and the home folks have long ago learned to run when we begin with ' Once upon a time,' so we have to spin our yarns to the stranger within our gates."

The major smiled, but the examiner only bowed coldly,

and abruptly quitted the bank. They saw him travel diagonally across the street in a straight line and enter the Stockmen's National Bank.

Major Tom sat down at his desk, and drew from his vest pocket the note Roy had given him. He had read it once, but hurriedly, and now, with something like a twinkle in his eyes, he read it again. These were the words he read:

DEAR TOM:

I hear there's one of Uncle Sam's grayhound's going through you, and that means that we'll catch him inside of a couple of hours, maybe. Now, I want you to do something for me. We've got just $2,200 in the bank, and the law requires that we have $20,000. I let Ross and Fisher have $18,000 late yesterday afternoon to buy up that Gibson bunch of cattle. They'll realize $40,000 in less than thirty days on the transaction, but that won't make my cash on hand look any prettier to that bank examiner. Now, I can't show him those notes, for they're just plain notes of hand without any security in sight, but you know very well that Pink Ross and Jim Fisher are two of the finest white men God ever made, and they'll do the square thing. You remember Jim Fisher—he was the one who shot that faro dealer in El Paso. I wired Sam Bradshaw's bank to send me $20,000, and it will get in on the narrow-gauge at 10.35. You can't let a bank examiner in to count $2,200 and close your doors. Tom, you hold that examiner. Hold him. Hold him if you have to rope him and sit on his head. Watch our front window after the narrow-gauge gets in, and when we've got the cash inside we'll pull down the shade for a signal. Don't turn him loose till then. I'm counting on you, Tom.

Your Old Pard,
BOB BUCKLEY,
Prest. Stockmen's National.

The major began to tear the note into small pieces and throw them into his waste basket. He gave a satisfied little chuckle as he did so.

"Confounded old reckless cowpuncher!" he growled, contentedly, "that pays him some on account for what he tried to do for me in the sheriff's office twenty years ago."

XIII

THE FOURTH IN SALVADOR

ON a summer's day, while the city was rocking with the din and red uproar of patriotism, Billy Casparis told me this story.

In his way, Billy is Ulysses, Jr. Like Satan, he comes from going to and fro upon the earth and walking up and down in it. To-morrow morning while you are cracking your breakfast egg he may be off with his little alligator grip to boom a town site in the middle of Lake Okeechobee or to trade horses with the Patagonians.

We sat at a little, round table, and between us were glasses holding big lumps of ice, and above us leaned an artificial palm. And because our scene was set with the properties of the one they recalled to his mind, Billy was stirred to narrative.

"It reminds me," said he, "of a Fourth I helped to celebrate down in Salvador. 'Twas while I was running an ice factory down there, after I unloaded that silver mine I had in Colorado. I had what they called a 'conditional concession.' They made me put up a thousand dollars cash forfeit that I would make ice continuously for six months. If I did that I could draw down my ante. If I failed to do so the government took the pot. So the inspectors kept dropping in, trying to catch me without the goods.

"One day when the thermometer was at 110, the clock at half-past one, and the calendar at July third, two of the little, brown, oily nosers in red trousers slid in to make an inspection. Now, the factory hadn't turned out a pound of ice in three

171

weeks, for a couple of reasons. The Salvador heathen wouldn't buy it; they said it made things cold they put it in. And I couldn't make any more, because I was broke. All I was holding on for was to get down my thousand so I could leave the country. The six months would be up on the sixth of July.

"Well, I showed 'em all the ice I had. I raised the lid of a darkish vat, and there was an elegant 100-pound block of ice, beautiful and convincing to the eye. I was about to close down the lid again when one of those brunette sleuths flops down on his red knees and lays a slanderous and violent hand on my guarantee of good faith. And in two minutes more they had dragged out on the floor that fine chunk of molded glass that had cost me fifty dollars to have shipped down from Frisco.

"' Ice-y? ' says the fellow that played me the dishonourable trick; ' verree warm ice-y. Yes. The day is that hot, señor. Yes. Maybeso it is of desirableness to leave him out to get the cool. Yes.'

"' Yes,' says I, ' yes,' for I knew they had me. ' Touching's believing, ain't it, boys? Yes. Now there's some might say the seats of your trousers are sky blue, but 'tis my opinion they are red. Let's apply the tests of the laying on of hands and feet.' And so I hoisted both those inspectors out the door on the toe of my shoe, and sat down to cool off on my block of disreputable glass.

"And, as I live without oats, while I sat there, homesick for money and without a cent to my ambition, there came on the breeze the most beautiful smell my nose had entered for a year. God knows where it came from in that backyard of a country — it was a bouquet of soaked lemon peel, cigar stumps, and stale beer — exactly the smell of Goldbrick Charley's place on Fourteenth Street where I used to play pinochle of afternoons with the third-rate actors. And that smell drove my troubles through me and clinched 'em at the back. I began to long for my country and feel sentiments about it; and I said words about Salvador that you wouldn't think could come legitimate out of an ice factory.

"And while I was sitting there, down through the blazing sunshine in his clean, white clothes comes Maximilian Jones, an American interested in rubber and rosewood.

"'Great carrambos!' says I, when he stepped in, for I was in a bad temper, 'didn't I have catastrophes enough? I know what you want. You want to tell me that story again about Johnny Ammiger and the widow on the train. You've told it nine times already this month.'

"'It must be the heat,' says Jones, stopping in the door, amazed. 'Poor Billy. He's got bugs. Sitting on ice, and calling his best friends pseudonyms. Hi! — *muchacho!*' Jones called my force of employees, who was sitting in the sun, playing with his toes, and told him to put on his trousers and run for the doctor.

"'Come back,' says I. 'Sit down, Maxy, and forget it. 'Tis not ice you see, nor a lunatic upon it. 'Tis only an exile full of homesickness sitting on a lump of glass that's just cost him a thousand dollars. Now, what was it Johnny said to the widow first? I'd like to hear it again, Maxy — honest. Don't mind what I said.'

"Maximilian Jones and I sat down and talked. He was about as sick of the country as I was, for the grafters were squeezing him for half the profits of his rosewood and rubber. Down in the bottom of a tank of water I had a dozen bottles of sticky Frisco beer; and I fished these up, and we fell to talking about home and the flag and Hail Columbia and home-fried potatoes; and the drivel we contributed would have sickened any man enjoying those blessings. But at that time we were out of 'em. You can't appreciate home till you've left it, money till it's spent, your wife till she's joined a woman's club, nor Old Glory till you see it hanging on a broomstick on the shanty of a consul in a foreign town.

"And sitting there me and Maximilian Jones, scratching at our prickly heat and kicking at the lizards on the floor, became afflicted with a dose of patriotism and affection for our country. There was me, Billy Casparis, reduced from a capitalist to a pauper by over-addiction to my glass (in the lump), declares my troubles off for the present and myself to be an uncrowned sovereign of the greatest country on earth. And Maximilian Jones pours out whole drug stores of his wrath on oligarchies and potentates in red trousers and calico shoes. And we issues a declaration of interference in which we guarantee that the fourth day of July shall be celebrated in Salvador with all the kinds of salutes, explosions, honours of war, oratory, and liquids known to tradition. Yes, neither me nor Jones breathed with soul so dead. There shall be rucuses in Salvador, we say, and the monkeys had better climb the tallest cocoanut trees and the fire department get out its red sashes and two tin buckets.

"About this time into the factory steps a native man incriminated by the name of General Mary Esperanza Dingo. He was some pumpkin both in politics and colour, and the friend of me and Jones. He was full of politeness and a kind of intelligence, having picked up the latter and managed to preserve the former during a two years' residence in Philadelphia studying medicine. For a Salvadorian he was not such a calamitous little man, though he always would play jack, queen, king, ace, deuce for a straight.

"General Mary sits with us and has a bottle. While he was in the States he had acquired a synopsis of the English language and the art of admiring our institutions. By and by the General gets up and tiptoes to the doors and windows and other stage entrances, remarking 'Hist!' at each one. They all do that in Salvador before they ask for a drink of water or the time of day, being conspirators from the cradle and matinee idols by proclamation.

" ' Hist! ' says General Dingo again, and then he lays his chest on the table quite like Gaspard the Miser. ' Good friends, señores, to-morrow will be the great day of Liberty and Independence. The hearts of Americans and Salvadorians should beat together. Of your history and your great Washington I know. Is it not so? '

" Now, me and Jones thought that nice of the General to remember when the Fourth came. It made us feel good. He must have heard the news going round in Philadelphia about that disturbance we had with England.

" ' Yes,' says me and Maxy together, ' we knew it. We were talking about it when you came in. And you can bet your bottom concession that there'll be fuss and feathers in the air to-morrow. We are few in numbers, but the welkin may as well reach out to push the button, for it's got to ring.'

" ' I, too, shall assist,' says the General, thumping his collar-bone. ' I, too, am on the side of Liberty. Noble Americans, we will make the day one to be never forgotten.'

" ' For us American whisky,' says Jones —' none of your Scotch smoke or anisada or Three Star Hennessey to-morrow. We'll borrow the consul's flag; old man Billfinger shall make orations, and we'll have a barbecue on the plaza.'

" ' Fireworks,' says I, ' will be scarce; but we'll have all the cartridges in the shops for our guns. I've got two navy sixes I brought from Denver.'

" ' There is one cannon,' said the General; ' one big cannon that will go " BOOM! " ' And three hundred men with rifles to shoot.'

" ' Oh, say! ' says Jones, ' Generalissimo, you're the real silk elastic. We'll make it a joint international celebration. Please, General, get a white horse and a blue sash and be grand marshal.'

" ' With my sword,' says the General, rolling his eyes. ' I shall ride at the head of the brave men who gather in the name of Liberty.'

" ' And you might,' we suggest ' see the commandante and advise him that we are going to prize things up a bit. We Americans, you know, are accustomed to using municipal regulations for gun wadding when we line up to help the eagle scream. He might suspend the rules for one day. We don't want to get in the calaboose for spanking his soldiers if they get in our way, do you see? '

" ' Hist!' says General Mary. ' The comandant is with us, heart and soul. He will aid us. He is one of us.'

" We made all the arrangements that afternoon. There was a buck coon from Georgia in Salvador who had drifted down there from a busted-up coloured colony that had been started on some possumless land in Mexico. As soon as he heard us say ' barbecue ' he wept for joy and groveled on the ground. He dug his trench on the plaza, and got half a beef on the coals for an all-night roast. Me and Maxy went to see the rest of the Americans in the town and they all sizzled like a seidlitz with joy at the idea of solemnizing an old-time Fourth.

" There were six of us all together — Martin Dillard, a coffee planter; Henry Barnes, a railroad man; old man Bill-finger, an educated tintype taker; me and Jonesy, and Jerry, the boss of the barbecue. There was also an Englishman in town named Sterrett, who was there to write a book on Domestic Architecture of the Insect World. We felt some bashfulness about inviting a Britisher to help crow over his own country, but we decided to risk it, out of our personal regard for him.

" We found Sterrett in pajamas working at his manuscript with a bottle of brandy for a paper weight.

" ' Englishman,' says Jones, ' let us interrupt your disquisition on bug houses for a moment. To-morrow is the Fourth of July. We don't want to hurt your feelings, but we're going to commemorate the day when we licked you by a little refined debauchery and nonsense — something that can be heard above five miles off. If you are broad-gauged enough to taste whisky at your own wake, we'd be pleased to have you join us.'

"'Do you know,' says Sterrett, setting his glasses on his nose, 'I like your cheek in asking me if I'll join you; blast me if I don't. You might have known I would, without asking. Not as a traitor to my own country, but for the intrinsic joy of a blooming row.'

"On the morning of the Fourth I woke up in that old shanty of an ice factory feeling sore. I looked around at the wreck of all I possessed, and my heart was full of bile. From where I lay on my cot I could look through the window and see the consul's old ragged Stars and Stripes hanging over his shack. 'You're all kinds of a fool, Billy Casparis,' I says to myself; 'and of all your crimes against sense it does look like this idea of celebrating the Fourth should receive the award of demerit. Your business is busted up, your thousand dollars is gone into the kitty of this corrupt country on that last bluff you made, you've got just fifteen Chili dollars left, worth forty-six cents each at bedtime last night and steadily going down. To-day you'll blow in your last cent hurrahing for that flag, and to-morrow you'll be living on bananas from the stalk and screwing your drinks out of your friends. What's the flag done for you? While you were under it you worked for what you got. You wore your finger nails down skinning suckers, and salting mines, and driving bears and alligators off your town lot additions. How much does patriotism count for on deposit when the little man with the green eye-shade in the savings-bank adds up your book? Suppose you were to get pinched over here in this irreligious country

for some little crime or other, and appealed to your country
for protection — what would it do for you? Turn your appeal over to a committee of one railroad man, an army officer,
a member of each labour union, and a coloured man to in-
vestigate whether any of your ancestors were ever related to
a cousin of Mark Hanna, and then file the papers in the
Smithsonian Institution until after the next election. That's
the kind of a sidetrack the Stars and Stripes would switch
you onto.'

"You can see that I was feeling like an indigo plant; but
after I washed my face in some cool water, and got out my
navys and ammunition, and started up to the Saloon of the
Immaculate Saints where we were to meet, I felt better. And
when I saw those other American boys come swaggering into
the trysting place — cool, easy, conspicuous fellows, ready to
risk any kind of a one-card draw, or to fight grizzlies, fire, or
extradition, I began to feel glad I was one of 'em. So, I
says to myself again: 'Billy, you've got fifteen dollars and
a country left this morning — blow in the dollars and blow
up the town as an American gentleman should on Independence Day.'

"It is my recollection that we began the day along conventional lines. The six of us — for Sterrett was along —
made progress among the cantinas, divesting the bars as we
went of all strong drink bearing American labels. We kept
informing the atmosphere as to the glory and preëminence of
the United States and its ability to subdue, outjump, and
eradicate the other nations of the earth. And, as the find-
ings of American labels grew more plentiful, we became more
contaminated with patriotism. Maximilian Jones hopes that
our late foe, Mr. Sterrett, will not take offense at our enthusiasm. He sets down his bottle and shakes Sterrett's hand.
'As white man to white man,' says he, 'denude our uproar of
the slightest taint of personality. Excuse us for Bunker Hill,

Patrick Henry, and Waldorf Astor, and such grievances as might lie between us as nations.'

" ' Fellow hoodlums,' says Sterrett, ' on behalf of the Queen I ask you to cheese it. It is an honour to be a guest at disturbing the peace under the American flag. Let us chant the passionate strains of " Yankee Doodle " while the señor behind the bar mitigates the occasion with another round of cochineal and aqua fortis.'

" Old Man Billfinger, being charged with a kind of rhetoric, makes speeches every time we stop. We explained to such citizens as we happened to step on that we were celebrating the dawn of our own private brand of liberty, and to please enter such inhumanities as we might commit on the list of unavoidable casualties.

" About eleven o'clock our bulletins read: ' A considerable rise in temperature, accompanied by thirst and other alarming symptoms.' We hooked arms and stretched our line across the narrow streets, all of us armed with Winchesters and navys for purposes of noise and without malice. We stopped on a street corner and fired a dozen or so rounds, and began a serial assortment of United States whoops and yells, probably the first ever heard in that town.

" When we made that noise things began to liven up. We heard a pattering up a side street, and here came General Mary Esperanza Dingo on a white horse with a couple of hundred brown boys following him in red undershirts and bare feet, dragging guns ten feet long. Jones and me had forgot all about General Mary and his promise to help us celebrate. We fired another salute and gave another yell, while the General shook hands with us and waved his sword.

" ' Oh, General,' shouts Jones, ' this is great. This will be a real pleasure to the eagle. Get down and have a drink.'

" ' Drink? ' says the general. ' No. There is no time to drink. *Viva la Libertad!* '

" ' Don't forget *E Pluribus Unum!* ' says Henry Barnes.

" ' *Viva* it good and strong,' says I. ' Likewise, *viva* George Washington. God save the Union, and,' I says, bowing to Sterrett, ' don't discard the Queen.'

" ' Thanks,' says Sterrett. ' The next round's mine. All in to the bar. Army, too.'

" But we were deprived of Sterrett's treat by a lot of gunshots several squares away, which General Dingo seemed to think he ought to look after. He spurred his old white plug up that way, and the soldiers scuttled along after him.

" ' Mary is a real tropical bird,' says Jones. ' He's turned out the Infantry to help us do honour to the Fourth. We'll get that cannon he spoke of after a while and fire some window-breakers with it. But just now I want some of that barbecued beef. Let us on to the plaza.'

" There we found the meat gloriously done, and Jerry waiting, anxious. We sat around on the grass, and got hunks of it on our tin plates. Maximilian Jones, always made tenderhearted by drink, cried some because George Washington couldn't be there to enjoy the day. ' There was a man I love, Billy,' he says, weeping on my shoulder. ' Poor George! To think he's gone, and missed the fireworks. A little more salt, please, Jerry.'

" From what we could hear, General Dingo seemed to be kindly contributing some noise while we feasted. There were guns going off around town, and pretty soon we heard that cannon go ' BOOM!' just as he said it would. And then men began to skim along the edge of the plaza, dodging in among the orange trees and houses. We certainly had things stirred up in Salvador. We felt proud of the occasion and grateful to General Dingo. Sterrett was about to take a bite off a juicy piece of rib when a bullet took it away from his mouth.

" ' Somebody's celebrating with ball cartridges,' says he,

reaching for another piece. 'Little over-zealous for a non-resident patriot, isn't it?'"

"'Don't mind it,' I says to him. ''Twas an accident. They happen, you know, on the Fourth. After one reading of the Declaration of Independence in New York I've known the S. R. O. sign to be hung out at all the hospitals and police stations.'

" But then Jerry gives a howl and jumps up with one hand clapped to the back of his leg where another bullet has acted over-zealous. And then comes a quantity of yells, and round a corner and across the plaza gallops General Mary Esperanza Dingo embracing the neck of his horse, with his men running behind him, mostly dropping their guns by way of discharging ballast. And chasing 'em all is a company of feverish little warriors wearing blue trousers and caps.

"'Assistance, amigos,' the General shouts, trying to stop his horse. 'Assistance, in the name of Liberty!'

"'That's the Compañía Azul, the President's bodyguard,' says Jones. 'What a shame! They've jumped on poor old Mary just because he was helping us to celebrate. Come on, boys, it's our Fourth; — do we let that little squad of A. D. T's break it up?'

"'I vote No,' says Martin Dillard, gathering his Winchester. 'It's the privilege of an American citizen to drink, drill, dress up, and be dreadful on the Fourth of July, no matter whose country he's in.'

"'Fellow citizens!' says old man Billfinger, 'In the darkest hour of Freedom's birth, when our brave forefathers promulgated the principles of undying liberty, they never expected that a bunch of blue jays like that should be allowed to bust up an anniversary. Let us preserve and protect the Constitution.'

" We made it unanimous, and then we gathered our guns and assaulted the blue troops in force. We fired over their

heads, and then charged 'em with a yell, and they broke and
ran. We were irritated at having our barbecue disturbed, and
we chased 'em a quarter of a mile. Some of 'em we caught
and kicked hard. The General rallied his troops and joined
in the chase. Finally they scattered in a thick banana grove,
and we couldn't flush a single one. So we sat down and rested.

"If I were to be put, severe, through the third degree, I
wouldn't be able to tell much about the rest of the day. I
mind that we pervaded the town considerable, calling upon
the people to bring out more armies for us to destroy. I remember seeing a crowd somewhere, and a tall man that wasn't
Billfinger making a Fourth of July speech from a balcony.
And that was about all.

"Somebody must have hauled the old ice factory up to
where I was, and put it around me, for there's where I was
when I woke up the next morning. As soon as I could recollect my name and address I got up and held an inquest. My
last cent was gone. I was all in.

"And then a neat black carriage drives to the door, and out
steps General Dingo and a bay man in a silk hat and tan shoes.

"'Yes,' says I to myself, 'I see it now. You're the Chief
de Policeos and High Lord Chamberlain of the Calaboosum:
and you want Billy Casparis for excess of patriotism and
assault with intent. All right. Might as well be in jail, anyhow.'

"But it seems that General Mary is smiling, and the bay
man shakes my hand, and speaks in the American dialect.

"'General Dingo has informed me, Señor Casparis, of
your gallant service in our cause. I desire to thank you with
my person. The bravery of you and the other señores Americanos turned the struggle for liberty in our favour. Our party
triumphed. The terrible battle will live forever in history.'

"'Battle?' says I; 'what battle?' and I ran my mind
back along history, trying to think.

"'Señor Casparis is modest,' says General Dingo. 'He led his brave compadres into the thickest of the fearful conflict. Yes. Without their aid the revolution would have failed.'

"'Why, now,' says I, 'don't tell me there was a revolution yesterday. That was only a Fourth of —'

"But right there I abbreviated. It seemed to me it might be best.

"'After the terrible struggle,' says the bay man, 'President Bolano was forced to fly. To-day Caballo is President by proclamation. Ah, yes. Beneath the new administration I am the head of the Department of Mercantile Concessions. On my file I find one report, Señor Casparis, that you have not made ice in accord with your contract.' And here the bay man smiles at me, 'cute.

"'Oh, well,' says I, 'I guess the report's straight. I know they caught me. That's all there is to it.'

"'Do not say so,' says the bay man. He pulls off a glove and goes over and lays his hand on that chunk of glass.

"'Ice,' says he, nodding his head, solemn.

"General Dingo also steps over and feels of it.

"'Ice,' says the General; 'I'll swear to it.'

"'If Señor Casparis,' says the bay man, 'will present himself to the treasury on the sixth day of this month he will receive back the thousand dollars he did deposit as a forfeit. Adios, señor.'

"The General and the bay man bowed themselves out, and I bowed as often as they did.

"And when the carriage rolls away through the sand I bows once more, deeper than ever, till my hat touches the ground. But this time 'twas not intended for them. For, over their heads, I saw the old flag fluttering in the breeze above the consul's roof; and 'twas to it I made my profoundest salute."

XIV

THE EMANCIPATION OF BILLY

In the old, old, square-porticoed mansion, with the wry window-shutters and the paint peeling off in discoloured flakes, lived one of the last of the war governors.

The South has forgotten the enmity of the great conflict, but it refuses to abandon its old traditions and idols. In "Governor" Pemberton, as he was still fondly called, the inhabitants of Elmville saw the relic of their state's ancient greatness and glory. In his day he had been a man large in the eye of his country. His state had pressed upon him every honour within its gift. And now when he was old, and enjoying a richly merited repose outside the swift current of public affairs, his townsmen loved to do him reverence for the sake of the past.

The Governor's decaying "mansion" stood upon the main street of Elmville within a few feet of its rickety paling-fence. Every morning the Governor would descend the steps with exterme care and deliberation — on account of his rheumatism — and then the click of his gold-headed cane would be heard as he slowly proceeded up the rugged brick sidewalk. He was now nearly seventy-eight, but he had grown old gracefully and beautifully. His rather long, smooth hair and flowing, parted whiskers were snow-white. His full-skirted frock-coat was always buttoned snugly about his tall, spare figure. He wore a high, well-kept silk hat — known as a "plug" in Elmville — and nearly always gloves. His manners were punctilious, and somewhat overcharged with courtesy.

The Governor's walks up Lee Avenue, the principal street, developed in their course into a sort of memorial, triumphant procession. Everyone he met saluted him with profound respect. Many would remove their hats. Those who were honoured with his personal friendship would pause to shake hands, and then you would see exemplified the genuine *beau ideal* Southern courtesy.

Upon reaching the corner of the second square from the mansion, the Governor would pause. Another street crossed the avenue there, and traffic, to the extent of sever farmers' wagons and a peddler's cart or two, would rage about the junction. Then the falcon eye of General Deffenbaugh would perceive the situation, and the General would hasten, with ponderous solicitude, from his office in the First National Bank building to the assistance of his old friend.

When the two exchanged greetings the decay of modern manners would become accusingly apparent. The General's bulky and commanding figure would bend lissomely at a point where you would have regarded its ability to do so with incredulity. The Governor's cherished rheumatism would be compelled, for the moment, to give way before a genuflexion brought down from the days of the cavaliers. The Governor would take the General's arm and be piloted safely between the hay-wagons and the sprinkling-cart to the other side of the street. Proceeding to the post-office in the care of his friend, the esteemed statesman would there hold an informal levée among the citizens who were come for their morning mail. Here, gathering two or three prominent in law, politics, or family, the pageant would make a stately progress along the Avenue, stopping at the Palace Hotel, where, perhaps, would be found upon the register the name of some guest deemed worthy of an introduction to the state's vener-

able and illustrious son. If any such were found, an hour or
two would be spent in recalling the faded glories of the Governor's long-vanished administration.

On the return march the General would invariably suggest that, His Excellency being no doubt fatigued, it would
be wise to recuperate for a few minutes at the Drug Emporium of Mr. Appleby R. Fentress (an elegant gentleman,
sir — one of the Chatham County Fentresses — so many of
our best-blooded families have had to go into trade, sir, since
the war).

Mr. Appleby R. Fentress was a *connoisseur* in fatigue. Indeed, if he had not been, his memory alone should have en-
abled him to prescribe, for the majestic invasion of his
pharmacy was a casual happening that had surprised him almost daily for years. Mr. Fentress knew the formula of,
and possessed the skill to compound, a certain potion antago-
nistic to fatigue, the salient ingredient of which he described
(no doubt in pharmaceutical terms) as " genuine old hand-
made Clover Leaf '59, Private Stock."

Nor did the ceremony of administering the potion ever
vary. Mr. Fentress would first compound two of the celebrated mixtures — one for the Governor, and the other for
the General to " sample." Then the Governor would make
this little speech in his high, piping, quavering voice:

" No, sir — not one drop until you have prepared one for
yourself and join us, Mr. Fentress. Your father, sir, was one
of my most valued supporters and friends during My Administration, and any mark of esteem I can confer upon his son
is not only a pleasure but a duty, sir."

Blushing with delight at the royal condescension, the druggist would obey, and all would drink to the General's toast:
" The prosperity of our grand old state, gentlemen — the
memory of her glorious past — the health of her Favourite
Son."

Some one of the Old Guard was always at hand to escort the Governor home. Sometimes the General's business duties denied him the privilege, and then Judge Broomfield or Colonel Titus, or one of the Ashford County Slaughters would be on hand to perform the rite.

Such were the observances attendant upon the Governor's morning stroll to the post-office. How much more magnificent, impressive, and spectacular, then, was the scene at public functions when the General would lead forth the silver-haired relic of former greatness, like some rare and fragile waxwork figure, and trumpet his pristine eminence to his fellow citizens!

General Deffenbaugh was the Voice of Elmville. Some said he was Elmville. At any rate, he had no competitor as the Mouthpiece. He owned enough stock in the *Daily Banner* to dictate its utterance, enough shares in the First National Bank to be the referee of its loans, and a war record that left him without a rival for first place at barbecues, school commencements, and Decoration Days. Besides these acquirements he was possessed with endowments. His personality was inspiring and triumphant. Undisputed sway, had moulded him to the likeness of a fatted Roman emperor. The tones of his voice were not otherwise than clarion. To say that the General was public-spirited would fall short of doing him justice. He had spirit enough for a dozen publics. And as a sure foundation for it all, he had a heart that was big and stanch. Yes; General Deffenbaugh was Elmville.

One little incident that usually occurred during the Governor's morning walk has had its chronicling delayed by more important matters. The procession was accustomed to halt before a small brick office on the Avenue, fronted by a short flight of steep wooden steps. A modest tin sign over the door bore the words: " Wm. B. Pemberton: Attorney-at-Law."

Looking inside, the General would roar: " Hello, Billy, my boy." The less-distinguished members of the escort would call: " Morning, Billy." The Governor would pipe: " Good-morning, William."

Then a patient-looking little man with hair turning gray along the temples would come down the steps and shake hands with each one of the party. All Elmville shook hands when it met.

The formalities concluded, the little man would go back to his table, heaped with law books and papers, while the procession would proceed.

Billy Pemberton was, as his sign declared, a lawyer by profession. By occupation and common consent he was the Son of his Father. This was the shadow in which Billy lived, the pit out of which he had unsuccessfully striven for years to climb and, he had come to believe, the grave in which his ambitions were destined to be buried. Filial respect and duty he paid beyond the habit of most sons, but he aspired to be known and appraised by his own deeds and worth.

After many years of tireless labour he had become known in certain quarters far from Elmville as a master of the principles of the law. Twice he had gone to Washington and argued cases before the highest tribunal with such acute logic and learning that the silken gowns on the bench had rustled from the force of it. His income from his practice had grown until he was able to support his father, in the old family mansion (which neither of them would have thought of abandoning, rickety as it was) in the comfort and almost the luxury of the old extravagant days. Yet, he remained to Elmville as only " Billy " Pemberton, the son of our distinguished and honoured fellow-townsman, " ex-Governor Pemberton." Thus was he introduced at public gatherings where he sometimes spoke, haltingly and prosily, for his talents were too serious and deep for extempore brilliancy; thus was he presented to strangers and to the lawyers who made the circuit of the courts; and so the *Daily Banner* referred to him in print. To be " the son of " was his doom. What ever he should accomplish would have to be sacrificed upon the altar of this magnificent but fatal parental precedence.

The peculiarity and the saddest thing about Billy's ambition was that the only world he thirsted to conquer was Elmville. His nature was diffident and unassuming. National or State honours might have oppressed him. But, above all things, he hungered for the appreciation of the friends among whom he had been born and raised. He would not have plucked one leaf from the garlands that were so lavishly bestowed upon his father, he merely rebelled against having his own wreaths woven from those dried and self-same branches. But Elmville " Billied " and " sonned " him to his concealed but lasting chagrin, until at length he grew more reserved and formal and studious than ever.

There came a morning when Billy found among his mail a letter from a very high source, tendering him the appointment to an important judicial position in the new island possessions of our country. The honour was a distinguished one, for the entire nation had discussed the probable recipients of these positions, and had agreed that the situation demanded only men of the highest character, ripe learning, and evenly balanced mind.

Billy could not subdue a certain exultation at this token of the success of his long and arduous labours, but, at the same time, a whimsical smile lingered around his mouth, for he foresaw in which column Elmville would place the credit. " We congratulate Governor Pemberton upon the mark of appreciation conferred upon his son "—" Elmville rejoices with our honoured citizen, Governor Pemberton, at his son's success "—" Put her there, Billy! "—" Judge Billy Pemberton, sir; son of our State's war hero and the people's pride! "—

these were the phrases, printed and oral, conjured up by Billy's prophetic fancy. Grandson of his State, and stepchild to Elmville — thus had fate fixed his kinship to the body politic.

Billy lived with his father in the old mansion. The two and an elderly lady — a distant relative — comprised the family. Perhaps, though, old Jeff, the Governor's ancient coloured body-servant, should be included. Without doubt, he would have claimed the honour. There were other servants, but Thomas Jefferson Pemberton, sah, was a member of " de fambly."

Jeff was the one Elmvillian who gave to Billy the gold of approval unmixed with the alloy of paternalism. To him "Mars William" was the greatest man in Talbot County. Beaten upon though he was by the shining light that emanates from an ex-war governor, and loyal as he remained to the old *régime,* his faith and admiration were Billy's. As valet to a hero, and a member of the family, he may have had superior opportunities for judging.

Jeff was the first one to whom Bill revealed the news. When he reached home for supper Jeff took his "plug" hat and smoothed it before hanging it upon the hall-rack.

" Dar now! " said the old man: " I knowed it was er comin'. I knowed it was gwine ter happen. Er Judge, you says, Mars William? Dem Yankees done made you er judge? It's high time, sah, dey was doin' somep'n to make up for dey rascality endurin' de war. I boun' dey holds a confab and says: ' Le's make Mars William Pemberton er judge, and dat'll settle it.' Does you have to go way down to dem Filly-pines, Mars William, or kin you judge 'em from here? "

" I'd have to live there most of the time, of course," said Billy.

" I wonder what de Gubnor gwine say 'bout dat," speculated Jeff.

Billy wondered too.

After supper, when the two sat in the library, according to their habit, the Governor smoking his clay pipe and Billy his cigar, the son dutifully confessed to having been tendered the appointment.

For a long time the Governor sat, smoking, without making any comment. Billy reclined in his favourite rocker, waiting, perhaps still flushed with satisfaction over the tender that had come to him, unsolicited, in his dingy little office, above the heads of the intriguing, time-serving, clamorous multitude.

At last the Governor spoke; and, though his words were seemingly irrelevant, they were to the point. His voice had a note of martyrdom running through its senile quaver.

" My rheumatism has been growing steadily worse these past months, William."

" I am sorry, father," said Billy, gently.

" And I am nearly seventy-eight. I am getting to be an old man. I can recall the names of but two or three who were in public life during My Administration. What did you say is the nature of this position that is offered you, William? "

" A Federal judgeship, father. I believe it is considered to be a somewhat flattering tender. It is outside of politics and wire-pulling, you know."

" No doubt, no doubt. Few of the Pembertons have engaged in professional life for nearly a century. None of them have ever held Federal positions. They have been land-holders, slave-owners, and planters on a large scale. One or two of the Derwents — your mother's family — were in the law. Have you decided to accept this appointment, William? "

" I am thinking it over," said Billy, slowly, regarding the ash of his cigar.

" You have been a good son to me," continued the Governor, stirring his pipe with the handle of a penholder.

" I've been **your** son all my life," said Billy, darkly.

" I am often gratified," piped the Governor, betraying a touch of complacency, " by being congratulated upon having a son with such sound and sterling qualities. Especially in this, our native town, is your name linked with mine in the talk of our citizens."

" I never knew anyone to forget the vinculum," murmured Billy, unintelligibly.

" Whatever prestige," pursued the parent, " I may be possessed of, by virtue of my name and services to the state, has been yours to draw upon freely. I have not hesitated to exert it in your behalf whenever opportunity offered. And you have deserved it, William. You've been the best of sons. And now this appointment comes to take you away from me. I have but a few years left to live. I am almost dependent upon others now, even in walking and dressing. What would I do without you, my son? "

The Governor's pipe dropped to the floor. A tear trickled from his eye. His voice had risen, and crumbled to a weakling falsetto, and ceased. He was an old, old man about to be bereft of the son that cherished him.

Billy rose, and laid his hand upon the Governor's shoulder.

" Don't worry, father," he said, cheerfully. " I'm not going to accept. Elmville is good enough for me. I'll write to-night and decline it."

At the next interchange of devoirs between the Governor and General Deffenbaugh on Lee Avenue, His Excellency, with a comfortable air of self-satisfaction, spoke of the appointment that had been tendered to Billy.

The General whistled.

" That's a plum for Billy," he shouted. " Who'd have thought that Billy — but, confound it, it's been in him all the time. It's a boost for Elmville. It'll send real estate up.

It's an honour to our state. It's a compliment to the South. We've all been blind about Billy. When does he leave? We must have a reception. Great Gatlings! that job's eight thousand a year! There's been a car-load of lead-pencils worn to stubs figuring on those appointments. Think of it! Our little, wood-sawing, mealy-mouthed Billy! Angel unawares doesn't begin to express it. Elmville is disgraced forever unless she lines up in a hurry for ratification and apology."

The venerable Moloch smiled fatuously. He carried the fire with which to consume all these tributes to Billy, the smoke of which would ascend as an incense to himself.

"William," said the Governor, with modest pride, "has declined the appointment. He refuses to leave me in my old age. He is a good son."

The General swung round, and laid a large forefinger upon the bosom of his friend. Much of the General's success had been due to his dexterity in establishing swift lines of communication between cause and effect.

"Governor," he said, with a keen look in his big, ox-like eyes, "you've been complaining to Billy about your rheumatism."

"My dear General," replied the Governor, stiffly, "my son is forty-two. He is quite capable of deciding such questions for himself. And I, as his parent, feel it my duty to state that your remark about — er — rheumatism is a mighty poor shot from a very small bore, sir, aimed at a purely personal and private affliction."

"If you will allow me," retorted the General, "you've afflicted the public with it for some time; and 'twas no small bore, at that."

This first tiff between the two old comrades might have grown into something more serious, but for the fortunate interruption caused by the ostentatious approach of Colonel

Titus and another one of the court retinue from the right county, to whom the General confided the coddled statesman and went his way.

After Billy had so effectually entombed his ambitions, and taken the veil, so to speak, in a sonnery, he was surprised to discover how much lighter of heart and happier he felt. He realized what a long, restless struggle he had maintained, and how much he had lost by failing to cull the simple but wholesome pleasures by the way. His heart warmed now to Elmville and the friends who had refused to set him upon a pedestal. It was better, he began to think, to be " Billy " and his father's son, and to be hailed familiarly by cheery neighbours and grown-up playmates, than to be " Your Honour," and sit among strangers, hearing, maybe, through the arguments of learned counsel, that old man's feeble voice crying: " What would I do without you, my son? "

Billy began to surprise his acquaintances by whistling as he walked up the street; others he astounded by slapping them disrespectfully upon their backs and raking up old anecdotes he had not had the time to recollect for years. Though he hammered away at his law cases as thoroughly as ever, he found more time for relaxation and the company of his friends. Some of the younger set were actually after him to join the golf club. A striking proof of his abandonment to obscurity was his adoption of a most undignified, rakish, little soft hat, reserving the " plug " for Sundays and state occasions. Billy was beginning to enjoy Elmville, though that irreverent burgh had neglected to crown him with bay and myrtle.

All the while uneventful peace pervaded Elmville. The Governor continued to make his triumphal parades to the post-office with the General as chief marshal, for the slight squall that had rippled their friendship had, to all indications, been forgotten by both.

But one day Elmville woke to sudden excitement. The news had come that a touring presidential party would honour Elmville by a twenty-minute stop. The Executive had promised a five-minute address from the balcony of the Palace Hotel.

Elmville arose as one man — that man being, of course, General Deffenbaugh — to receive becomingly the chieftain of all the clans. The train with the tiny Stars and Stripes fluttering from the engine pilot arrived. Elmville had done her best. There were bands, flowers, carriages, uniforms, banners, and committees without end. High-school girls in white frocks impeded the steps of the party with roses strewn nervously in bunches. The chieftain had seen it all before — scores of times. He could have pictured it exactly in advance, from the Blue-and-Gray speech down to the smallest rosebud. Yet his kindly smile of interest greeted Elmville's display as if it had been the only and original.

In the upper rotunda of the Palace Hotel the town's most illustrious were assembled for the honour of being presented to the distinguished guests previous to the expected address. Outside, Elmville's inglorious but patriotic masses filled the streets.

Here, in the hotel General Deffenbaugh was holding in reserve Elmville's trump card. Elmville knew; for the trump was a fixed one, and its lead consecrated by archaic custom.

At the proper moment Governor Pemberton, beautifully venerable, magnificently antique, tall, paramount, stepped forward upon the arm of the General.

Elmville watched and harked with bated breath. Never until now — when a Northern President of the United States should clasp hands with ex-war-Governor Pemberton would the breach be entirely closed — would the country be made one and indivisible — no North, not much South, very little East, and no West to speak of. So Elmville excitedly scraped kalsomine from the walls of the Palace Hotel with its Sunday best, and waited for the Voice to speak.

And Billy! We had nearly forgotten Billy. He was cast for Son, and he waited patiently for his cue. He carried his "plug" in his hand, and felt serene. He admired his father's striking air and pose. After all, it was a great deal to be son of a man who could so gallantly hold the position of a cynosure for three generations.

General Deffenbaugh cleared his throat. Elmville opened its mouth, and squirmed. The chieftain with the kindly, fateful face was holding out his hand, smiling. Ex-war-Governor Pemberton extended his own across the chasm. But what was this the General was saying?

"Mr. President, allow me to present to you one who has the honour to be the father of our foremost, distinguished citizen, learned and honoured jurist, beloved townsman, and model Southern gentleman — the Honourable William B. Pemberton."

XV

THE ENCHANTED KISS

BUT a clerk in the Cut-rate Drug Store was Samuel Tansey, yet his slender frame was a pad that enfolded the passion of Romeo, the gloom of Lara, the romance of D'Artagnan, and the desperate inspiration of Melnotte. Pity, then, that he had been denied expression, that he was doomed to the burden of utter timidity and diffidence, that Fate had set him tongue-tied and scarlet before the muslin-clad angels whom he adored and vainly longed to rescue, clasp, comfort, and subdue.

The clock's hands were pointing close upon the hour of ten while Tansey was playing billiards with a number of his friends. On alternate evenings he was released from duty at the store after seven o'clock. Even among his fellow-men Tansey was timorous and constrained. In his imagination he had done valiant deeds and performed acts of distinguished gallantry; but in fact he was a sallow youth of twenty-three, with an over-modest demeanor and scant vocabulary.

When the clock struck ten, Tansey hastily laid down his cue and struck sharply upon the show-case with a coin for the attendant to come and receive the pay for his score.

"What's your hurry, Tansey?" called one. "Got another engagement?"

"Tansey got an engagement!" echoed another. "Not on your life. Tansey's got to get home at Motten by her Peek's orders."

"It's no such thing," chimed in a pale youth, taking a large cigar from his mouth; "Tansey's afraid to be late because Miss Katie might come down stairs to unlock the door, and kiss him in the hall."

This last delicate piece of raillery sent a fiery tingle into Tansey's blood, for the indictment was true — barring the kiss. That was a thing to dream of; to wildly hope for; but too remote and sacred a thing to think of lightly.

Casting a cold and contemptuous look at the speaker — a punishment commensurate with his own diffident spirit — Tansey left the room, descending the stairs into the street.

For two years he had silently adored Miss Peek, worshipping her from a spiritual distance through which her attractions took on stellar brightness and mystery. Mrs. Peek kept a few choice boarders, among whom was Tansey. The other young men romped with Katie, chased her with crickets in their fingers, and "jollied" her with an irreverent freedom that turned Tansey's heart into cold lead in his bosom. The signs of his adoration were few — a tremulous "Good morning," stealthy glances at her during meals, and occasionally (Oh, rapture!) a blushing, delirious game of cribbage with her in the parlour on some rare evening when a miraculous lack of engagement kept her at home. Kiss him in the hall! Aye, he feared it, but it was an ecstatic fear such as Elijah must have felt when the chariot lifted him into the unknown.

But to-night the gibes of his associates had stung him to a feeling of forward, lawless mutiny; a defiant, challenging, atavistic recklessness. Spirit of corsair, adventurer, lover, poet, bohemian, possessed him. The stars he saw above him seemed no more unattainable, no less high, than the favour of Miss Peek or the fearsome sweetness of her delectable lips. His fate seemed to him strangly dramatic and pathetic, and to call for a solace consonant with its extremity. A saloon was near by, and to this he flitted, calling for absinthe —

beyond doubt the drink most adequate to his mood — the tipple of the roué, the abandoned, the vainly sighing lover.

Once he drank of it, and again, and then again until he felt a strange, exalted sense of non-participation in worldly affairs pervade him. Tansey was no drinker; his consumption of three absinthe anisettes within almost as few minutes proclaimed his unproficiency in the art; Tansey was merely flooding with unproven liquor his sorrows; which record and tradition alleged to be drownable.

Coming out upon the sidewalk, he snapped his fingers defiantly in the direction of the Peek homestead, turned the other way, and voyaged, Columbus-like into the wilds of an enchanted street. Nor is the figure exorbitant, for, beyond his store the foot of Tansey had scarcely been set for years — store and boarding-house; between these ports he was chartered to run, and contrary currents had rarely deflected his prow.

Tansey aimlessly protracted his walk, and, whether it was his unfamiliarity with the district, his recent accession of audacious errantry, or the sophistical whisper of a certain green-eyed fairy, he came at last to tread a shuttered, blank, and echoing thoroughfare, dark and unpeopled. And, suddenly, this way came to an end (as many streets do in the Spanish-built, archaic town of San Antone), butting its head against an imminent, high, brick wall. No — the street still lived! To the right and to the left it breathed through slender tubes of exit — narrow, somnolent ravines, cobble paved and unlighted. Accommodating a rise in the street to the right was reared a phantom flight of five luminous steps of limestone, flanked by a wall of the same height and of the same material.

Upon one of these steps Tansey seated himself and bethought him of his love, and how she might never know she was his love. And of Mother Peek, fat, vigilant and kind;

not unpleased, Tansey thought, that he and Katie should play cribbage in the parlour together. For the Cut-rate had not cut his salary, which, sordidly speaking, ranked him star boarder at the Peek's. And he thought of Captain Peek, Katie's father, a man he dreaded and abhorred; a genteel loafer and spendthrift, battening upon the labour of his women-folk; a very queer fish, and, according to repute, not of the freshest.

The night had turned chill and foggy. The heart of the town, with its noises, was left behind. Reflected from the high vapours, its distant lights were manifest in quivering, cone-shaped streamers, in questionable blushes of unnamed colours, in unstable, ghostly waves of far, electric flashes. Now that the darkness was become more friendly, the wall against which the street splintered developed a stone coping topped with an armature of spikes. Beyond it loomed what appeared to be the acute angles of mountain peaks, pierced here and there by little lambent parallelograms. Considering this vista, Tansey at length persuaded himself that the seeming mountains were, in fact, the convent of Santa Mercedes, with which ancient and bulky pile he was better familiar from different coigns of view. A pleasant noise of singing in his ears reënforced his opinion. High, sweet, holy carolling, far and harmonious and uprising, as of sanctified nuns at their responses. At what hour did the Sisters sing? He tried to think — was it six, eight, twelve? Tansey leaned his back against the limestone wall and wondered. Strange things followed. The air was full of white, fluttering pigeons that circled about, and settled upon the convent wall. The wall blossomed with a quantity of shining green eyes that blinked and peered at him from the solid masonry. A pink, classic nymph came from an excavation in the cavernous road and danced, barefoot and airy, upon the ragged flints. The sky was traversed by a company of beribboned cats, marching in stupendous, aërial procession. The noise of singing grew louder; an illumination of unseasonable fireflies danced past, and strange whispers came out of the dark without meaning or excuse.

Without amazement Tansey took note of these phenomena. He was on some new plane of understanding, though his mind seemed to him clear and, indeed, happily tranquil.

A desire for movement and exploration seized him: he rose and turned into the black gash of street to his right. For a time the high wall formed one of its boundaries; but further on, two rows of black-windowed houses closed it in.

Here was the city's quarter once given over to the Spaniard. Here were still his forbidding abodes of concrete and adobe, standing cold and indomitable against the century. From the murky fissure, the eye saw, flung against the sky, the tangled filigree of his Moorish balconies. Through stone archways breaths of dead, vault-chilled air coughed upon him; his feet struck jingling iron rings in staples stone-buried for half a cycle. Along these paltry avenues had swaggered the arrogant Don, had caracoled and serenaded and blustered while the tomahawk and the pioneer's rifle were already uplifted to expel him from a continent. And Tansey, stumbling through this old-world dust, looked up, dark as it was, and saw Andalusian beauties glimmering on the balconies. Some of them were laughing and listening to the goblin music that still followed; others harked fearfully through the night, trying to catch the hoof beats of caballeros whose last echoes from those stones had died away a century ago. Those women were silent, but Tansey heard the jangle of horseless bridle-bits, the whirr of riderless rowels, and, now and then, a muttered malediction in a foreign tongue. But he was not frightened. Shadows, nor shadows of sounds could daunt him. Afraid? No. Afraid of Mother Peek? Afraid to face the girl of his heart? Afraid of tipsy Captain Peek? Nay! nor of these apparitions, nor of that spectral singing that always pursued him. Singing! He would show them! He lifted up a strong and untuneful voice:

"When you hear them bells go tingalingling,"

serving notice upon those mysterious agencies that if it should come to a face-to-face encounter

"There'll be a hot time
In the old town
To-night!"

How long Tansey consumed in treading this haunted byway was not clear to him, but in time he emerged into a more commodious avenue. When within a few yards of the corner he perceived, through a window, that a small confectionery of mean appearance was set in the angle. His same glance that estimated its meagre equipment, its cheap soda-water fountain and stock of tobacco and sweets, took cognizance of Captain Peek within lighting a cigar at a swinging gaslight.

As Tansey rounded the corner Captain Peek came out, and they met *vis-a-vis*. An exultant joy filled Tansey when he found himself sustaining the encounter with implicit courage. Peek, indeed! He raised his hand, and snapped his fingers loudly.

It was Peek himself who quailed guiltily before the valiant mien of the drug clerk. Sharp surprise and a palpable fear bourgeoned upon the Captain's face. And, verily, that face was one to rather call up such expressions upon the faces of others. The face of a libidinous heathen idol, small eyed, with carven folds in the heavy jowls, and a consuming, pagan license in its expression. In the gutter just beyond the store Tansey saw a closed carriage standing with its back toward him and a motionless driver perched in his place.

"Why, it's Tansey!" exclaimed Captain Peek. "How are you, Tansey? H-have a cigar, Tansey?"

" Why, it's Peek! " cried Tansey, jubilant at his own temerity. " What deviltry are you up to now, Peek? Back streets and a closed carriage! Fie! Peek! "

" There's no one in the carriage," said the Captain, smoothly.

" Everybody out of it is in luck," continued Tansey, aggressively. " I'd love for you to know, Peek, that I'm not stuck on you. You're a bottle-nosed scoundrel."

" Why, the little rat's drunk! " cried the Captain, joyfully; " only drunk, and I thought he was on! Go home, Tansey, and quit bothering grown persons on the street."

But just then a white-clad figure sprang out of the carriage, and a shrill voice — Katie's voice — sliced the air: " Sam! Sam! — help me, Sam! "

Tansey sprang toward her, but Captain Peek interposed his bulky form. Wonder of wonders! the whilom spiritless youth struck out with his right, and the hulking Captain went over in a swearing heap. Tansey flew to Katie, and took her in his arms like a conquering knight. She raised her face, and he kissed her — violets! electricity! caramels! champagne! Here was the attainment of a dream that brought no disenchantment.

" Oh, Sam," cried Katie, when she could, " I knew you would come to rescue me. What do you suppose the mean things were going to do with me? "

" Have your picture taken," said Tansey, wondering at the foolishness of his remark.

" No, they were going to eat me. I heard them talking about it."

" Eat you! " said Tansey, after pondering a moment. " That can't be; there's no plates."

But a sudden noise warned him to turn. Down upon him were bearing the Captain and a monstrous long-bearded dwarf in a spangled cloak and red trunk-hose. The dwarf leaped twenty feet and clutched him. The Captain seized Katie and hurled her, shrieking, back into the carriage, himself followed, and the vehicle dashed away. The dwarf lifted Tansey high above his head and ran with him into the store. Holding him with one hand, he raised the lid of an enormous chest half filled with cakes of ice, flung Tansey inside, and closed down the cover.

The force of the fall must have been great, for Tansey lost consciousness. When his faculties revived his first sensation was one of severe cold along his back and limbs. Opening his eyes, he found himself to be seated upon the limestone steps still facing the wall and convent of Santa Mercedes. His first thought was of the ecstatic kiss from Katie. The outrageous villainy of Captain Peek, the unnatural mystery of the situation, his preposterous conflict with the improbable dwarf — these things roused and angered him, but left no impression of the unreal.

" I'll go back there to-morrow," he grumbled aloud, " and knock the head off that comic-opera squab. Running out and picking up perfect strangers, and shoving them into cold storage ! "

But the kiss remained uppermost in his mind. " I might have done that long ago," he mused. " She liked it, too. She called me ' Sam ' four times. I'll not go up that street again. Too much scrapping. Guess I'll move down the other way. Wonder what she meant by saying they were going to eat her ! "

Tansey began to feel sleepy, but after a while he decided to move along again. This time he ventured into the street to his left. It ran level for a distance, and then dipped gently downward, opening into a vast, dim, barren space — the old Military Plaza. To his left, some hundred yards distant, he saw a cluster of flickering lights along the Plaza's border. He knew the locality at once.

Huddled within narrow confines were the remnants of the

once-famous purveyors of the celebrated Mexican national cookery. A few years before, their nightly encampments upon the historic Alamo Plaza, in the heart of the city, had been a carnival, a saturnalia that was renowned throughout the land. Then the caterers numbered hundreds; the patrons thousands. Drawn by the coquettish *señoritas,* the music of the weird Spanish minstrels, and the strange piquant Mexican dishes served at a hundred competing tables, crowds thronged the Alamo Plaza all night. Travellers, rancheros, family parties, gay gasconading rounders, sightseers and prowlers of polyglot, owlish San Antone mingled there at the centre of the city's fun and frolic. The popping of corks, pistols, and questions; the glitter of eyes, jewels and daggers; the ring of laughter and coin — these were the order of the night.

But now no longer. To some half-dozen tents, fires, and tables had dwindled the picturesque festival, and these had been relegated to an ancient disused plaza.

Often had Tansey strolled down to these stands at night to partake of the delectable *chili-con-carne,* a dish evolved by the genius of Mexico, composed of delicate meats minced with aromatic herbs and the poignant *chili colorado* — a compound full of singular savour and a fiery zest delightful to the Southron's palate.

The titillating odour of this concoction came now, on the breeze, to the nostrils of Tansey, awakening in him hunger for it. As he turned in that direction he saw a carriage dash up to the Mexicans' tents out of the gloom of the Plaza. Some figures moved back and forward in the uncertain light of the lanterns, and then the carriage was driven swiftly away.

Tansey approached, and sat at one of the tables covered with gaudy oil-cloth. Traffic was dull at the moment. A few half-grown boys noisily fared at another table; the Mexicans hung listless and phlegmatic about their wares. And

it was still. The night hum of the city crowded to the wall
of dark buildings surrounding the Plaza, and subsided to an
indefinite buzz through which sharply perforated the crackle
of the languid fires and the rattle of fork and spoon. A
sedative wind blew from the southeast. The starless firmament pressed down upon the earth like a leaden cover.

In all that quiet Tansey turned his head suddenly, and
saw, without disquietude, a troop of spectral horsemen deploy
into the Plaza and charge a luminous line of infantry that
advanced to sustain the shock. He saw the fierce flame of
cannon and small arms, but heard no sound. The careless
victuallers lounged vacantly, not deigning to view the conflict. Tansey mildly wondered to what nations these mute
combatants might belong; turned his back to them and ordered his chili and coffee from the Mexican woman who advanced to serve him. This woman was old and careworn;
her face was lined like the rind of a cantaloupe. She fetched
the viands from a vessel set by the smouldering fire, and then
retired to a tent, dark within, that stood near by.

Presently Tansey heard a turmoil in the tent; a wailing,
broken-hearted pleading in the harmonious Spanish tongue,
and then two figures tumbled out into the light of the lanterns. One was the old woman; the other was a man clothed
with a sumptuous and flashing splendour. The woman seemed
to clutch and beseech from him something against his will.
The man broke from her and struck her brutally back into
the tent, where she lay, whimpering and invisible. Observing
Tansey, he walked rapidly to the table where he sat. Tansey
recognized him to be Ramon Torres, a Mexican, the proprietor
of the stand he was patronizing.

Torres was a handsome, nearly full-blooded descendant of
the Spanish, seemingly about thirty years of age, and of a
haughty, but extremely courteous demeanour. To-night he
was dressed with signal magnificence. His costume was that

of a triumphant *matador,* made of purple velvet almost hidden by jeweled embroidery. Diamonds of enormous size flashed upon his garb and his hands. He reached for a chair, and, seating himself at the opposite side of the table, began to roll a finical cigarette.

"Ah, Meester Tansee," he said, with a sultry fire in his silky, black eyes, "I give myself pleasure to see you this evening. Meester Tansee, you have many times come to eat at my table. I theenk you a safe man — a verree good friend. How much would it please you to leeve forever?"

"Not come back any more?" inquired Tansey.

"No; not leave — *leeve;* the not-to-die."

"I would call that," said Tansey, "a snap."

Torres leaned his elbows upon the table, swallowed a mouthful of smoke, and spake — each word being projected in a little puff of gray.

"How old do you theenk I am, Meester Tansee?"

"Oh, twenty-eight or thirty."

"Thees day," said the Mexican, "ees my birthday. I am four hundred and three years of old to-day."

"Another proof," said Tansey, airily, "of the healthfulness of our climate."

"Eet is not the air. I am to relate to you a secret of verree fine value. Listen me, Meester Tansee. At the age of twenty-three I arrive in Mexico from Spain. When? In the year fifteen hundred nineteen, with the *soldados* of Hernando Cortez. I come to thees country seventeen fifteen. I saw your Alamo reduced. It was like yesterday to me. Three hundred ninety-six year ago I learn the secret always to leeve. Look at these clothes I wear — at these *diamantes.* Do you theenk I buy them with the money I make with selling the *chili-con-carne,* Meester Tansee?"

"I should think not," said Tansey, promptly. Torres laughed loudly.

" *Valgame Dios!* but I do. But it not the kind you eating now. I make a deeferent kind, the eating of which makes men to always leeve. What do you think! One thousand people I supply — *diez pesos* each one pays me the month. You see! ten thousand *pesos* everee month! *Que diable!* Low not I wear the fine *ropa!* You see that old woman try to hold me back a little while ago? That ees my wife. When I marry her she is young — seventeen year — *bonita.* Like the rest she ees become old and — what you say! — tough? I am the same — young all the time. To-night I resolve to dress myself and find another wife befitting my age. This old woman try to scr-r-ratch my face. Ha! ha! Meester Tansee — same way they do *entre los Americanos.*"

" And this health-food you spoke of? " said Tansey.

" Hear me," said Torres, leaning over the table until he lay flat upon it; " eet is the *chili-con-carne* made not from the beef or the chicken, but from the flesh of the *señorita* — young and tender. That ees the secret. Everee month you must eat of it, having care to do so before the moon is full, and you will not die any times. See how I trust you, friend Tansee! To-night I have bought one young ladee — verree pretty — so *fina, gorda, blandita!* To-morrow the *chili* will be ready. *Ahora si!* One thousand dollars I pay for thees young ladee. From an *Americano* I have bought — a verree tip-top man — *el Capitan Peek — que es, Señor?* "

For Tansey had sprung to his feet, upsetting the chair. The words of Katie reverberated in his ears: " They're going to eat me, Sam." This, then, was the monstrous fate to which she had been delivered by her unnatural parent. The carriage he had seen drive up from the Plaza was Captain Peck's. Where was Katie? Perhaps already —

Before he could decide what to do a loud scream came from the tent. The old Mexican woman ran out, a flashing knife in her hand. " I have released her," she cried. " You shall kill no more. They will hang you — *ingrato* — *encantador!* "

Torres, with a hissing exclamation, sprang at her.

" Ramoncito! " she shrieked; " once you loved me."

The Mexican's arm raised and descended. " You are old,"
he cried; and she fell and lay motionless.

Another scream; the flaps of the tent were flung aside, and
there stood Katie, white with fear, her wrists still bound with
a cruel cord.

" Sam! " she cried, " save me again! "

Tansey rounded the table, and flung himself, with superb
nerve, upon the Mexican. Just then a clangour began; the
clocks of the city were tolling the midnight hour. Tansey
clutched at Torres, and, for a moment, felt in his grasp
the crunch of velvet and the cold facets of the glittering
gems. The next instant, the bedecked caballero turned in his
hands to a shrunken, leather-visaged, white-bearded, old, old,
screaming mummy, sandalled, ragged, and four hundred and
three. The Mexican woman was crawling to her feet, and
laughing. She shook her brown hand in the face of the
whining *viejo*.

" Go, now," she cried, " and seek your señorita. It was
I, Ramoncito, who brought you to this. Within each moon
you eat of the life-giving *chili*. It was I that kept the wrong
time for you. You should have eaten *yesterday* instead of
to-morrow. It is too late. Off with you, *hombre!* You are
too old for me! "

" This," decided Tansey, releasing his hold of the gray-
beard, " is a private family matter concerning age, and no
business of mine."

With one of the table knives he hastened to saw asunder
the fetters of the fair captive; and then, for the second time
that night he kissed Katie Peek — tasted again the sweetness,
the wonder, the thrill of it, attained once more the maximum
of his incessant dreams.

The next instant an icy blade was driven deep between his shoulders; he felt his blood slowly congeal; heard the senile cackle of the perennial Spaniard; saw the Plaza rise and reel till the zenith crashed into the horizon — and knew no more.

When Tansey opened his eyes again he was sitting upon those self-same steps gazing upon the dark bulk of the sleeping convent. In the middle of his back was still the acute, chilling pain. How had he been conveyed back there again? He got stiffly to his feet and stretched his cramped limbs. Supporting himself against the stonework he revolved in his mind the extravagant adventures that had befallen him each time he had strayed from the steps that night. In reviewing them certain features strained his credulity. Had he really met Captain Peek or Katie or the unparalleled Mexican in his wanderings — had he really encountered them under commonplace conditions and his over-stimulated brain had supplied the incongruities? However that might be, a sudden, elating thought caused him an intense joy. Nearly all of us have, at some point in our lives — either to excuse our own stupidity or placate our consciences — promulgated some theory of fatalism. We have set up an intelligent Fate that works by codes and signals. Tansey had done likewise; and now he read, through the night's incidents, the finger-prints of destiny. Each excursion that he had made had led to the one paramount finale — to Katie and that kiss, which survived and grew strong and intoxicating in his memory. Clearly, Fate was holding up to him the mirror that night, calling him to observe what awaited him at the end of whichever road he might take. He immediately turned, and hurried homeward.

Clothed in an elaborate, pale blue wrapper, cut to fit, Miss Katie Peek reclined in an armchair before a waning fire in her room. Her little, bare feet were thrust into house-shoes rimmed with swan's down. By the light of a small lamp she was attacking the society news of the latest Sunday paper. Some happy substance, seemingly indestructible, was being rhythmically crushed between her small white teeth. Miss Katie read of functions and furbelows, but she kept a vigilant ear for outside sounds and a frequent eye upon the clock over the mantel. At every footstep upon the asphalt sidewalk her smooth, round chin would cease for a moment its regular rise and fall, and a frown of listening would pucker her pretty brows.

At last she heard the latch of the iron gate click. She sprang up, tripped swiftly to the mirror, where she made a few of those feminine, flickering passes at her front hair and throat which are warranted to hypnotize the approaching guest.

The door-bell rang. Miss Katie, in her haste, turned the blaze of the lamp lower instead of higher, and hastened noiselessly down stairs into the hall. She turned the key, the door opened, and Mr. Tansey side-stepped in.

"Why, the i-de-a!" exclaimed Miss Katie, "is this you, Mr. Tansey? It's after midnight. Aren't you ashamed to wake me up at such an hour to let you in? You're just *awful!*"

"I was late," said Tansey, brilliantly.

"I should think you were! Ma was awfully worried about you. When you weren't in by ten, that hateful Tom McGill said you were out calling on another — said you were out calling on some young lady. I just despise Mr. McGill. Well, I'm not going to scold you any more, Mr. Tansey, if it *is* a little late — Oh! I turned it the wrong way!"

Miss Katie gave a little scream. Absent-mindedly she had turned the blaze of the lamp entirely out instead of higher. It was very dark.

Tansey heard a musical, soft giggle, and breathed an entrancing odour of heliotrope. A groping light hand touched his arm.

"How awkward I was! Can you find your way — Sam?"

"I — I think I have a match, Miss K-Katie."

A scratching sound; a flame; a glow of light held at arm's length by the recreant follower of Destiny illuminating a tableau which shall end the ignominious chronicle — a maid with unkissed, curling, contemptuous lips slowly lifting the lamp chimney and allowing the wick to ignite; then waving a scornful and abjuring hand toward the staircase — the unhappy Tansey, erstwhile champion in the prophetic lists of fortune, ingloriously ascending to his just and certain doom, while (let us imagine) half within the wings stands the imminent figure of Fate jerking wildly at the wrong strings, and mixing things up in her usual able manner.

XVI

A DEPARTMENTAL CASE

IN Texas you may travel a thousand miles in a straight
line. If your course is a crooked one, it is likely that both
the distance and your rate of speed may be vastly increased.
Clouds there sail serenely against the wind. The whip-poor-
will delivers its disconsolate cry with the notes exactly reversed from those of his Northern brother. Given a drought
and a subsequently lively rain, and lo! from a glazed and
stony soil will spring in a single night blossomed lilies, mir-
aculously fair. Tom Green County was once the standard
of measurement. I have forgotten how many New Jerseys
and Rhode Islands it was that could have been stowed away
and lost in its chaparral. But the legislative axe has slashed
Tom Green into a handful of counties hardly larger than
European kingdoms. The legislature convenes at Austin, near
the centre of the state; and, while the representative from the
Rio Grande country is gathering his palm-leaf fan and his
linen duster to set out for the capital, the Pan-handle solon
winds his muffler above his well-buttoned overcoat and kicks
the snow from his well-greased boots ready for the same journey. All this merely to hint that the big ex-republic of the
Southwest forms a sizable star on the flag, and to prepare for
the corollary that things sometimes happen there uncut to
pattern and unfettered by metes and bounds.

The Commissioner of Insurance, Statistics, and History of
the State of Texas was an official of no very great or very
small importance. The past tense is used, for now he is

Commissioner of Insurance alone. Statistics and history are no longer proper nouns in the government records.

In the year 188–, the governor appointed Luke Coonrod Standifer to be the head of this department. Standifer was then fifty-five years of age, and a Texan to the core. His father had been one of the state's earliest settlers and pioneers. Standifer himself had served the commonwealth as Indian fighter, soldier, ranger, and legislator. Much learning he did not claim, but he had drank pretty deep of the spring of experience.

If other grounds were less abundant, Texas should be well up in the lists of glory as the grateful republic. For both as republic and state, it has busily heaped honours and solid rewards upon its sons who rescued it from the wilderness.

Wherefore and therefore, Luke Coonrod Standifer, son of Ezra Standifer, ex-Terry ranger, simon-pure democrat, and lucky dweller in an unrepresented portion of the politico-geographical map, was appointed Commissioner of Insurance, Statistics, and History.

Standifer accepted the honour with some doubt as to the nature of the office he was to fill and his capacity for filling it — but he accepted, and by wire. He immediately set out from the little country town where he maintained (and was scarcely maintained by) a somnolent and unfruitful office of surveying and map-drawing. Before departing, he had looked up under the I's, S's and H's in the " Encyclopædia Britannica " what information and preparation toward his official duties that those weighty volumes afforded.

A few weeks of incumbency diminished the new commissioner's awe of the great and important office he had been called upon to conduct. An increasing familiarity with its workings soon restored him to his accustomed placid course of life. In his office was an old, spectacled clerk — a consecrated, informed, able machine, who held his desk regardless of changes of administrative heads. Old Kauffman instructed his new chief gradually in the knowledge of the department without seeming to do so, and kept the wheels revolving without the slip of a cog.

Indeed, the Department of Insurance, Statistics, and History carried no great heft of the burden of state. Its main work was the regulating of the business done in the state by foreign insurance companies, and the letter of the law was its guide. As for statistics — well, you wrote letters to county officers, and scissored other people's reports, and each year you got out a report of your own about the corn crop and the cotton crop and pecans and pigs and black and white population, and a great many columns of figures headed " bushels " and " acres " and " square miles," etc.— and there you were. History? The branch was purely a receptive one. Old ladies interested in the science bothered you some with long reports of proceedings of their historical societies. Some twenty or thirty people would write you each year that they had secured Sam Houston's pocket-knife or Santa Ana's whisky-flask or Davy Crockett's rifle — all absolutely authenticated — and demanded legislative appropriation to purchase. Most of the work in the history branch went into pigeon-holes.

One sizzling August afternoon the commissioner reclined in his office chair, with his feet upon the long, official table covered with green billiard cloth. The commissioner was smoking a cigar, and dreamily regarding the quivering landscape framed by the window that looked upon the treeless capitol grounds. Perhaps he was thinking of the rough and ready life he had led, of the old days of breathless adventure and movement, of the comrades who now trod other paths or had ceased to tread any, of the changes civilization and peace had brought, and, maybe, complacently, of the snug and comfortable camp pitched for him under the dome of the capitol of the state that had not forgotten his services.

The business of the department was lax. Insurance was easy. Statistics were not in demand. History was dead. Old Kauffman, the efficient and perpetual clerk, had requested an infrequent half-holiday, incited to the unusual dissipation by the joy of having successfully twisted the tail of a Connecticut insurance company that was trying to do business contrary to the edicts of the great Lone Star State.

The office was very still. A few subdued noises trickled in through the open door from the other departments — a dull tinkling crash from the treasurer's office adjoining, as a clerk tossed a bag of silver to the floor of the vault — the vague, intermittent clatter of a dilatory typewriter — a dull tapping from the state geologist's quarters as if some woodpecker had flown in to bore for his prey in the cool of the massive building — and then a faint rustle and the light shuffling of the well-worn shoes along the hall, the sounds ceasing at the door toward which the commissioner's lethargic back was presented. Following this, the sound of a gentle voice speaking words unintelligible to the commissioner's somewhat dormant comprehension, but giving evidence of bewilderment and hesitation.

The voice was feminine; the commissioner was of the race of cavaliers who make salaam before the trail of a skirt without considering the quality of its cloth.

There stood in the door a faded woman, one of the numerous sisterhood of the unhappy. She was dressed all in black — poverty's perpetual mourning for lost joys. Her face had the contours of twenty and the lines of forty. She may have lived that intervening score of years in a twelvemonth. There was about her yet an aurum of indignant, unappeased, protesting youth that shone faintly through the premature veil of unearned decline.

"I beg your pardon, ma'am," said the commissioner, gaining his feet to the accompaniment of a great creaking and sliding of his chair.

"Are you the governor, sir?" asked the vision of melancholy.

The commissioner hesitated at the end of his best bow, with his hand in the bosom of his double-breasted "frock." Truth at last conquered.

"Well, no, ma'am. I am not the governor. I have the honour to be Commissioner of Insurance, Statistics and History. Is there anything, ma'am, I can do for you? Won't you have a chair, ma'am?"

The lady subsided into the chair handed her, probably from purely physical reasons. She wielded a cheap fan — last token of gentility to be abandoned. Her clothing seemed to indicate a reduction almost to extreme poverty. She looked at the man who was not the governor, and saw kindliness and simplicity and a rugged, unadorned courtliness emanating from a countenance tanned and toughened by forty years of outdoor life. Also, she saw that his eyes were clear and strong and blue. Just so they had been when he used them to skim the horizon for raiding Kiowas and Sioux. His mouth was as set and firm as it had been on that day when he bearded the old Lion Sam Houston himself, and defied him during that season when secession was the theme. Now, in bearing and dress, Luke Coonrod Standifer endeavoured to do credit to the important arts and sciences of Insurance, Statistics, and History. He had abandoned the careless dress of his country home. Now, his broad-brimmed black slouch hat, and his long-tailed "frock" made him not the least imposing of the official family, even if his office was reckoned to stand at the tail of the list.

"You wanted to see the governor, ma'am?" asked the commissioner, with a deferential manner he always used toward the fair sex.

" I hardly know," said the lady, hesitatingly. " I suppose
so." And then, suddenly drawn by the sympathetic look of
the other, she poured forth the story of her need.

It was a story so common that the public has come to look
at its monotony instead of its pity. The old tale of an unhappy married life — made so by a brutal, conscienceless husband, a robber, a spendthrift, a moral coward and a bully,
who failed to provide even the means of the barest existence.
Yes, he had come down in the scale so low as to strike her.
It happened only the day before — there was the bruise on
one temple — she had offended his highness by asking for
a little money to live on. And yet she must needs, woman-
like, append a plea for her tyrant — he was drinking; he had
rarely abused her thus when sober.

" I thought," mourned this pale sister of sorrow " that maybe the state might be willing to give me some relief. I've
heard of such things being done for the families of old settlers.
I've heard tell that the state used to give land to the men who
fought for it against Mexico, and settled up the country, and
helped drive out the Indians. My father did all of that, and
he never received anything. He never would take it. I
thought the governor would be the one to see, and that's why I
came. If father was entitled to anything, they might let it
come to me."

" It's possible, ma'am," said Standifer, " that such might
be the case. But 'most all the veterans and settlers got their
land certificates issued, and located long ago. Still, we can
look that up in the land office, and be sure. Your father's
name, now, was —"

" Amos Colvin, sir."

" Good Lord! " exclaimed Standifer, rising and unbutton-
ing his tight coat, excitedly. " Are you Amos Colvin's
daughter? Why, ma'am, Amos Colvin and me were thicker
than two hoss thieves for more than ten years! We fought

Kiowas, drove cattle, and rangered side by side nearly all over Texas. I remember seeing you once before, now. You were a kid, about seven, a-riding a little yellow pony up and down. Amos and me stopped at your home for a little grub when we were trailing that band of Mexican cattle thieves down through Karnes and Bee. Great tarantulas! and you're Amos Colvin's little girl! Did you ever hear your father mention Luke Standifer — just kind of casually — as if he'd met me once or twice?"

A little pale smile flitted across the lady's white face.

"It seems to me," she said, "that I don't remember hearing him talk about much else. Every day there was some story he had to tell about what he and you had done. Mighty near the last thing I heard him tell was about the time when the Indians wounded him, and you crawled out to him through the grass, with a canteen of water, while they —"

"Yes, yes — well — oh, that wasn't anything," said Standifer, "hemming" loudly and buttoning his coat again, briskly. "And now, ma'am, who was the infernal skunk — I beg your pardon, ma'am — who was the gentleman you married?"

"Benton Sharp."

The commissioner plumped down again into his chair, with a groan. This gentle, sad little woman, in the rusty black gown, the daughter of his oldest friend, the wife of Benton Sharp! Benton Sharp, one of the most noted "bad" men in that part of the state — a man who had been a cattle thief, an outlaw, a desperado, and was now a gambler, a swaggering bully, who plied his trade in the larger frontier towns, relying upon his record and the quickness of his gun play to maintain his supremacy. Seldom did any one take the risk of going "up against" Benton Sharp. Even the law officers were content to let him make his own terms of peace. Sharp was a ready and an accurate shot, and as lucky as a brand-new penny at coming clear from his scrapes. Standifer wondered how this pillaging eagle ever came to be mated with Amos Colvin's little dove, and expressed his wonder.

Mrs. Sharp sighed.

"You see, Mr. Standifer, we didn't know anything about him, and he can be very pleasant and kind when he wants to. We lived down in the little town of Goliad. Benton came riding down that way, and stopped there a while. I reckon I was some better looking then than I am now. He was good to me for a whole year after we were married. He insured his life for me for five thousand dollars. But for the last six months he has done everything but kill me. I often wish he had done that, too. He got out of money for a while, and abused me shamefully for not having anything he could spend. Then father died, and left me the little home in Goliad. My husband made me sell that, and turned me out into the world. I've barely been able to live, for I'm not strong enough to work. Lately, I heard he was making money in San Antonio, so I went there, and found him, and asked for a little help. This," touching the livid bruise on her temple, "is what he gave me. So I came on to Austin to see the governor. I once heard father say that there was some land, or a pension, coming to him from the state that he never would ask for."

Luke Standifer rose to his feet, and pushed his chair back. He looked rather perplexedly around the big office, with its handsome furniture.

"It's a long trail to follow," he said, slowly, "trying to get back dues from the government. There's red tape and lawyers and rulings and evidences and courts to keep you waiting. I'm not certain," continued the commissioner, with a profoundly meditative frown, "whether this department that I'm the boss of has any jurisdiction or not. It's only Insurance, Statistics, and History, ma'am, and it don't sound as if it would cover the case. But sometimes a saddle blanket can be made to stretch. You keep your seat, just for a few minutes, ma'am, till I step into the next room and see about it."

The state treasurer was seated within his massive, complicated railings, reading a newspaper. Business for the day was about over. The clerks lolled at their desks, awaiting the closing hour. The Commissioner of Insurance, Statistics, and History entered, and leaned in at the window.

The treasurer, a little, brisk old man, with snow-white moustache and beard, jumped up youthfully and came forward to greet Standifer. They were friends of old.

"Uncle Frank," said the commissioner, using the familiar name by which the historic treasurer was addressed by every Texan, "how much money have you got on hand?"

The treasurer named the sum of the last balance down to the odd cents — something more than a million dollars.

The commissioner whistled lowly, and his eyes grew hopefully bright.

"You know, or else you've heard of, Amos Colvin, Uncle Frank?"

"Knew him well," said the treasurer, promptly. "A good man. A valuable citizen. One of the first settlers in the Southwest."

"His daughter," said Standifer, "is sitting in my office. She's penniless. She's married to Benton Sharp, a coyote and a murderer. He's reduced her to want, and broken her heart. Her father helped build up this state, and it's the state's turn to help his child. A couple of thousand dollars will buy back her home and let her live in peace. The State of Texas can't afford to refuse it. Give me the money, Uncle Frank, and I'll give it to her right away. We'll fix up the red-tape business afterward."

The treasurer looked a little bewildered.

"Why, Standifer," he said, "you know I can't pay a cent out of the treasury without a warrant from the comptroller. I can't disburse a dollar without a voucher to show for it."

The commissioner betrayed a slight impatience.

"I'll give you a voucher," he declared. "What's this job they've given me for? Am I just a knot on a mesquite stump? Can't my office stand for it? Charge it up to Insurance and the other two sideshows. Don't Statistics show that Amos Colvin came to this state when it was in the hands of Greasers and rattlesnakes and Comanches, and fought day and night to make a white man's country of it? Don't they show that Amos Colvin's daughter is brought to ruin by a villain who's trying to pull down what you and I and old Texans shed our blood to build up? Don't History show that the Lone Star State never yet failed to grant relief to the suffering and oppressed children of the men who made her the grandest commonwealth in the Union? If Statistics and History don't bear out the claim of Amos Colvin's child I'll ask the next legislature to abolish my office. Come, now, Uncle Frank, let her have the money. I'll sign the papers officially, if you say so; and then if the governor or the comptroller or the janitor or anybody else makes a kick, by the Lord I'll refer the matter to the people, and see if they won't indorse the act."

The treasurer looked sympathetic but shocked. The commissioner's voice had grown louder as he rounded off the sentences that, however praiseworthy they might be in sentiment, reflected somewhat upon the capacity of the head of a more or less important department of state. The clerks were beginning to listen.

"Now, Standifer," said the treasurer, soothingly, "you know I'd like to help in this matter, but stop and think a moment, please. Every cent in the treasury is expended only by appropriation made by the legislature, and drawn out by checks issued by the comptroller. I can't control the use of a cent of it. Neither can you. Your department isn't disbursive — it isn't even administrative — it's purely clerical. The only way for the lady to obtain relief is to petition the legislature, and —"

" To the devil with the legislature," said Standifer, turning away.

The treasurer called him back.

" I'd be glad, Standifer, to contribute a hundred dollars personally toward the immediate expenses of Colvin's daughter." He reached for his pocketbook.

" Never mind, Uncle Frank," said the commissioner, in a softer tone. " There's no need of that. She hasn't asked for anything of that sort yet. Besides, her case is in my hands. I see now what a little, rag-tag, bob-tail, gotch-eared department I've been put in charge of. It seems to be about as important as an almanac or a hotel register. But while I'm running it, it won't turn away any daughters of Amos Colvin without stretching its jurisdiction to cover, if possible. You want to keep your eye on the Department of Insurance, Statistics, and History."

The commissioner returned to his office, looking thoughtful. He opened and closed an inkstand on his desk many times with extreme and undue attention before he spoke. " Why don't you get a divorce? " he asked, suddenly.

" I haven't the money to pay for it," answered the lady.

" Just at present," announced the commissioner, in a formal tone, " the powers of my department appear to be considerably string-halted. Statistics seem to be overdrawn at the bank, and History isn't good for a square meal. But you've come to the right place, ma'am. The department will see you through. Where did you say your husband is, ma'am? "

" He was in San Antonio yesterday. He is living there now."

Suddenly the commissioner abandoned his official air. He took the faded little woman's hands in his, and spoke in the old voice he used on the trail and around campfires.

" Your name's Amanda, isn't it? "

" Yes, sir."

" I thought so. I've heard your dad say it often enough. Well, Amanda, here's your father's best friend, the head of a big office in the state government, that's going to help you out of your troubles. And here's the old bushwhacker and cow-puncher that your father has helped out of scrapes time and time again wants to ask you a question. Amanda, have you got money enough to run you for the next two or three days? "

Mrs. Sharp's white face flushed the least bit.

" Plenty, sir — for a few days."

" All right, then, ma'am. Now you go back where you are stopping here, and you come to the office again the day after to-morrow at four o'clock in the afternoon. Very likely by that time there will be something definite to report to you." The commissioner hesitated, and looked a trifle embarrassed. " You said your husband had insured his life for $5,000. Do you know whether the premiums have been kept paid upon it or not? "

" He paid for a whole year in advance about five months ago," said Mrs. Sharp. " I have the policy and receipts in my trunk."

" Oh, that's all right, then," said Standifer. " It's best to look after things of that sort. Some day they may come in handy."

Mrs. Sharp departed, and soon afterward Luke Standifer went down to the little hotel where he boarded and looked up the railroad time-table in the daily paper. Half an hour later he removed his coat and vest, and strapped a peculiarly constructed pistol holster across his shoulders, leaving the receptacle close under his left armpit. Into the holster he shoved a short-barrelled .44 calibre revolver. Putting on his clothes again, he strolled down to the station and caught the five-twenty afternoon train for San Antonio.

The San Antonio *Express* of the following morning contained this sensational piece of news:

BENTON SHARP MEETS HIS MATCH

THE MOST NOTED DESPERADO IN SOUTHWEST TEXAS SHOT TO DEATH IN THE GOLD FRONT RESTAURANT — PROMINENT STATE OFFICIAL SUCCESSFULLY DEFENDS HIMSELF AGAINST THE NOTED BULLY — MAGNIFICENT EXHIBITION OF QUICK GUN PLAY.

Last night about eleven o'clock Benton Sharp, with two other men, entered the Gold Front Restaurant and seated themselves at a table. Sharp had been drinking, and was loud and boisterous, as he always was when under the influence of liquor. Five minutes after the party was seated a tall, well-dressed, elderly gentleman entered the restaurant. Few present recognized the Honorable Luke Standifer, the recently appointed Commissioner of Insurance, Statistics, and History.

Going over to the same side where Sharp was, Mr. Standifer prepared to take a seat at the next table. In hanging his hat upon one of the hooks along the wall he let it fall upon Sharp's head. Sharp turned, being in an especially ugly humour, and cursed the other roundly. Mr. Standifer apologized calmly for the accident, but Sharp continued his vituperations. Mr. Standifer was observed to draw near and speak a few sentences to the desperado in so low a tone that no one else caught the words. Sharp sprang up, wild with rage. In the meantime Mr. Standifer had stepped some yards away, and was standing quietly with his arms folded across the breast of his loosely hanging coat.

With that impetuous and deadly rapidity that made Sharp so dreaded, he reached for the gun he always carried in his hip pocket — a movement that has preceded the death of at least a dozen men at his hands. Quick as the motion was, the bystanders assert that it was met by the most beautiful exhibition of lightning gun-pulling ever witnessed in the Southwest. As Sharp's pistol was being raised — and the act was really quicker than the eye could follow — a glittering .44 appeared as if by some conjuring trick in the right hand of Mr. Standifer, who, without a perceptible movement of his arm, shot Benton Sharp through the heart. It seems that the new Commissioner of Insurance, Statistics, and History has been an old-time Indian fighter and ranger for many years, which accounts for the happy knack he has of handling a .44.

It is not believed that Mr. Standifer will be put to any inconvenience beyond a necessary formal hearing to-day, as all the witnesses who were present unite in declaring that the deed was done in self-defence.

When Mrs. Sharp appeared at the office of the commissioner, according to appointment, she found that gentleman calmly eating a golden russet apple. He greeted her without embarrassment and without hesitation at approaching the subject that was the topic of the day.

" I had to do it, ma'am," he said, simply, " or get it myself. Mr. Kauffman," he added, turning to the old clerk, " please look up the records of the Security Life Insurance Company and see if they are all right."

" No need to look," grunted Kauffman, who had everything in his head. " It's all O. K. They pay all losses within ten days."

Mrs. Sharp soon rose to depart. She had arranged to remain in town until the policy was paid. The commissioner did not detain her. She was a woman, and he did not know just what to say to her at present. Rest and time would bring her what she needed.

But, as she was leaving, Luke Standifer indulged himself in an official remark:

" The Department of Insurance, Statistics, and History, ma'am, has done the best it could with your case. 'Twas a case hard to cover according to red tape. Statistics failed, and History missed fire, but, if I may be permitted to say it, we came out particularly strong on Insurance."

XVII

THE RENAISSANCE AT CHARLEROI

GRANDEMONT CHARLES was a little Creole gentleman, aged thirty-four, with a bald spot on the top of his head and the manners of a prince. By day he was a clerk in a cotton broker's office in one of those cold, rancid mountains of oozy brick, down near the levee in New Orleans. By night, in his three-story-high *chambre garnier* in the old French Quarter he was again the last male descendant of the Charles family, that noble house that had lorded it in France, and had pushed its way smiling, rapiered, and courtly into Louisiana's early and brilliant days. Of late years the Charleses had subsided into the more republican but scarcely less royally carried magnificence and ease of plantation life along the Mississippi. Perhaps Grandemont was even Marquis de Brassé. There was that title in the family. But a Marquis on seventy-five dollars per month! *Vraiment!* Still, it has been done on less.

Grandemont had saved out of his salary the sum of six hundred dollars. Enough, you would say, for any man to marry on. So, after a silence of two years on that subject, he reopened that most hazardous question to Mlle. Adèle Fauquier, riding down to Meade d'Or, her father's plantation. Her answer was the same that it had been any time during the last ten years: "First find my brother, Monsieur Charles."

This time he had stood before her, perhaps discouraged by a love so long and hopeless, being dependent upon a contingency so unreasonable, and demanded to be told in simple words whether she loved him or no.

Adèle looked at him steadily out of her gray eyes that betrayed no secrets and answered, a little more softly:

" Grandemont, you have no right to ask that question unless you can do what I ask of you. Either bring back brother Victor to us or the proof that he died."

Somehow, though five times thus rejected, his heart was not so heavy when he left. She had not denied that she loved. Upon what shallow waters can the bark of passion remain afloat! Or, shall we play the doctrinaire, and hint that at thirty-four the tides of life are calmer and cognizant of many sources instead of but one — as at four-and-twenty?

Victor Fauquier would never be found. In those early days of his disappearance there was money to the Charles name, and Grandemont had spent the dollars as if they were picayunes in trying to find the lost youth. Even then he had had small hope of success, for the Mississippi gives up a victim from its oily tangles only at the whim of its malign will.

A thousand times had Grandemont conned in his mind the scene of Victor's disappearance. And, at each time that Adèle had set her stubborn but pitiful alternative against his suit, still clearer it repeated itself in his brain.

The boy had been the family favourite; daring, winning, reckless. His unwise fancy had been captured by a girl on the plantation — the daughter of an overseer. Victor's family was in ignorance of the intrigue, as far as it had gone. To save them the inevitable pain that his course promised, Grandemont strove to prevent it. Omnipotent money smoothed the way. The overseer and his daughter left, between a sunset and dawn, for an undesignated bourne. Grandemont was confident that this stroke would bring the boy to reason. He rode over to Meade d'Or to talk with him. The two strolled out of the house and grounds, crossed the road, and, mounting the levee, walked its broad path while they conversed. A thunder-cloud was hanging, imminent, above, but, as yet, no rain fell. At Grandemont's disclosure of his interference in the clandestine romance, Victor attacked him, in a wild and sudden fury. Grandemont, though of slight frame, possessed muscles of iron. He caught the wrists amid a shower of blows descending upon him, bent the lad backward and stretched him upon the levee path. In a little while the gust of passion was spent, and he was allowed to rise. Calm now, but a powder mine where he had been but a whiff of the tantrums, Victor extended his hand toward the dwelling house of Meade d'Or.

"You and they," he cried, "have conspired to destroy my happiness. None of you shall ever look upon my face again."

Turning, he ran swiftly down the levee, disappearing in the darkness. Grandemont followed as well as he could, calling to him, but in vain. For longer than an hour he pursued the search. Descending the side of the levee, he penetrated the rank density of weeds and willows that undergrew the trees until the river's edge, shouting Victor's name. There was never an answer, though once he thought he heard a bubbling scream from the dun waters sliding past. Then the storm broke, and he returned to the house drenched and dejected.

There he explained the boy's absence sufficiently, he thought, not speaking of the tangle that had led to it, for he hoped that Victor would return as soon as his anger had cooled. Afterward, when the threat was made good and they saw his face no more, he found it difficult to alter his explanations of that night, and there clung a certain mystery to the boy's reasons for vanishing as well as to the manner of it.

It was on that night that Grandemont first perceived a new and singular expression in Adèle's eyes whenever she looked at him. And through the years following that expression was always there. He could not read it, for it was born of a thought she would never otherwise reveal.

Perhaps, if he had known that Adèle had stood at the gate
on that unlucky night, where she had followed, lingering, to
await the return of her brother and lover, wondering why
they had chosen so tempestuous an hour and so black a spot
to hold converse — if he had known that a sudden flash of
lightning had revealed to her sight that short, sharp struggle
as Victor was sinking under his hands, he might have explained everything, and she —

I know not what she would have done. But one thing is
clear — there was something besides her brother's disappearance between Grandemont's pleadings for her hand and
Adèle's "yes." Ten years had passed, and what she had
seen during the space of that lightning flash remained an in-
delible picture. She had loved her brother, but was she holding out for the solution of that mystery or for the " Truth "?
Women have been known to reverence it, even as an abstract
principle. It is said there have been a few who, in the matter
of their affections, have considered a life to be a small thing
as compared with a lie. That I do not know. But, I wonder,
had Grandemont cast himself at her feet crying that his hand
had sent Victor to the bottom of that inscrutable river, and
that he could no longer sully his love with a lie, I wonder if
— I wonder what she would have done!

But, Grandemont Charles, Arcadian little gentleman, never
guessed the meaning of that look in Adèle's eyes; and from
this last bootless payment of his devoirs he rode away as rich
as ever in honour and love, but poor in hope.

That was in September. It was during the first winter
month that Grandemont conceived his idea of the *renaissance*.
Since Adèle would never be his, and wealth without her were
useless trumpery, why need he add to that hoard of slowly
harvested dollars? Why should he even retain that hoard?

Hundreds were the cigarettes he consumed over his claret,
sitting at the little polished tables in the Royal street cafés

while thinking over his plan. By and by he had it perfect.
It would cost, beyond doubt, all the money he had, but —
le jeu vaut la chandelle — for some hours he would be once
more a Charles of Charleroi. Once again should the nineteenth of January, that most significant day in the fortunes
of the house of Charles, be fittingly observed. On that date
the French king had seated a Charles by his side at table; on
that date Armand Charles, Marquis de Brassé, landed, like a
brilliant meteor, in New Orleans; it was the date of his
mother's wedding; of Grandemont's birth. Since Grandemont could remember until the breaking up of the family that
anniversary had been the synonym for feasting, hospitality,
and proud commemoration.

Charleroi was the old family plantation, lying some twenty
miles down the river. Years ago the estate had been sold to
discharge the debts of its too-bountiful owners. Once again
it had changed hands, and now the must and mildew of liti-
gation had settled upon it. A question of heirship was in the
courts, and the dwelling house of Charleroi, unless the tales
told of ghostly powdered and laced Charleses haunting its
unechoing chambers were true, stood uninhabited.

Grandemont found the solicitor in chancery who held the
keys pending the decision. He proved to be an old friend of
the family. Grandemont explained briefly that he desired to
rent the house for two or three days. He wanted to give a
dinner at his old home to a few friends. That was all.

"Take it for a week — a month, if you will," said the
solicitor; "but do not speak to me of rental." With a sigh
he concluded: "The dinners I have eaten under that roof,
mon fils!"

There came to many of the old, established dealers in
furniture, china, silverware, decorations and household fittings
at their stores on Canal, Chartres, St. Charles, and Royal
Streets, a quiet young man with a little bald spot on the top

of his head, distinguished manners, and the eye of a *connoisseur,* who explained what he wanted. To hire the complete and elegant equipment of a dining-room, hall, reception-room, and cloak-rooms. The goods were to be packed and sent, by boat, to the Charleroi landing, and would be returned within three or four days. All damage or loss to be promptly paid for.

Many of those old merchants knew Grandemont by sight, and the Charleses of old by association. Some of them were of Creole stock and felt a thrill of responsive sympathy with the magnificently indiscreet design of this impoverished clerk who would revive but for a moment the ancient flame of glory with the fuel of his savings.

"Choose what you want," they said to him. "Handle everything carefully. See that the damage bill is kept low, and the charges for the loan will not oppress you."

To the wine merchants next; and here a doleful slice was lopped from the six hundred. It was an exquisite pleasure to Grandemont once more to pick among the precious vintages. The champagne bins lured him like the abodes of sirens, but these he was forced to pass. With his six hundred he stood before them as a child with a penny stands before a French doll. But he bought with taste and discretion of other wines — Chablis, Moselle, Château d'Or, Hochheimer, and port of right age and pedigree.

The matter of the cuisine gave him some studious hours until he suddenly recollected André — André, their old *chef* — the most sublime master of French Creole cookery in the Mississippi Valley. Perhaps he was yet somewhere about the plantation. The solicitor had told him that the place was still being cultivated, in accordance with a compromise agreement between the litigants.

On the next Sunday after the thought Grandemont rode, horseback, down to Charleroi. The big, square house with its two long ells looked blank and cheerless with its closed shutters and doors.

The shrubbery in the yard was ragged and riotous. Fallen leaves from the grove littered the walks and porches. Turning down the lane at the side of the house, Grandemont rode on to the quarters of the plantation hands. He found the workers just streaming back from church, careless, happy, and bedecked in gay yellows, reds, and blues.

Yes, André was still there; his wool a little grayer; his mouth as wide; his laughter as ready as ever. Grandemont told him of his plan, and the old *chef* swayed with pride and delight. With a sigh of relief, knowing that he need have no further concern until the serving of that dinner was announced, he placed in André's hands a liberal sum for the cost of it, giving *carte blanche* for its creation.

Among the blacks were also a number of the old house servants. Absalom, the former major domo, and a half-dozen of the younger men, once waiters and attachés of the kitchen, pantry, and other domestic departments crowded around to greet " *M'shi Grande.*" Absalom guaranteed to marshal, of these, a corps of assistants that would perform with credit the serving of the dinner.

After distributing a liberal largesse among the faithful, Grandemont rode back to town well pleased. There were many other smaller details to think of and provide for, but eventually the scheme was complete, and now there remained only the issuance of the invitations to his guests.

Along the river within the scope of a score of miles dwelt some half-dozen families with whose princely hospitality that of the Charleses had been contemporaneous. They were the proudest and most august of the old régime. Their small circle had been a brilliant one; their social relations close and warm; their houses full of rare welcome and discriminating bounty. Those friends, said Grandemont, should once more, if never again, sit at Charleroi on a nineteenth of January to celebrate the festal day of his house.

Grandemont had his cards of invitation engraved. They were expensive, but beautiful. In one particular their good taste might have been disputed; but the Creole allowed himself that one feather in the cap of his fugacious splendour. Might he not be allowed, for the one day of the *renaissance*, to be "Grandemont du Puy Charles, of Charleroi"? He sent the invitations out early in January so that the guests might not fail to receive due notice.

At eight o'clock on the morning of the nineteenth, the lower coast steamboat *River Belle* gingerly approached the long unused landing at Charleroi. The bridge was lowered, and a swarm of the plantation hands streamed along the rotting pier, bearing ashore a strange assortment of freight. Great shapeless bundles and bales and packets swathed in cloths and bound with ropes; tubs and urns of palms, evergreens, and tropical flowers; tables, mirrors, chairs, couches, carpets, and pictures — all carefully bound and padded against the dangers of transit.

Grandemont was among them, the busiest there. To the safe conveyance of certain large hampers eloquent with printed cautions to delicate handling he gave his superintendence, for they contained the fragile china and glassware. The dropping of one of those hampers would have cost him more than he could have saved in a year.

The last article unloaded, the *River Belle* backed off and continued her course down stream. In less than an hour everything had been conveyed to the house. And came then Absalom's task, directing the placing of the furniture and wares. There was plenty of help, for that day was always a holiday at Charleroi, and the Negroes did not suffer the old traditions to lapse. Almost the entire population of the quarters volunteered their aid. A score of piccaninnies were sweeping at the leaves in the yard. In the big kitchen at the rear André was lording it with his old-time magnificence over his numerous sub-cooks and scullions. Shutters were flung wide; dust spun in clouds; the house echoed to voices and the tread of busy feet. The prince had come again, and Charleroi woke from its long sleep.

The full moon, as she rose across the river that night and peeped above the levee saw a sight that had been long missing from her orbit. The old plantation house shed a soft and alluring radiance from every window. Of its two-score rooms only four had been refurnished — the large reception chamber, the dining hall, and two smaller rooms for the convenience of the expected guests. But lighted wax candles were set in the windows of every room.

The dining hall was the *chef d'œuvre*. The long table, set with twenty-five covers, sparkled like a winter landscape with its snowy napery and china and the icy gleam of crystal. The chaste beauty of the room had required small adornment. The polished floor burned to a glowing ruby with the reflection of candle light. The rich wainscoting reached half way to the ceiling. Along and above this had been set the relieving lightness of a few water-colour sketches of fruit and flower.

The reception chamber was fitted in a simple but elegant style. Its arrangement suggested nothing of the fact that on the morrow the room would again be cleared and abandoned to the dust and the spider. The entrance hall was imposing with palms and ferns and the light of an immense candelabrum.

At seven o'clock Grandemont, in evening dress, with pearls — a family passion — in his spotless linen, emerged from somewhere. The invitations had specified eight as the dining hour. He drew an armchair upon the porch, and sat there, smoking cigarettes and half dreaming.

The moon was an hour high. Fifty yards back from the gate stood the house, under its noble grove. The road ran in front, and then came the grass-grown levee and the insatiate river beyond. Just above the levee top a tiny red light was creeping down and a tiny green one was creeping up. Then the passing steamers saluted, and the hoarse din startled the drowsy silence of the melancholy lowlands. The stillness returned, save for the little voices of the night — the owl's recitative, the capriccio of the crickets, the concerto of the frogs in the grass. The piccaninnies and the dawdlers from the quarters had been dismissed to their confines, and the melée of the day was reduced to an orderly and intelligent silence. The six coloured waiters, in their white jackets, paced, cat-footed, about the table, pretending to arrange where all was beyond betterment. Absalom, in black and shining pumps posed, superior, here and there where the lights set off his grandeur. And Grandemont rested in his chair, waiting for his guests.

He must have drifted into a dream — and an extravagant one — for he was master of Charleroi and Adèle was his wife. She was coming out to him now; he could hear her steps; he could feel her hand upon his shoulder —

"*Pardon moi, M'shi Grande*"— it was Absalom's hand touching him, it was Absalom's voice, speaking the *patois* of the blacks —"but it is eight o'clock."

Eight o'clock. Grandemont sprang up. In the moonlight he could see the row of hitching-posts outside the gate. Long ago the horses of the guests should have stood there. They were vacant.

A chanted roar of indignation, a just, waxing bellow of affront and dishonoured genius came from André's kitchen, filling the house with rhythmic protest. The beautiful dinner, the pearl of a dinner, the little excellent superb jewel of a dinner! But one moment more of waiting and not even the thousand thunders of black pigs of the quarters would touch it!

" They are a little late," said Grandemont, calmly. " They will come soon. Tell André to hold back dinner. And ask him if, by some chance, a bull from the pastures has broken, roaring, into the house."

He seated himself again to his cigarettes. Though he had said it, he scarcely believed Charleroi would entertain company that night. For the first time in history the invitation of a Charles had been ignored. So simple in courtesy and honour was Grandemont and, perhaps, so serenely confident in the prestige of his name, that the most likely reasons for his vacant board did not occur to him.

Charleroi stood by a road travelled daily by people from those plantations whither his invitations had gone. No doubt even on the day before the sudden reanimation of the old house they had driven past and observed the evidences of long desertion and decay. They had looked at the corpse of Charleroi and then at Grandemont's invitations, and, though the puzzle or tasteless hoax or whatever the thing meant left them perplexed, they would not seek its solution by the folly of a visit to that deserted house.

The moon was now above the grove, and the yard was pied with deep shadows save where they lightened in the tender glow of outpouring candle light. A crisp breeze from the river hinted at the possibility of frost when the night should have become older. The grass at one side of the steps was specked with the white stubs of Grandemont's cigarettes. The cotton-broker's clerk sat in his chair with the smoke spiralling above him. I doubt that he once thought of the little fortune he had so impotently squandered. Perhaps it was compensation enough for him to sit thus at Charleroi for a few retrieved hours. Idly his mind wandered in and out many fanciful paths of memory. He smiled to himself as a paraphrased line of Scripture strayed into his mind: "A certain *poor* man made a feast."

He heard the sound of Absalom coughing a note of summons. Grandemont stirred. This time he had not been asleep — only drowsing.

"Nine o'clock, *M'shi Grande*," said Absalom in the uninflected voice of a good servant who states a fact unqualified by personal opinion.

Grandemont rose to his feet. In their time all the Charleses had been proven, and they were gallant losers.

"Serve dinner," he said calmly. And then he checked Absalom's movement to obey, for something clicked the gate latch and was coming down the walk toward the house. Something that shuffled its feet and muttered to itself as it came. It stopped in the current of light at the foot of the steps and spake, in the universal whine of the gadding mendicant.

"Kind sir, could you spare a poor, hungry man, out of luck, a little to eat? And to sleep in the corner of a shed? For "— the thing concluded, irrelevantly —" I can sleep now. There are no mountains to dance reels in the night; and the copper kettles are all scoured bright. The iron band is still around my ankle, and a link, if it is your desire I should be chained."

It set a foot upon the step and drew up the rags that hung upon the limb. Above the distorted shoe, caked with the dust of a hundred leagues, they saw the link and the iron band. The clothes of the tramp were wreaked to piebald tatters by sun and rain and wear. A mat of brown, tangled hair and beard covered his head and face, out of which his eyes stared distractedly. Grandemont noticed that he carried in one hand a white, square card.

"What is that?" he asked.

"I picked it up, sir, at the side of the road." The vagabond handed the card to Grandemont. "Just a little to eat, sir. A little parched corn, a *tortilla,* or a handful of beans. Goat's meat I cannot eat. When I cut their throats they cry like children."

Grandemont held up the card. It was one of his own invitations to dinner. No doubt some one had cast it away from a passing carriage after comparing it with the tenantless house of Charleroi.

" From the hedges and highways bid them come," he said to himself, softly smiling. And then to Absalom: " Send Louis to me."

Louis, once his own body-servant, came promptly, in his white jacket.

" This gentleman," said Grandemont, "will dine with me. Furnish him with bath and clothes. In twenty minutes have him ready and dinner served."

Louis approached the disreputable guest with the suavity due to a visitor to Charleroi, and spirited him away to inner regions.

Promptly, in twenty minutes, Absalom announced dinner, and, a moment later, the guest was ushered into the dining hall where Grandemont waited, standing, at the head of the table. The attentions of Louis had transformed the stranger into something resembling the polite animal. Clean linen and an old evening suit that had been sent down from town to clothe a waiter had worked a miracle with his exterior. Brush and comb had partially subdued the wild disorder of his hair. Now he might have passed for no more extravagant a thing than one of those *poseurs* in art and music who affect such oddity of guise. The man's countenance and demeanour, as he approached the table, exhibited nothing of the awkwardness or confusion to be expected from his Arabian Nights change. He allowed Absalom to seat him at Grandemont's right hand with the manner of one thus accustomed to be waited upon.

"It grieves me," said Grandemont, "to be obliged to ex-change names with a guest. My own name is Charles."

"In the mountains," said the wayfarer, "they call me Gringo. Along the roads they call me Jack."

"I prefer the latter," said Grandemont. "A glass of wine with you, Mr. Jack."

Course after course was served by the supernumerous wait-ers. Grandemont, inspired by the results of André's ex-quisite skill in cookery and his own in the selection of wines became the model host, talkative, witty, and genial. The guest was fitful in conversation. His mind seemed to be sus-taining a succession of waves of dementia followed by inter-vals of comparative lucidity. There was the glassy bright-ness of recent fever in his eyes. A long course of it must have been the cause of his emaciation and weakness, his dis-tracted mind, and the dull pallor that showed even through the tan of wind and sun.

"Charles," he said to Grandemont — for thus he seemed to interpret his name —"you never saw the mountains dance, did you?"

"No, Mr. Jack," answered Grandemont, gravely, "the spectacle has been denied me. But, I assure you, I can under-stand it must be a diverting sight. The big ones, you know, white with snow on the tops, waltzing — *décolleté*, we may say."

"You first scour the kettles," said Mr. Jack, leaning to-ward him excitedly, "to cook the beans in the morning, and you lie down on a blanket and keep quite still. Then they come out and dance for you. You would go out and dance with them but you are chained every night to the centre pole of the hut. You believe the mountains dance, don't you, Charlie?"

"I contradict no traveller's tales," said Grandemont, with a smile.

Mr. Jack laughed loudly. He dropped his voice to a confidential whisper.

"You are a fool to believe it," he went on. "They don't really dance. It's the fever in your head. It's the hard work and the bad water that does it. You are sick for weeks and there is no medicine. The fever comes on every evening, and then you are as strong as two men. One night the *compañia* are lying drunk with *mescal*. They have brought back sacks of silver dollars from a ride, and they drink to celebrate. In the night you file the chain in two and go down the mountain. You walk for miles — hundreds of them. By and by the mountains are all gone, and you come to the prairies. They do not dance at night; they are merciful, and you sleep. Then you come to the river, and it says things to you. You follow it down, down, but you can't find what you are looking for."

Mr. Jack leaned back in his chair, and his eyes slowly closed. The food and wine had steeped him in a deep calm. The tense strain had been smoothed from his face. The languor of repletion was claiming him. Drowsily he spoke again.

"It's bad manners — I know — to go to sleep — at table — but — that was — such a good dinner — Grande, old fellow."

Grande! The owner of the name started and set down his glass. How should this wretched tatterdemalion whom he had invited, Caliph-like, to sit at his feast know his name?

Not at first, but soon, little by little, the suspicion, wild and unreasonable as it was, stole into his brain. He drew out his watch with hands that almost balked him by their trembling, and opened the back case. There was a picture there — a photograph fixed to the inner side.

Rising, Grandemont shook Mr. Jack by the shoulder. The weary guest opened his eyes. Grandemont held the watch.

" Look at this picture, Mr. Jack.   Have you ever —"

" *My sister Adèle!* "

The vagrant's voice rang loud and sudden through the room.   He started to his feet, but Grandemont's arms were about him, and Grandemont was calling him " Victor! — Victor Fauquier! *Merci, merci, mon Dieu!* "

Too far overcome by sleep and fatigue was the lost one to talk that night.   Days afterward, when the tropic *calentura* had cooled in his veins, the disordered fragments he had spoken were completed in shape and sequence.   He told the story of his angry flight, of toils and calamities on sea and shore, of his ebbing and flowing fortune in southern lands, and of his latest peril when, held a captive, he served menially in a stronghold of bandits in the Sonora Mountains of Mexico.   And of the fever that seized him there and his escape and delirium, during which he strayed, perhaps led by some marvellous instinct, back to the river on whose bank he had been born.   And of the proud and stubborn thing in his blood that had kept him silent through all those years, clouding the honour of one, though he knew it not, and keeping apart two loving hearts.   "What a thing is love!" you may say.   And if I grant it, you shall say, with me: " What a thing is pride! "

On a couch in the reception chamber Victor lay, with a dawning understanding in his heavy eyes and peace in his softened countenance.   Absalom was preparing a lounge for the transient master of Charleroi, who, to-morrow, would be again the clerk of a cotton broker, but also —

" To-morrow," Grandemont was saying, as he stood by the couch of his guest, speaking the words with his face shining as must have shone the face of Elijah's charioteer when he announced the glories of that heavenly journey — " To-morrow I will take you to Her."

XVIII

ON BEHALF OF THE MANAGEMENT

THIS is the story of the man manager, and how he held his own until the very last paragraph.

I had it from Sully Magoon, *viva voce*. The words are indeed his; and if they do not constitute truthful fiction my memory should be taxed with the blame.

It is not deemed amiss to point out, in the beginning, the stress that is laid upon the masculinity of the manager. For, according to Sully, the term when applied to the feminine division of mankind has precisely an opposite meaning. The woman manager (he says) economizes, saves, oppresses her household with bargains and contrivances, and looks sourly upon any pence that are cast to the fiddler for even a single jig-step on life's arid march. Wherefore her men-folk call her blessed, and praise her; and then sneak out the backdoor to see the Gilhooly Sisters do a buck-and-wing dance.

Now, the man manager (I still quote Sully) is a Cæsar without a Brutus. He is an autocrat without responsibility, a player who imperils no stake of his own. His office is to enact, to reverberate, to boom, to expand, to out-coruscate — profitably, if he can. Bill-paying and growing gray hairs over results belong to his principals. It is his to guide the risk, to be the Apotheosis of Front, the three-tailed Bashaw of Bluff, the Essential Oil of Razzle-Dazzle.

We sat at luncheon, and Sully Magoon told me. I asked for particulars.

"My old friend Denver Galloway was a born manager,"

said Sully. "He first saw the light of day in New York at three years of age. He was born in Pittsburg, but his parents moved East the third summer afterward.

"When Denver grew up, he went into the managing business. At the age of eight he managed a news-stand for the Dago that owned it. After that he was manager at different times of a skating-rink, a livery-stable, a policy game, a restaurant, a dancing academy, a walking match, a burlesque company, a dry-goods store, a dozen hotels and summer resorts, an insurance company, and a district leader's campaign. That campaign, when Coughlin was elected on the East Side, gave Denver a boost. It got him a job as manager of a Broadway hotel, and for a while he managed Senator O'Grady's campaign in the nineteenth.

"Denver was a New Yorker all over. I think he was out of the city just twice before the time I'm going to tell you about. Once he went rabbit-shooting in Yonkers. The other time I met him just landing from a North River ferry. 'Been out West on a big trip, Sully, old boy,' says he. 'Gad! Sully, I had no idea we had such a big country. It's immense. Never conceived of the magnificence of the West before. It's gorgeous and glorious and infinite. Makes the East seem cramped and little. It's a grand thing to travel and get an idea of the extent and resources of our country.'

"I'd made several little runs out to California and down to Mexico and up through Alaska, so I sits down with Denver for a chat about the things he saw.

"'Took in the Yosemite, out there, of course?' I asks.

"'Well — no,' says Denver, 'I don't think so. At least, I don't recollect it. You see, I only had three days, and I didn't get any farther west than Youngstown, Ohio.'

"About two years ago I dropped into New York with a little fly-paper proposition about a Tennessee mica mine that I wanted to spread out in a nice, sunny window, in the hopes of catching a few. I was coming out of a printing-shop one afternoon with a batch of fine, sticky prospectuses when I ran against Denver coming around a corner. I never saw him looking so much like a tiger-lily. He was as beautiful and new as a trellis of sweet peas, and as rollicking as a clarinet solo. We shook hands, and he asked me what I was doing, and I gave him the outlines of the scandal I was try- ing to create in mica.

" ' Pooh, pooh! for your mica,' says Denver. ' Don't you know better, Sully, than to bump up against the coffers of little old New York with anything as transparent as mica? Now, you come with me over to the Hotel Brunswick. You're just the man I was hoping for. I've got something there in sepia and curled hair that I want you to look at.'

" ' You putting up at the Brunswick? ' I asks.

" ' Not a cent,' says Denver, cheerful. ' The syndicate that owns the hotel puts up. I'm manager.'

" The Brunswick wasn't one of them Broadway pot-houses all full of palms and hyphens and flowers and costumes — kind of a mixture of lawns and laundries. It was on one of the East Side avenues; but it was a solid, old-time cara- vansary such as the Mayor of Skaneateles or the Governor of Missouri might stop at. Eight stories high it stalked up, with new striped awnings, and the electrics had it as light as day.

" ' I've been manager here for a year,' says Denver, as we drew nigh. ' When I took charge,' says he, ' nobody nor nothing ever stopped at the Brunswick. The clock over the clerks' desk used to run for weeks without winding. A man fell dead with heart-disease on the sidewalk in front of it one day, and when they went to pick him up he was two blocks away. I figured out a scheme to catch the West In- dies and South American trade. I persuaded the owners to invest a few more thousands, and I put every cent of it in electric lights, cayenne pepper, gold-leaf, and garlic. I got a Spanish-speaking force of employees and a string band; and there was talk going around of a cockfight in the basement every Sunday. Maybe I didn't catch the nut-brown gang! From Havana to Patagonia the Don Señors knew about the Brunswick. We get the highfliers from Cuba and Mexico and the couple of Americas farther south; and they've simply got the boodle to bombard every bullfinch in the bush with.'

When we get to the hotel, Denver stops me at the door.

" ' There's a little liver-coloured man,' says he, ' sitting in a big leather chair to your right, inside. You sit down and watch him for a few minutes, and then tell me what you think.'

" I took a chair, while Denver circulates around in the big rotunda. The room was about full of curly-headed Cubans and South American brunettes of different shades; and the atmosphere was international with cigarette smoke, lit up by diamond rings and edged off with a whisper of garlic.

" That Denver Galloway was sure a relief to the eye. Six feet two he was, red-headed, and pink-gilled as a sun-perch. And the air he had! Court of Saint James, Chauncey Olcott, Kentucky colonels, Count of Monte Cristo, grand opera — all these things he reminded you of when he was doing the honours. When he raised his finger the hotel porters and bell-boys skated across the floor like cockroaches, and even the clerk behind the desk looked as meek and unimportant as Andy Carnegie.

" Denver passed around, shaking hands with his guests, and saying over the two or three Spanish words he knew until it was like a coronation rehearsal or a Bryan barbecue in Texas.

" I watched the little man he told me to. 'Twas a little foreign person in a double-breasted frock-coat, trying to touch the floor with his toes. He was the colour of vici kid, and his whiskers was like excelsior made out of mahogany wood. He breathed hard, and he never once took his eyes off of Denver. There was a look of admiration and respect on his face like you see on a boy that's following a champion base-ball team, or the Kaiser William looking at himself in a glass.

" After Denver goes his rounds he takes me into his private office.

" ' What's your report on the dingy I told you to watch? ' he asks.

" ' Well,' says I, ' if you was as big a man as he takes you to be, nine rooms and bath in the Hall of Fame, rent free till October 1st, would be about your size.'

" ' You've caught the idea,' says Denver. ' I've given him the wizard grip and the cabalistic eye. The glamour that emanates from yours truly has enveloped him like a North River fog. He seems to think that Señor Galloway is the man who. I guess they don't raise 74-inch sorrel-tops with romping ways down in his precinct. Now, Sully,' goes on Denver, ' if you was asked, what would you take the little man to be? '

" ' Why,' says I, ' the barber around the corner; or, if he's royal, the king of the boot-blacks.'

" ' Never judge by looks,' says Denver; ' he's the dark-horse candidate for president of a South American republic.'

" ' Well,' says I, ' he didn't look quite that bad to me.'

" Then Denver draws his chair up close and gives out his scheme.

" ' Sully,' says he, with seriousness and levity, ' I've been a manager of one thing and another for over twenty years. That's what I was cut out for — to have somebody else to put up the money and look after the repairs and the police and taxes while I run the business. I never had a dollar of

my own invested in my life. I wouldn't know how it felt
to have the dealer rake in a coin of mine. But I can handle
other people's stuff and manage other people's enterprises.
I've had an ambition to get hold of something big — something
higher than hotels and lumber-yards and local politics. I
want to be manager of something way up — like a railroad
or a diamond trust or an automobile factory. Now here
comes this little man from the tropics with just what I want,
and he's offered me the job.'

"'What job?' I asks. 'Is he going to revive the Georgia
Minstrels or open a cigar store?'

"'He's no 'coon,' says Denver, severe. 'He's General
Rompiro — General Josey Alfonso Sapolio Jew-Ann Rompiro — he has his cards printed by a news-ticker. He's the
real thing, Sully, and he wants me to manage his campaign —
he wants Denver C. Galloway for a president-maker. Think
of that, Sully! Old Denver romping down to the tropics,
plucking lotos-flowers and pineapples with one hand and
making presidents with the other; Won't it make Uncle Mark
Hanna mad? And I want you to go too, Sully. You can
help me more than any man I know. I've been herding that
brown man for a month in the hotel so he wouldn't stray
down around Fourteenth Street and get roped in by that
crowd of refugee tamale-eaters down there. And he's landed,
and D. C. G. is manager of General J. A. S. J. Rompiro's
presidential campaign in the great republic of — what's its
name?'

"Denver gets down an atlas from a shelf, and we have a
look at the afflicted country. 'Twas a dark blue one, on the
west coast, about the size of a special delivery stamp.

"'From what the General tells me,' says Denver, 'and
from what I can gather from the encyclopædia and by con-
versing with the janitor of the Astor Library, it'll be as easy
to handle the vote of that country as it would be for Tam-

many to get a man named Geoghan appointed on the White Wings force.'

"'Why don't General Rumptyro stay at home,' says I, 'and manage his own canvass?'

"'You don't understand South American politics,' says Denver, getting out the cigars. 'It's this way. General Rompiro had the misfortune of becoming a popular idol. He distinguished himself by leading the army in pursuit of a couple of sailors who had stolen the plaza — or the carramba, or something belonging to the government. The people called him a hero and the government got jealous. The president sends for the chief of the Department of Public Edifices. "Find me a nice, clean adobe wall," says he, "and stand Señor Rompiro up against it. Then call out a file of soldiers and — then let him be up against it." Something,' goes on Denver, 'like the way they've treated Hobson and Carrie Nation in our country. So the General had to flee. But he was thoughtful enough to bring along his roll. He's got sinews of war enough to buy a battleship and float her off in the christening fluid.'

"'What chance has he got to be president?'

"'Wasn't I just giving you his rating?' says Denver. 'His country is one of the few in South America where the presidents are elected by popular ballot. The General can't go there just now. It hurts to be shot against a wall. He needs a campaign manager to go down and whoop things up for him — to get the boys in line and the new two-dollar bills afloat and the babies kissed and the machine in running order. Sully, I don't want to brag, but you remember how I brought Coughlin under the wire for leader of the nineteenth? Ours was the banner district. Don't you suppose I know how to manage a little monkey-cage of a country like that? Why, with the dough the General's willing to turn loose I could put two more coats of Japan varnish on him and have him elected Governor of Georgia. New York has got the finest lot of campaign managers in the world, Sully, and you give me a feeling of hauteur when you cast doubts on my ability to handle the political situation in a country so small that they have to print the names of the towns in the appendix and footnotes."

"I argued with Denver some. I told him that politics down in that tropical hemisphere was bound to be different from the nineteenth district; but I might just as well have been a Congressman from North Dakota trying to get an appropriation for a lighthouse and a coast survey. Denver Galloway had ambitions in the manager line, and what I said didn't amount to as much as a fig-leaf at the National Dressmakers' Convention. 'I'll give you three days to cogitate about going,' says Denver; 'and I'll introduce you to General Rompiro to-morrow, so you can get his ideas drawn right from the rosewood.'

"I put on my best reception-to-Booker-Washington manner, the next day and tapped the distinguished rubber-plant for what he knew.

"General Rompiro wasn't so gloomy inside as he appeared on the surface. He was polite enough; and he exuded a number of sounds that made a fair stagger at arranging themselves into language. It was English he aimed at, and when his system of syntax reached your mind it wasn't past you to understand it. If you took a college professor's magazine essay and a Chinese laundryman's explanation of a lost shirt and jumbled 'em together, you'd have about what the General handed you out for conversation. He told me all about his bleeding country, and what they were trying to do for it before the doctor came. But he mostly talked of Denver C. Galloway.

"'Ah, señor,' says he, 'that is the most fine of mans. Never I have seen one man so magnifico, so gr-r-rand, so

conformable to make done things so swiftly by other mans.
He shall make other mans do the acts and himself to order
and regulate, until we arrive at seeing accomplishments of a
suddenly. Oh, yes, señor. In my countree there is not such
mans of so beegness, so good talk, so compliments, so strong-
ness of sense and such. Ah, that Señor Galloway!'

" ' Yes,' says I, ' old Denver is the boy you want. He's
managed every kind of business here except filibustering, and
he might as well complete the list.'

" Before the three days was up I decided to join Denver
in his campaign. Denver got three months' vacation from
his hotel owners. For a week we lived in a room with the
General, and got all the pointers about his country that we
could interpret from the noises he made. When we got ready
to start, Denver had a pocket full of memorandums, and
letters from the General to his friends, and a list of names
and addresses of loyal politicians who would help along the
boom of the exiled popular idol. Besides these liabilities we
carried assets to the amount of $20,000 in assorted United
States currency. General Rompiro looked like a burnt ef-
figy, but he was Br'er Fox himself when it came to the real
science of politics.

" ' Here is moneys,' says the General, ' of a small amount.
There is more with me — moocho more. Plentee moneys shall
you be supplied, Señor Galloway. More I shall send you at
all times that you need. I shall desire to pay ifeefty — one
hundred thousand pesos, if necessario, to be elect. How no?
Sacramento! If that I am president and do not make one
meelion dolla in the one year you shall keek me on that side!
— *valgame Dios!* '

" Denver got a Cuban cigar-maker to fix up a little cipher
code with English and Spanish words, and gave the General
a copy, so we could cable him bulletins about the election, or
for more money, and then we were ready to start. General

Rompiro escorted us to the steamer. On the pier he hugged Denver around the waist and sobbed. 'Noble mans,' says he, 'General Rompiro propels into you his confidence and trust. Go, in the hands of the saints to do the work for your friend. *Viva la libertad!* '

"' Sure,' says Denver. 'And viva la liberality an' la soap-erino and hoch der land of the lotus and the vote us. Don't worry, General. We'll have you elected as sure as bananas grow upside down.'

"' Make pictures on me,' pleads the General —' make pictures on me for money as it is needful.'

"' Does he want to be tattooed, would you think?' asks Denver, wrinkling up his eyes.

"' Stupid!' says I. 'He wants you to draw on him for election expenses. It'll be worse than tattooing. More like an autopsy.'

"Me and Denver steamed down to Panama, and then hiked across the Isthmus, and then by steamer again down to the town of Espiritu on the coast of the General's country.

"That was a town to send J. Howard Payne to the growler. I'll tell you how you could make one like it. Take a lot of Filipino huts and a couple of hundred brick-kilns and arrange 'em in squares in a cemetery. Cart down all the conservatory plants in the Astor and Vanderbilt greenhouses, and stick 'em about wherever there's room. Turn all the Bellevue patients and the barbers' convention and the Tuskegee school loose in the streets, and run the thermometer up to 120 in the shade. Set a fringe of the Rocky Mountains around the rear, let it rain, and set the whole business on Rockaway Beach in the middle of January — and you'd have a good imitation of Espiritu.

"It took me and Denver about a week to get acclimated. Denver sent out the letters the General had given him, and notified the rest of the gang that there was something doing at the captain's office. We set up headquarters in an old 'dobe house on a side street where the grass was waist high. The election was only four weeks off; but there wasn't any excitement. The home candidate for president was named Roadrickeys. This town of Espiritu wasn't the capital any more than Cleveland, Ohio, is the capital of the United States, but it was the political centre where they cooked up revolutions, and made up the slates.

"At the end of the week Denver says the machine is started running.

"'Sully,' says he, 'we've got a walkover. Just because General Rompiro ain't Don Juan-on-the-spot the other crowd ain't at work. They're as full of apathy as a territorial delegate during the chaplain's prayer. Now, we want to introduce a little hot stuff in the way of campaigning, and we'll surprise 'em at the polls.'

"'How are you going to go about it?' I asks.

"'Why, the usual way,' says Denver, surprised. 'We'll get the orators on our side out every night to make speeches in the native lingo, and have torch-light parades under the shade of the palms, and free drinks, and buy up all the brass bands, of course, and — well, I'll turn the baby-kissing over to you, Sully — I've seen a lot of 'em.'

"'What else?' says I.

"'Why, you know,' says Denver. 'We get the heelers out with the crackly two-spots, and coal-tickets, and orders for groceries, and have a couple of picnics out under the banyan-trees, and dances in the Firemen's Hall — and the usual things. But first of all, Sully, I'm going to have the biggest clam-bake down on the beach that was ever seen south of the tropic of Capricorn. I figured that out from the start. We'll stuff the whole town and the jungle folk for miles around with clams. That's the first thing on the programme. Suppose you go out now, and make the arrangements for that.

I want to look over the estimates the General made of the vote in the coast districts.'

"I had learned some Spanish in Mexico, so I goes out, as Denver says, and in fifteen minutes I come back to head-quarters.

"'If there ever was a clam in this country nobody ever saw it,' I says.

"'Great sky-rockets!' says Denver, with his mouth and eyes open. 'No clams? How in the — who ever saw a country without clams? What kind of a — how's an election to be pulled off without a clam-bake, I'd like to know? Are you sure there's no clams, Sully?'

"'Not even a can,' says I.

"'Then for God's sake go out and try to find what the people here do eat. We've got to fill 'em up with grub of some kind.'

"I went out again. Sully was manager. In half an hour I gets back.

"'They eat,' says I, 'tortillas, cassava, carne de chivo, arroz con pollo, aquacates, zapates, yucca, and huevos fritos.'

"'A man that would eat them things,' says Denver, getting a little mad, 'ought to have his vote challenged.'

"In a few more days the campaign managers from the other towns came sliding into Espiritu. Our headquarters was a busy place. We had an interpreter, and ice-water, and drinks, and cigars, and Denver flashed the General's roll so often that it got so small you couldn't have bought a Republican vote in Ohio with it.

"And then Denver cabled to General Rompiro for ten thousand dollars more and got it.

"There were a number of Americans in Espiritu, but they were all in business or grafts of some kind, and wouldn't take any hand in politics, which was sensible enough. But they showed me and Denver a fine time, and fixed us up so we сould get decent things to eat and drink. There was one American, named Hicks, used to come and loaf at the headquarters. Hicks had had fourteen years of Espiritu. He was six feet four and weighed in at 135. Cocoa was his line; and coast fever and the climate had taken all the life out of him. They said he hadn't smiled in eight years. His face was three feet long, and it never moved except when he opened it to take quinine. He used to sit in our headquarters and kill fleas and talk sarcastic.

" ' I don't take much interest in politics,' says Hicks, one day, ' but I'd like you to tell me what you're trying to do down here, Galloway? '

" ' We're boosting General Rompiro, of course,' says Denver. ' We're going to put him in the presidential chair. I'm his manager.'

" ' Well,' says Hicks, ' if I was you I'd be a little slower about it. You've got a long time ahead of you, you know.'

" ' Not any longer than I need,' says Denver.

" Denver went ahead and worked things smooth. He dealt out money on the quiet to his lieutenants, and they were always coming after it. There was free drinks for everybody in town, and bands playing every night, and fireworks, and there was a lot of heelers going around buying up votes day and night for the new style of politics in Espiritu, and everybody liked it.

" The day set for the election was November 4th. On the night before Denver and me were smoking our pipes in headquarters, and in comes Hicks and unjoints himself, and sits in a chair, mournful. Denver is cheerful and confident. ' Rompiro will win in a romp,' says he. ' We'll carry the country by 10,000. It's all over but the vivas. To-morrow will tell the tale.'

" ' What's going to happen to-morrow? ' asks Hicks.

" ' Why, the presidential election, of course,' says Denver.

"'Say,' says Hicks, looking kind of funny, 'didn't any-body tell you fellows that the election was held a week be-fore you came? Congress changed the date to July 27th. Roadrickeys was elected by 17,000. I thought you was boom-ing old Rompiro for next term, two years from now. Won-dered if you was going to keep up such a hot lick that long.'

"I dropped my pipe on the floor. Denver bit the stem off of his. Neither of us said anything.

"And then I heard a sound like somebody ripping a clap-board off of a barn-roof. 'Twas Hicks laughing for the first time in eight years."

Sully Magoon paused while the waiter poured us black cof-fee.

"Your friend was, indeed, something of a manager," I said.

"Wait a minute," said Sully, "I haven't given you any idea of what he could do yet. That's all to come.

"When we got back to New York there was General Rom-piro waiting for us on the pier. He was dancing like a cinnamon bear, all impatient for the news, for Denver had just cabled him when we would arrive and nothing more.

"'Am I elect?' he shouts. 'Am I elect, friend of mine? Is it that mine country have demand General Rompiro for the president? The last dollar of mine have I sent you that last time. It is necessario that I am elect. I have not more money. Am I elect, Señor Galloway?'

"Denver turns to me.

"'Leave me with old Rompey, Sully,' he says. 'I've got to break it to him gently. 'Twould be indecent for other eyes to witness the operation. This is the time, Sully,' says he, 'when old Denver has got to make good as a jollier and a silver-tongued sorcerer, or else give up all the medals he's earned.'

"A couple of days later I went around to the hotel. There

was Denver in his old place, looking like the hero of two historical novels, and telling 'em what a fine time he'd had down on his orange plantation in Florida.

"'Did you fix things up with the General?' I asks him.

"'Did I?' says Denver. 'Come and see.'

"He takes me by the arm and walks me to the dining-room door. There was a little chocolate-brown fat man in a dress suit, with his face shining with joy as he swelled himself and skipped about the floor. Danged if Denver hadn't made General Rompiro head waiter of the Hotel Brunswick!"

"Is Mr. Galloway still in the managing business?" I asked, as Mr. Magoon ceased.

Sully shook his head.

"Denver married an auburn-haired widow that owns a big hotel in Harlem. He just helps around the place."

XIX

WHISTLING DICK'S CHRISTMAS STOCKING

IT was with much caution that Whistling Dick slid back the door of the box-car, for Article 5716, City Ordinances, authorized (perhaps unconstitutionally) arrest on suspicion, and he was familiar of old with this ordinance. So, before climbing out, he surveyed the field with all the care of a good general.

He saw no change since his last visit to this big, almsgiving, long-suffering city of the South, the cold weather paradise of the tramps. The levee where his freight-car stood was pimpled with dark bulks of merchandise. The breeze reeked with the well-remembered, sickening smell of the old tarpaulins that covered bales and barrels. The dun river slipped along among the shipping with an oily gurgle. Far down toward Chalmette he could see the great bend in the stream outlined by the row of electric lights. Across the river Algiers lay, a long, irregular blot, made darker by the dawn which lightened the sky beyond. An industrious tug or two, coming for some early sailing ship, gave a few appalling toots, that seemed to be the signal for breaking day. The Italian luggers were creeping nearer their landing, laden with early vegetables and shellfish. A vague roar, subterranean in quality, from dray wheels and street cars, began to make itself heard and felt; and the ferryboats, the Mary Anns of water craft, stirred sullenly to their menial morning tasks.

Whistling Dick's red head popped suddenly back into the car. A sight too imposing and magnificent for his gaze had

258

been added to the scene. A vast, incomparable policeman rounded a pile of rice sacks and stood within twenty yards of the car. The daily miracle of the dawn, now being performed above Algiers, received the flattering attention of this specimen of municipal official splendour. He gazed with unbiased dignity at the faintly glowing colours until, at last, he turned to them his broad back, as if convinced that legal interference was not needed, and the sunrise might proceed unchecked. So he turned his face to the rice bags, and, drawing a flat flask from an inside pocket, he placed it to his lips and regarded the firmament.

Whistling Dick, professional tramp, possessed a half-friendly acquaintance with this officer. They had met several times before on the levee at night, for the officer, himself a lover of music, had been attracted by the exquisite whistling of the shiftless vagabond. Still, he did not care, under the present circumstances, to renew the acquaintance. There is a difference between meeting a policeman upon a lonely wharf and whistling a few operatic airs with him, and being caught by him crawling out of a freight-car. So Dick waited, as even a New Orleans policeman must move on some time — perhaps it is a retributive law of nature — and before long " Big Fritz " majestically disappeared between the trains of cars.

Whistling Dick waited as long as his judgment advised, and then slid swiftly to the ground. Assuming as far as possible the air of an honest labourer who seeks his daily toil, he moved across the network of railway lines, with the intention of making his way by quiet Girod Street to a certain bench in Lafayette Square, where, according to appointment, he hoped to rejoin a pal known as " Slick," this adventurous pilgrim having preceded him by one day in a cattle-car into which a loose slat had enticed him.

As Whistling Dick picked his way where night still lingered

among the big, reeking, musty warehouses, he gave way to the habit that had won for him his title. Subdued, yet clear, with each note as true and liquid as a bobolink's, his whistle tinkled about the dim, cold mountains of brick like drops of rain falling into a hidden pool. He followed an air, but it swam mistily into a swirling current of improvisation. You could cull out the trill of mountain brooks, the staccato of green rushes shivering above chilly lagoons, the pipe of sleepy birds.

Rounding a corner, the whistler collided with a mountain of blue and brass.

"So," observed the mountain calmly, "You are already pack. Und dere vill not pe frost before two veeks yet! Und you haf forgotten how to vistle. Dere was a valse note in dot last bar."

"Watcher know about it?" said Whistling Dick, with tentative familiarity; "you wit yer little Gherman-band nix-cumrous chunes. Watcher know about music? Pick yer ears, and listen agin. Here's de way I whistled it — see?"

He puckered his lips, but the big policeman held up his hand.

"Shtop," he said, "und learn der right way. Und learn also dot a rolling shtone can't vistle for a cent."

Big Fritz's heavy moustache rounded into a circle, and from its depths came a sound deep and mellow as that from a flute. He repeated a few bars of the air the tramp had been whistling. The rendition was cold, but correct, and he emphasized the note he had taken exception to.

"Dot p is p natural, und not p vlat. Py der vay, you petter pe glad I meet you. Von hour later, und I vould haf to put you in a gage to vistle mit der chail pirds. Der orders are to bull all der pums after sunrise."

"To which?"

" To bull der pums — eferybody mitout fisible means. Dirty days is der price, or fifteen tollars."

" Is dat straight, or a game you givin' me? "

" It's der pest tip you efer had. I gif it to you pecause I pelief you are not so bad as der rest. Und pecause you gan visl ' Der Freischütz ' bezzer dan I myself gan. Don't run against any more bolicemans aroundt der corners, but go away from town a few tays. Goot-pye."

So Madame Orleans had at last grown weary of the strange and ruffled brood that came yearly to nestle beneath her charitable pinions.

After the big policeman had departed, Whistling Dick stood for an irresolute minute, feeling all the outraged indignation of a delinquent tenant who is ordered to vacate his premises. He had pictured to himself a day of dreamful ease when he should have joined his pal; a day of lounging on the wharf, munching the bananas and cocoanuts scattered in unloading the fruit steamers; and then a feast along the free-lunch counters from which the easy-going owners were too good-natured or too generous to drive him away, and afterward a pipe in one of the little flowery parks and a snooze in some shady corner of the wharf. But here was a stern order to exile, and one that he knew must be obeyed. So, with a wary eye open from the gleam of brass buttons, he began his retreat toward a rural refuge. A few days in the country need not necessarily prove disastrous. Beyond the possibility of a slight nip of frost, there was no formidable evil to be looked for.

However, it was with a depressed spirit that Whistling Dick passed the old French market on his chosen route down the river. For safety's sake he still presented to the world his portrayal of the part of the worthy artisan on his way to labour. A stall-keeper in the market, undeceived, hailed him by the generic name of his ilk, and " Jack " halted, taken by surprise. The vender, melted by this proof of his own acuteness, bestowed a foot of Frankfurter and half a loaf, and thus the problem of breakfast was solved.

When the streets, from topographical reasons, began to shun the river bank the exile mounted to the top of the levee, and on its well-trodden path pursued his way. The suburban eye regarded him with cold suspicion, individuals reflected the stern spirit of the city's heartless edict. He missed the seclusion of the crowded town and the safety he could always find in the multitude.

At Chalmette, six miles upon his desultory way, there suddenly menaced him a vast and bewildering industry. A new port was being established; the dock was being built, compresses were going up; picks and shovels and barrows struck at him like serpents from every side. An arrogant foreman bore down upon him, estimating his muscles with the eye of a recruiting-sergeant. Brown men and black men all about him were toiling away. He fled in terror.

By noon he had reached the country of the plantations, the great, sad, silent levels bordering the mighty river. He overlooked fields of sugar-cane so vast that their farthest limits melted into the sky. The sugar-making season was well advanced, and the cutters were at work; the waggons creaked drearily after them; the Negro teamsters inspired the mules to greater speed with mellow and sonorous imprecations. Dark-green groves, blurred by the blue of distance, showed where the plantation-houses stood. The tall chimneys of the sugar-mills caught the eye miles distant, like lighthouses at sea.

At a certain point Whistling Dick's unerring nose caught the scent of frying fish. Like a pointer to a quail, he made his way down the levee side straight to the camp of a credulous and ancient fisherman, whom he charmed with song and story, so that he dined like an admiral, and then like a philosopher annihilated the worst three hours of the day by a nap under the trees.

When he awoke and again continued his hegira, a frosty sparkle in the air had succeeded the drowsy warmth of the day, and as this portent of a chilly night translated itself to the brain of Sir Peregrine, he lengthened his stride and bethought him of shelter. He travelled a road that faithfully followed the convolutions of the levee, running along its base, but whither he knew not. Bushes and rank grass crowded it to the wheel ruts, and out of this ambuscade the pests of the lowlands swarmed after him, humming a keen, vicious soprano. And as the night grew nearer, although colder, the whine of the mosquitoes became a greedy, petulant snarl that shut out all other sounds. To his right, against the heavens, he saw a green light moving, and, accompanying it, the masts and funnels of a big incoming steamer, moving as upon a screen at a magic-lantern show. And there were mysterious marshes at his left, out of which came queer gurgling cries and a choked croaking. The whistling vagrant struck up a merry warble to offset these melancholy influences, and it is likely that never before, since Pan himself jigged it on his reeds, had such sounds been heard in those depressing solitudes.

A distant clatter in the rear quickly developed into the swift beat of horses' hoofs, and Whistling Dick stepped aside into the dew-wet grass to clear the track. Turning his head, he saw approaching a fine team of stylish grays drawing a double surrey. A stout man with a white moustache occupied the front seat, giving all his attention to the rigid lines in his hands. Behind him sat a placid, middle-aged lady and a brilliant-looking girl hardly arrived at young ladyhood. The lap-robe had slipped partly from the knees of the gentleman driving, and Whistling Dick saw two stout canvas bags between his feet — bags such as, while loafing in cities, he had seen warily transferred between express wag-gons and bank doors. The remaining space in the vehicle was filled with parcels of various sizes and shapes.

As the surrey swept even with the sidetracked tramp, the bright-eyed girl, seized by some merry, madcap impulse, leaned out toward him with a sweet, dazzling smile, and cried, "Mer-ry Christ-mas!" in a shrill, plaintive treble.

Such a thing had not often happened to Whistling Dick, and he felt handicapped in devising the correct response. But lacking time for reflection, he let his instinct decide, and snatching off his battered derby, he rapidly extended it at arm's length, and drew it back with a continuous motion, and shouted a loud, but ceremonious, "Ah, there!" after the flying surrey.

The sudden movement of the girl had caused one of the parcels to become unwrapped, and something limp and black fell from it into the road. The tramp picked it up, and found it to be a new black silk stocking, long and fine and slender. It crunched crisply, and yet with a luxurious soft-ness, between his fingers.

"Ther bloomin' little skeezicks!" said Whistling Dick, with a broad grin bisecting his freckled face. "W'ot d' yer think of dat, now! Mer-ry Chris-mus! Sounded like a cuckoo clock, dat's what she did. Dem guys is swells, too, bet yer life, an' der old 'un stacks dem sacks of dough down under his trotters like dey was common as dried apples. Been shoppin' fer Chrismus, and de kid's lost one of her new socks w'ot she was goin' to hold up Santy wid. De bloomin' little skeezicks! Wit' her 'Mer-ry Chris-mus!' W'ot d' yer t'ink! Same as to say, 'Hello, Jack, how goes it?' and as swell as Fift' Av'noo, and as easy as a blowout in Cincinnat.'"

Whistling Dick folded the stocking carefully, and stuffed it into his pocket.

It was nearly two hours later when he came upon signs of habitation. The buildings of an extensive plantation were brought into view by a turn in the road. He easily selected the planter's residence in a large square building with two wings, with numerous good-sized, well-lighted windows, and broad verandas running around its full extent. It was set upon a smooth lawn, which was faintly lit by the far-reaching rays of the lamps within. A noble grove surrounded it, and old-fashioned shrubbery grew thickly about the walks and fences. The quarters of the hands and the mill buildings were situated at a distance in the rear.

The road was now enclosed on each side by a fence, and presently, as Whistling Dick drew nearer the houses, he suddenly stopped and sniffed the air.

" If dere ain't a hobo stew cookin' somewhere in dis immediate precinct," he said to himself, " me nose has quit tellin' de trut'."

Without hesitation he climbed the fence to windward. He found himself in an apparently disused lot, where piles of old bricks were stacked, and rejected, decaying lumber. In a corner he saw the faint glow of a fire that had become little more than a bed of living coals, and he thought he could see some dim human forms sitting or lying about it. He drew nearer, and by the light of a little blaze that suddenly flared up he saw plainly the fat figure of a ragged man in an old brown sweater and cap.

" Dat man," said Whistling Dick to himself softly, " is a dead ringer for Boston Harry. I'll try him wit de high sign."

He whistled one or two bars of a rag-time melody, and the air was immediately taken up, and then quickly ended with a peculiar run. The first whistler walked confidently up to the fire. The fat man looked up, and spake in a loud, asthmatic wheeze:

" Gents, the unexpected but welcome addition to our circle is Mr. Whistling Dick, an old friend of mine for whom I fully vouches. The waiter will lay another cover at once. Mr. W. D. will join us at supper, during which function he will enlighten us in regard to the circumstances that give us the pleasure of his company."

" Chewin' de stuffin' ou 'n de dictionary, as usual, Boston," said Whistling Dick; " but t'anks all de same for de invitashun. I guess I finds meself here about de same way as yous guys. A cop gimme de tip dis mornin'. Yous workin' on dis farm? "

" A guest," said Boston sternly, " shouldn't never insult his entertainers until he's filled up wid grub. 'Tain't good business sense. Workin'! — but I will restrain myself. We five — me, Deaf Pete, Blinky, Goggles, and Indiana Tom — got put on to this scheme of Noo Orleans to work visiting gentlemen upon her dirty streets, and we hit the road last evening just as the tender hues of twilight had flopped down upon the daisies and things. Blinky, pass the empty oyster-can at your left to the empty gentleman at your right."

For the next ten minutes the gang of roadsters paid their undivided attention to the supper. In an old five-gallon kerosene can they had cooked a stew of potatoes, meat, and onions, which they partook of from smaller cans they had found scattered about the vacant lot.

Whistling Dick had known Boston Harry of old, and knew him to be one of the shrewdest and most successful of his brotherhood. He looked like a prosperous stock-drover or a solid merchant from some country village. He was stout and hale, with a ruddy, always smoothly shaven face. His clothes were strong and neat, and he gave special attention to his decent-appearing shoes. During the past ten years he had acquired a reputation for working a larger number of successfully managed confidence games than any of his acquaintances, and he had not a day's work to be counted against him. It was rumoured among his associates that he had saved a considerable amount of money. The four other men were fair specimens of the slinking, ill-clad, noisome genus who carried their labels of " suspicious " in plain view.

After the bottom of the large can had been scraped, and pipes lit at the coals, two of the men called Boston aside and spake with him lowly and mysteriously. He nodded decisively, and then said aloud to Whistling Dick:

" Listen, sonny, to some plain talky-talk. We five are on a lay. I've guaranteed you to be square, and you're to come in on the profits equal with the boys, and you've got to help. Two hundred hands on this plantation are expecting to be paid a week's wages to-morrow morning. To-morrow's Christmas, and they want to lay off. Says the boss: ' Work from five to nine in the morning to get a train load of sugar off, and I'll pay every man cash down for the week and a day extra.' They say: ' Hooray for the boss! It goes.' He drives to Noo Orleans to-day, and fetches back the cold dollars. Two thousand and seventy-four fifty is the amount. I got the figures from a man who talks too much, who got 'em from the bookkeeper. The boss of this plantation thinks he's going to pay this wealth to the hands. He's got it down wrong; he's going to pay it to us. It's going to stay in the leisure class, where it belongs. Now, half of this haul goes to me, and the other half the rest of you may divide. Why the difference? I represent the brains. It's my scheme. Here's the way we're going to get it. There's some company at supper in the house, but they'll leave about nine. They've just happened in for an hour or so. If they don't go pretty soon, we'll work the scheme anyhow. We want all night to get away good with the dollars. They're heavy. About nine o'clock Deaf Pete and Blinky'll go down the road about a quarter beyond the house, and set fire to a big cane-field there that the cutters haven't touched yet. The wind's just right to have it roaring in two minutes. The alarm'll be given, and every man Jack about the place will be down there in ten minutes, fighting fire. That'll leave the money sacks and the women alone in the house for us to handle. You've heard cane burn? Well, there's mighty few women can screech loud enough to be heard above its crackling. The thing's dead safe. The only danger is in being caught be-fore we can get far enough away with the money. Now, if you —"

" Boston," interrupted Whistling Dick, rising to his feet, " T'anks for de grub yous fellers has given me, but I'll be movin' on now."

" What do you mean? " asked Boston, also rising.

" W'y, you can count me outer dis deal. You oughter know that. I'm on de bum all right enough, but dat other t'ing don't go wit' me. Burglary is no good. I'll say good night and many t'anks fer —"

Whistling Dick had moved away a few steps as he spoke, but he stopped very suddenly. Boston had covered him with a short revolver of roomy calibre.

" Take your seat," said the tramp leader. " I'd feel mighty proud of myself if I let you go and spoil the game. You'll stick right in this camp until we finish the job. The end of that brick pile is your limit. You go two inches beyond that, and I'll have to shoot. Better take it easy, now."

" It's my way of doin'," said Whistling Dick. " Easy goes. You can depress de muzzle of dat twelve-incher, and run 'er back on de trucks. I remains, as de newspapers says, ' in yer midst.' "

"All right," said Boston, lowering his piece, as the other returned and took his seat again on a projecting plank in a pile of timber. "Don't try to leave; that's all. I wouldn't miss this chance even if I had to shoot an old acquaintance to make it go. I don't want to hurt anybody specially, but this thousand dollars I'm going to get will fix me for fair. I'm going to drop the road, and start a saloon in a little town I know about. I'm tired of being kicked around."

Boston Harry took from his pocket a cheap silver watch, and held it near the fire.

"It's a quarter to nine," he said. "Pete, you and Blinky start. Go down the road past the house, and fire the cane in a dozen places. Then strike for the levee, and come back on it, instead of the road, so you won't meet anybody. By the time you get back the men will all be striking out for the fire, and we'll break for the house and collar the dollars. Everybody cough up what matches he's got."

The two surly tramps made a collection of all the matches in the party, Whistling Dick contributing his quota with propitiatory alacrity, and then they departed in the dim starlight in the direction of the road.

Of the three remaining vagrants, two, Goggles and Indiana Tom, reclined lazily upon convenient lumber and regarded Whistling Dick with undisguised disfavour. Boston, observing that the dissenting recruit was disposed to remain peaceably, relaxed a little of his vigilance. Whistling Dick arose presently and strolled leisurely up and down keeping carefully within the territory assigned him.

"Dis planter chap," he said, pausing before Boston Harry, "w'ot makes yer t'ink he's got de tin in de house wit' 'im?"

"I'm advised of the facts in the case," said Boston. "He drove to Noo Orleans and got it, I say, to-day. Want to change your mind now and come in?"

" Naw, I was just askin'. Wot kind o' team did de boss drive ? "

" Pair of grays."

" Double surrey ? "

" Yep."

" Women folks along ? '

" Wife and kid. Say, what morning paper are you trying to pump news for ? "

" I was just conversin' to pass de time away. I guess dat team passed me in de road dis evenin'. Dat's all."

As Whistling Dick put his hands into his pockets and continued his curtailed beat up and down by the fire, he felt the silk stocking he had picked up in the road.

" Ther bloomin' little skeezicks," he muttered, with a grin.

As he walked up and down he could see, through a sort of natural opening or lane among the trees, the planter's residence some seventy-five yards distant. The side of the house toward him exhibited spacious, well-lighted windows through which a soft radiance streamed, illuminating the broad veranda and some extent of the lawn beneath.

" What's that you said ? " asked Boston, sharply.

" Oh, nuttin' 't all," said Whistling Dick, lounging carelessly, and kicking meditatively at a little stone on the ground.

" Just as easy," continued the warbling vagrant softly to himself, " an' sociable an' swell an' sassy, wit' her ' Mer-ry Chris-mus,' Wot d'yer t'ink, now ! "

Dinner, two hours late, was being served in the Bellemeade plantation dining-room.

The dining-room and all its appurtenances spoke of an old regime that was here continued rather than suggested to the memory. The plate was rich to the extent that its age and quaintness alone saved it from being showy; there were interesting names signed in the corners of the pictures on the

walls; the viands were of the kind that bring a shine into
the eyes of gourmets. The service was swift, silent, lavish,
as in the days when the waiters were assets like the plate.
The names by which the planter's family and their visitors
addressed one another were historic in the annals of two nations. Their manners and conversation had that most difficult kind of ease — the kind that still preserves punctilio.
The planter himself seemed to be the dynamo that generated
the larger portion of the gaiety and wit. The younger ones
at the board found it more than difficult to turn back on
him his guns of raillery and banter. It is true, the young
men attempted to storm his works repeatedly, incited by the
hope of gaining the approbation of their fair companions;
but even when they sped a well-aimed shaft, the planter
forced them to feel defeat by the tremendous discomfiting
thunder of the laughter with which he accompanied his re-
torts. At the head of the table, serene, matronly, benevolent,
reigned the mistress of the house, placing here and there the
right smile, the right word, the encouraging glance.

The talk of the party was too desultory, too evanescent to
follow, but at last they came to the subject of the tramp
nuisance, one that had of late vexed the plantations for many
miles around. The planter seized the occasion to direct his
good-natured fire of raillery at the mistress, accusing her of
encouraging the plague. "They swarm up and down the
river every winter," he said. "They overrun New Orleans,
and we catch the surplus, which is generally the worst part.
And, a day or two ago, Madame New Orleans, suddenly discovering that she can't go shopping without brushing her
skirts against great rows of the vagabonds sunning themselves on the banquettes, says to the police: 'Catch 'em all,'
and the police catch a dozen or two, and the remaining three
or four thousand overflow up and down the levees, and madame there"— pointing tragically with the carving-knife at

her —" feeds them. They won't work; they defy my over-
seers, and they make friends with my dogs; and you, madame,
feed them before my eyes, and intimidate me when I would interfere. Tell us, please, how many to-day did you thus incite
to future laziness and depredation? "

" Six, I think," said madame, with a reflective smile; " but
you know two of them offered to work, for you heard them
yourself."

The planter's disconcerting laugh rang out again.

" Yes, at their own trades. And one was an artificial-
flower maker, and the other a glass-blower. Oh, they were
looking for work! Not a hand would they consent to lift to
labour of any other kind."

" And another one," continued the soft-hearted mistress,
" used quite good language. It was really extraordinary for
one of his class. And he carried a watch. And had lived in
Boston. I don't believe they are all bad. They have always
seemed to me to rather lack development. I always look
upon them as children with whom wisdom has remained at a
standstill while whiskers have continued to grow. We passed
one this evening as we were driving home who had a face as
good as it was incompetent. He was whistling the inter-
mezzo from ' Cavalleria ' and blowing the spirit of Mascagni
himself into it."

A bright-eyed young girl who sat at the left of the mistress leaned over, and said in a confidential undertone:

" I wonder, mamma, if that tramp we passed on the road
found my stocking, and do you think he will hang it up to-
night? Now I can hang up but one. Do you know why I
wanted a new pair of silk stockings when I have plenty?
Well, old Aunt Judy says, if you hang up two that have
never been worn, Santa Claus will fill one with good things,
and Monsieur Pambe will place in the other payment for all
the words you have spoken — good or bad — on the day be-

fore Christmas. That's why I've been unusually nice and polite to everyone to-day. Monsieur Pambe, you know, is a witch gentleman; he —"

The words of the young girl were interrupted by a startling thing.

Like the wraith of some burned-out shooting star, a black streak came crashing through the window-pane and upon the table, where it shivered into fragments a dozen pieces of crystal and china ware, and then glanced between the heads of the guests to the wall, imprinting therein a deep, round indentation, at which, to-day, the visitor to Bellemeade marvels as he gazes upon it and listens to this tale as it is told.

The women screamed in many keys, and the men sprang to their feet, and would have laid their hands upon their swords had not the verities of chronology forbidden.

The planter was the first to act; he sprang to the intruding missile, and held it up to view.

" By Jupiter! " he cried. " A meteoric shower of hoisery! Has communication at last been established with Mars? "

" I should say — ahem! — Venus," ventured a young-gentleman visitor, looking hopefully for approbation toward the unresponsive young-lady visitors.

The planter held at arm's length the unceremonious visitor — a long dangling black stocking. " It's loaded," he announced.

As he spoke he reversed the stocking, holding it by the toe, and down from it dropped a roundish stone, wrapped about by a piece of yellowish paper. " Now for the first interstellar message of the century! " he cried; and nodding to the company, who had crowded about him, he adjusted his glasses with provoking deliberation, and examined it closely. When he finished, he had changed from the jolly host to the practical, decisive man of business. He immediately struck a bell, and said to the silent-footed mulatto man who responded:

" Go and tell Mr. Wesley to get Reeves and Maurice and about ten stout hands they can rely upon, and come to the hall door at once. Tell him to have the men arm themselves, and bring plenty of ropes and plough lines. Tell him to hurry." And then he read aloud from the paper these words:

To THE GENT OF DE HOUS:

Dere is five tuff hoboes xcept meself in the vaken lot near de road war de old brick piles is. Dey got me stuck up wid a gun see and 1 taken dis means of comunikaten. 2 of der lads is gone down to set fire to de cain field below de hous and when yous fellers goes to turn de hoes on it de hole gang is goin to rob de hous of de money yoo gotto pay off wit say git a move on ye say de kid dropt dis sock in der rode tel her mery crismus de same as she told me. Ketch de bums down de rode first and den sen a relefe core to get me out of soke youres truly, WHISTLEN DICK.

There was some quiet, but rapid, manœuvring at Bellemeade during the ensuing half hour, which ended in five disgusted and sullen tramps being captured, and locked securely in an outhouse pending the coming of the morning and retribution. For another result, the visiting young gentlemen had secured the unqualified worship of the visiting young ladies by their distinguished and heroic conduct. For still another, behold Whistling Dick, the hero, seated at the planter's table, feasting upon viands his experience had never before included, and waited upon by admiring femininity in shapes of such beauty and " swellness " that even his ever-full mouth could scarcely prevent him from whistling. He was made to disclose in detail his adventure with the evil gang of Boston Harry, and how he cunningly wrote the note and wrapped it around the stone and placed it in the toe of the stocking, and, watching his chance, sent it silently, with a wonderful centrifugal momentum, like a comet, at one of the big lighted windows of the dining-room.

The planter vowed that the wanderer should wander no

more; that his was a goodness and an honesty that should be rewarded, and that a debt of gratitude had been made that must be paid; for had he not saved them from a doubtless imminent loss, and maybe a greater calamity? He assured Whistling Dick that he might consider himself a charge upon the honour of Bellemeade; that a position suited to his powers would be found for him at once, and hinted that the way would be heartily smoothed for him to rise to as high places of emolument and trust as the plantation afforded.

But now, they said, he must be weary, and the immediate thing to consider was rest and sleep. So the mistress spoke to a servant, and Whistling Dick was conducted to a room in the wing of the house occupied by the servants. To this room, in a few minutes, was brought a portable tin bathtub filled with water, which was placed on a piece of oiled cloth upon the floor. There the vagrant was left to pass the night.

By the light of a candle he examined the room. A bed, with the covers neatly turned back, revealed snowy pillows and sheets. A worn, but clean, red carpet covered the floor. There was a dresser with a beveled mirror, a washstand with a flowered bowl and pitcher; the two or three chairs were softly upholstered. A little table held books, papers, and a day-old cluster of roses in a jar. There were towels on a rack and soap in a white dish.

Whistling Dick set his candle on a chair and placed his hat carefully under the table. After satisfying what we must suppose to have been his curiosity by a sober scrutiny, he remov' his coat, folded it, and laid it upon the floor, near the wall, as far as possible from the unused bathtub. Taking his coat for a pillow, he stretched himself luxuriously upon the carpet.

When, on Christmas morning, the first streaks of dawn broke above the marshes, Whistling Dick awoke, and reached instinctively for his hat. Then he remembered that the skirts

of Fortune had swept him into their folds on the night previous, and he went to the window and raised it, to let the
fresh breath of the morning cool his brow and fix the yet
dream-like memory of his good luck within his brain.

As he stood there, certain dread and ominous sounds pierced
the fearful hollow of his ear.

The force of plantation workers, eager to complete the
shortened task allotted to them, were all astir. The mighty
din of the ogre Labour shook the earth, and the poor tattered
and forever disguised Prince in search of his fortune held
tight to the window-sill even in the enchanted castle, and
trembled.

Already from the bosom of the mill came the thunder of
rolling barrels of sugar, and (prison-like sounds) there was
a great rattling of chains as the mules were harried with stimu-
lant imprecations to their places by the waggon-tongues. A
little vicious " dummy " engine, with a train of flat cars in
tow, stewed and fumed on the plantation tap of the narrow-
gauge railroad, and a toiling, hurrying, hallooing stream of
workers were dimly seen in the half darkness loading the
train with the weekly output of sugar. Here was a poem;
an epic — nay, a tragedy — with work, the curse of the world,
for its theme.

The December air was frosty, but the sweat broke out upon
Whistling Dick's face. He thrust his head out of the window, and looked down. Fifteen feet below him, against the
wall of the house, he could make out that a border of flowers grew, and by that token he overhung a bed of soft earth.

Softly as a burglar goes, he clambered out upon the sill,
lowered himself until he hung by his hands alone, and then
dropped safely. No one seemed to be about upon this side
of the house. He dodged low, and skimmed swiftly across
the yard to the low fence. It was an easy matter to vault
this, for a terror urged him such as lifts the gazelle over

the thorn bush when the lion pursues. A crash through the dew-drenched weeds on the roadside, a clutching, slippery rush up the grassy side of the levee to the footpath at the summit, and — he was free!

The east was blushing and brightening. The wind, himself a vagrant rover, saluted his brother upon the cheek. Some wild geese, high above, gave cry. A rabbit skipped along the path before him, free to turn to the right or to the left as his mood should send him. The river slid past, and certainly no one could tell the ultimate abiding place of its waters.

A small, ruffled, brown-breasted bird, sitting upon a dogwood sapling, began a soft, throaty, tender little piping in praise of the dew which entices foolish worms from their holes; but suddenly he stopped, and sat with his head turned sidewise, listening.

From the path along the levee there burst forth a jubilant, stirring, buoyant, thrilling whistle, loud and keen and clear as the cleanest notes of the piccolo. The soaring sound rippled and trilled and arpeggioed as the songs of wild birds do not; but it had a wild free grace that, in a way, reminded the small, brown bird of something familiar, but exactly what he could not tell. There was in it the bird call, or reveille, that all birds know; but a great waste of lavish, unmeaning things that art had added and arranged, besides, and that were quite puzzling and strange; and the little brown bird sat with his head on one side until the sound died away in the distance.

The little bird did not know that the part of that strange warbling that he understood was just what kept the warbler without his breakfast; but he knew very well that the part he did not understand did not concern him, so he gave a little flutter of his wings and swooped down like a brown bullet upon a big fat worm that was wriggling along the levee path.

XX

THE HALBERDIER OF THE LITTLE RHEIN-SCHLOSS

I GO sometimes into the *Bierhalle* and restaurant called Old Munich. Not long ago it was a resort of interesting Bohemians, but now only artists and musicians and literary folk frequent it. But the Pilsner is yet good, and I take some diversion from the conversation of Waiter No. 18.

For many years the customers of Old Munich have accepted the place as a faithful copy from the ancient German town. The big hall with its smoky rafters, rows of imported steins, portrait of Goethe, and verses painted on the walls — translated into German from the original of the Cincinnati poets — seems atmospherically correct when viewed through the bottom of a glass.

But not long ago the proprietors added the room above, called it the Little Rheinschloss, and built in a stairway. Up there was an imitation stone parapet, ivy-covered, and the walls were painted to represent depth and distance, with the Rhine winding at the base of the vineyarded slopes, and the castle of Ehrenbreitstein looming directly opposite the entrance. Of course there were tables and chairs; and you could have beer and food brought you, as you naturally would on the top of a castle on the Rhine.

I went into Old Munich one afternoon when there were few customers, and sat at my usual table near the stairway. I was shocked and almost displeased to perceive that the glass cigar-case by the orchestra stand had been smashed to

278

smithereens. I did not like things to happen in Old Munich. Nothing had ever happened there before.

Waiter No. 18 came and breathed on my neck. I was his by right of discovery. Eighteen's brain was built like a corral. It was full of ideas which, when he opened the gate, came huddling out like a flock of sheep that might get together afterward or might not. I did not shine as a shepherd. As a type Eighteen fitted nowhere. I did not find out if he had a nationality, family, creed, grievance, hobby, soul, preference, home, or vote. He only came always to my table and, as long as his leisure would permit, let words flutter from him like swallows leaving a barn at daylight.

"How did the cigar-case come to be broken, Eighteen?" I asked, with a certain feeling of personal grievance.

"I can tell you about that, sir," said he, resting his foot on the chair next to mine. "Did you ever have anybody hand you a double handful of good luck while both your hands was full of bad luck, and stop to notice how your fingers behaved?"

"No riddles, Eighteen," said I. "Leave out palmistry and manicuring."

"You remember," said Eighteen, "the guy in the hammered brass Prince Albert and the oroide gold pants and the amalgamated copper hat, that carried the combination meataxe, ice-pick, and liberty-pole, and used to stand on the first landing as you go up to the Little Rindslosh?"

"Why, yes," said I. "The halberdier. I never noticed him particularly. I remember I thought he was only a suit of armour. He had a perfect poise."

"He had more than that," said Eighteen. "He was me friend. He was an advertisement. The boss hired him to stand on the stairs for a kind of scenery to show there was something doing in the has-been line upstairs. What did you call him — a what kind of a beer?"

"A halberdier," said I. "That was an ancient man-at-arms of many hundred years ago."

"Some mistake," said Eighteen. "This one wasn't that old. He wasn't over twenty-three or four.

"It was the boss's idea, rigging a man up in an ante-bellum suit of tinware and standing him on the landing of the slosh. He bought the goods at a Fourth Avenue antique store, and hung a sign out: "Able-bodied hal — halberdier wanted. Costume furnished.'

"The same morning a young man with wrecked good clothes and a hungry look comes in, bringing the sign with him. I was filling the mustard-pots at my station.

"'I'm it,' says he, 'whatever it is. But I never halberdiered in a restaurant. Put me on. Is it a masquerade?'

"'I hear talk in the kitchen of a fishball,' says I.

"'Bully for you, Eighteen," says he. 'You and I'll get on. Show me the boss's desk.'

"Well, the boss tries the Harveyized pajamas on him, and they fitted him like the scales on a baked redsnapper, and he gets the job. You've seen what it is — he stood straight up in the corner of the first landing with his halberd to his shoulder, looking right ahead and guarding the Portugals of the castle. The boss is nutty about having the true Old-World flavour to his joint. 'Halberdiers goes with Rind-sloshes,' says he, 'just as rats goes with rathskellers and white cotton stockings with Tyrolean villages.' The boss is a kind of a antiologist, and is all posted up on data and such information.

"From 8 P.M. to two in the morning was the halberdier's hours. He got two meals with us help and a dollar a night. I eat with him at the table. He liked me. He never told his name. He was travelling impromptu, like kings, I guess. The first time at supper I says to him: 'Have some more of the spuds, Mr. Frelinghuysen.' 'Oh, don't be so formal and offish, Eighteen,' says he. 'Call me Hal — that's short for halberdier.' 'Oh, don't think I wanted to pry for names,' says I. 'I know all about the dizzy fall from wealth and greatness. We've got a count washing dishes in the kitchen; and the third bartender used to be a Pullman conductor. And they *work*, Sir Percival,' says I, sarcastic.

"'Eighteen,' says he, 'as a friendly devil in a cabbage-scented hell, would you mind cutting up this piece of steak for me? I don't say that it's got more muscle than I have, but —' And then he shows me the insides of his hands. They was blistered and cut and corned and swelled up till they looked like a couple of flank steaks criss-crossed with a knife — the kind the butchers hide and take home, knowing what is the best.

"'Shoveling coal,' says he, 'and piling bricks and loading drays. But they gave out, and I had to resign. I was born for a halberdier, and I've been educated for twenty-four years to fill the position. Now, quit knocking my profession, and pass along a lot more of that ham. I'm holding the closing exercises,' says he, 'of a forty-eight-hour fast.'

"The second night he was on the job he walks down from his corner to the cigar-case and calls for cigarettes. The customers at the tables all snicker out loud to show their acquaintance with history. The boss is on.

"'An '— let's see — oh, yes —'An anarchism,' says the boss. 'Cigarettes was not made at the time when halberdiers was invented.'

"'The ones you sell was,' says Sir Percival. 'Caporal wins from chronology by the length of a cork tip.' So he gets 'em and lights one, and puts the box in his brass helmet, and goes back to patroling the Rindslosh.

"He made a big hit, 'specially with the ladies. Some of 'em would poke him with their fingers to see if he was real or only a kind of a stuffed figure like they burn in elegy.

And when he'd move they'd squeak, and make eyes at him as they went up to the slosh. He looked fine in his halber- dashery. He slept at $2 a week in a hall-room on Third Avenue. He invited me up there one night. He had a little book on the washstand that he read instead of shopping in the saloons after hours. 'I'm on to that,' says I, 'from read- ing about it in novels. All the heroes on the bum carry the little book. It's either Tantalus or Liver or Horace, and its printed in Latin, and you're a college man. And I wouldn't be surprised,' says I, 'if you wasn't educated, too.' But it was only the batting averages of the League for the last ten years.

"One night, about half past eleven, there comes in a party of these high-rollers that are always hunting up new places to eat in and poke fun at. There was a swell girl in a 40 H.-P. auto tan coat and veil, and a fat old man with white side-whiskers, and a young chap that couldn't keep his feet off the tail of the girl's coat, and an oldish lady that looked upon life as immoral and unnecessary. 'How perfectly de- lightful,' they says, 'to sup in a slosh.' Up the stairs they go; and in half a minute back down comes the girl, her skirts swishing like the waves on the beach. She stops on the landing and looks our halberdier in the eye.

"'You!' she says, with a smile that reminded me of lemon sherbet. I was waiting up-stairs in the slosh, then, and I was right down here by the door, putting some vinegar and cayenne into an empty bottle of tabasco, and I heard all they said.

"'It,' says Sir Percival, without moving. 'I'm only local colour. Are my hauberk, helmet, and halberd on straight?''

"'Is there an explanation to this?' says she. 'Is it a practical joke such as men play in those Griddle-cake and Lamb Clubs? I'm afraid I don't see the point. I heard, vaguely, that you were away. For three months I — we have not seen you or heard from you.'

" ' I'm halberdiering for my living,' says the statue. 'I'm working,' says he. 'I don't suppose you know what work means.'

" ' Have you — have you lost your money? ' she asks.

" Sir Percival studies a minute.

" ' I am poorer,' says he, 'than the poorest sandwich man on the streets — if I don't earn my living.'

" ' You call this work? ' says she. 'I thought a man worked with his hands or his head instead of becoming a mountebank.'

" ' The calling of a halberdier,' says he, 'is an ancient and honourable one. Sometimes,' says he, 'the man-at-arms at the door has saved the castle while the plumed knights were cake-walking in the banquet-halls above.'

" ' I see you're not ashamed,' says she, 'of your peculiar tastes. I wonder, though, that the manhood I used to think I saw in you didn't prompt you to draw water or hew wood instead of publicly flaunting your ignominy in this disgraceful masquerade.'

" Sir Percival kind of rattles his armour and says: ' Helen, will you suspend sentence in this matter for just a little while? You don't understand," says he. 'I've got to hold this job down a bit longer.'

" ' You like being a harlequin — or halberdier, as you call it? ' says she.

" ' I wouldn't get thrown out of the job just now,' says he, with a grin, 'to be appointed Minister to the Court of St. James's.'

" And then the 40 H.-P. girl's eyes sparkled as hard as diamonds.

" ' Very well,' says she. 'You shall have full run of your serving-man's tastes this night.' And she swims over to the boss's desk and gives him a smile that knocks the specks off his nose.

"'I think your Rindslosh,' says she, 'is as beautiful as a dream. It is a little slice of the Old World set down in New York. We shall have a nice supper up there; but if you will grant us one favour the illusion will be perfect — give us your halberdier to wait on our table.'

"That hit the boss's antiology hobby just right. 'Sure,' says he, 'dot vill be fine. Und der orchestra shall blay "Die Wacht am Rhein" all der time.' And he goes over and tells the halberdier to go upstairs and hustle the grub at the swells' table.

"'I'm on the job," says Sir Percival, taking off his helmet and hanging it on his halberd and leaning 'em in the corner. The girl goes up and takes her seat and I see her jaw squared tight under her smile. 'We're going to be waited on by a real halberdier,' says she, 'one who is proud of his profession. Isn't it sweet?'

"'Ripping,' says the swell young man. 'Much prefer a waiter,' says the fat old gent. 'I hope he doesn't come from a cheap museum,' says the old lady; 'he might have microbes in his costume.'

"Before he goes to the table, Sir Percival takes me by the arm. 'Eighteen,' says he, 'I've got to pull off this job without a blunder. You coach me straight or I'll take that halberd and make hash out of you.' And then he goes up to the table with his coat of mail on and a napkin over his arm and waits for the order.

"'Why, it's Deering!' says the young swell. 'Hello, old man. What the —'

"'Beg pardon, sir,' interrupts the halberdier, 'I'm waiting on the table.'

"The old man looks at him grim, like a Boston bull. 'So, Deering,' he says, 'you're at work yet.'

"' Yes, sir,' says Sir Percival, quiet and gentlemanly as I could have been myself, ' for almost three months, now.' ' You haven't been discharged during the time? ' asks the old man. ' Not once, sir,' says he, ' though I've had to change my work several times.'

"' Waiter,' orders the girl, short and sharp, ' another napkin.' He brings her one, respectful.

" I never saw more devil, if I may say it, stirred up in a lady. There was two bright red spots on her cheeks, and her eyes looked exactly like a wildcat's I'd seen in the zoo. Her foot kept slapping the floor all the time.

"' Waiter,' she orders, ' bring me filtered water without ice. Bring me a footstool. Take away this empty salt-cellar.' She kept him on the jump. She was sure giving the halberdier his.

" There wasn't but a few customers up in the slosh at that time, so I hung out near the door so I could help Sir Percival serve.

" He got along fine with the olives and celery and the bluepoints. They was easy. And then the consommé came up the dumb-waiter all in one big silver tureen. Instead of serving it from the side-table he picks it up between his hands and starts to the dining-table with it. When nearly there he drops the tureen smash on the floor, and the soup soaks all the lower part of that girl's swell silk dress.

"' Stupid — incompetent,' says she, giving him a look. ' Standing in a corner with a halberd seems to be your mission in life.'

"' Pardon me, lady,' says he. ' It was just a little bit hotter than blazes. I couldn't help it.'

" The old man pulls out a memorandum book and hunts in it. ' The 25th of April, Deering,' says he. ' I know it,' says Sir Percival. ' And ten minutes to twelve o'clock,' says the old man. ' By Jupiter! you haven't won yet.' And he

pounds the table with his fist and yells to me: 'Waiter, call
the manager at once — tell him to hurry here as fast as he
can.' I go after the boss, and old Brockmann hikes up to the
slosh on the jump.

"'I want this man discharged at once,' roars the old guy.
'Look what he's done. Ruined my daughter's dress. It cost
at least $600. Discharge this awkward lout at once or I'll sue
you for the price of it.'

"'Dis is bad pizness,' says the boss. 'Six hundred dollars is much. I reckon I vill haf to —'

"'Wait a minute, Herr Brockmann,' says Sir Percival, easy
and smiling. But he was worked up under his tin suitings;
I could see that. And then he made the finest, neatest little
speech I ever listened to. I can't give you the words, of
course. He give the millionaires a lovely roast in a sarcastic
way, describing their automobiles and opera-boxes and diamonds; and then he got around to the working-classes and
the kind of grub they eat and the long hours they work —
and all that sort of stuff — bunkum, of course. 'The restless rich,' says he, 'never content with their luxuries, always
prowling among the haunts of the poor and humble, amusing
themselves with the imperfections and misfortunes of their
fellow men and women. And even here, Herr Brockmann,'
he says, 'in this beautiful Rindslosh, a grand and enlighten-
ing reproduction of Old-World history and architecture, they
come to disturb its symmetry and picturesqueness by demand-
ing in their arrogance that the halberdier of the castle wait
upon their table! I have faithfuly and conscientiously,' says
he, 'performed my duties as a halberdier. I know nothing
of a waiter's duties. It was the insolent whim of these transient, pampered aristocrats that I should be detailed to serve
them food. Must I be blamed — must I be deprived of the
means of a livelihood,' he goes on, 'on account of an accident that was the result of their own presumption and

haughtiness? But what hurts me more than all,' says Sir
Percival, 'is the desecration that has been done to this splendid Rindslosh — the confiscation of its halberdier to serve
menially at the banquet board.'

" Even I could see that this stuff was piffle; but it caught
the boss.

" ' Mein Gott,' says he, ' you vas right. Ein halberdier
have not got der right to dish up soup. Him I vill not discharge. Have anoder waiter if you like, und let mein halberdier go back und stand mit his halberd. But, gentlemen,'
he says, pointing to the old man, ' you go ahead and sue mit
der dress. Sue me for $600 or $6,000. I stand der suit.'
And the boss puffs off down-stairs. Old Brockmann was an
all-right Dutchman.

" Just then the clock strikes twelve, and the old guy laughs
loud. ' You win, Deering,' says he. ' Let me explain to
all,' he goes on. ' Some time ago Mr. Deering asked me for
something that I did not want to give him.' (I looks at the
girl, and she turns as red as a pickled beet.) ' I told him,'
says the old guy, ' if he would earn his own living for three
months without once being discharged for incompetence, I
would give him what he wanted. It seems that the time was
up at twelve o'clock to-night. I came near fetching you,
though, Deering, on that soup question,' says the old boy,
standing up and grabbing Sir Percival's hand.

" The halberdier lets out a yell and jumps three feet high.

" ' Look out for those hands,' says he, and he holds 'em
up. You never saw such hands except on a labourer in a
limestone quarry.

" ' Heavens, boy!' says old side-whiskers, ' what have you
been doing to 'em? '

" ' Oh,' says Sir Percival, ' little chores like hauling coal
and excavating rock till they went back on me. And when
I couldn't hold a pick or a whip I took up halberdiering to

give 'em a rest. Tureens full of hot soup don't seem to be a particularly soothing treatment.'

" I would have bet on that girl. That high-tempered kind always go as far the other way, according to my experience. She whizzes round the table like a cyclone and catches both his hands in hers. ' Poor hands — dear hands,' she sings out, and sheds tears on 'em and holds 'em close to her bosom. Well, sir, with all that Rindslosh scenery it was just like a play. And the halberdier sits down at the table at the girl's side, and I served the rest of the supper. And that was about all, except that when they left he shed his hardware store and went with 'em."

I dislike to be side-tracked from an original proposition.

" But you haven't told me, Eighteen," said I, " how the cigar-case came to be broken."

" Oh, that was last night," said Eighteen. " Sir Percival and the girl drove up in a cream-coloured motor-car, and had dinner in the Rindslosh. ' The same table, Billy,' I heard her say as they went up. I waited on 'em. We've got a new halberdier now, a bow-legged guy with a face like a sheep. As they came down-stairs Sir Percival passes him a ten-case note. The new halberdier drops his halberd, and it falls on the cigar-case. That's how that happened."

XXI

TWO RENEGADES

IN the Gate City of the South the Confederate Veterans were reuniting; and I stood to see them march, beneath the tangled flags of the great conflict, to the hall of their oratory and commemoration.

While the irregular and halting line was passing I made onslaught upon it and dragged forth from the ranks my friend Barnard O'Keefe, who had no right to be there. For he was a Northerner born and bred; and what should he be doing hallooing for the Stars and Bars among those gray and moribund veterans? And why should he be trudging, with his shining, martial, humorous, broad face, among those warriors of a previous and alien generation?

I say I dragged him forth, and held him till the last hickory leg and waving goatee had stumbled past. And then I hustled him out of the crowd into a cool interior; for the Gate City was stirred that day, and the hand-organs wisely eliminated " Marching Through Georgia " from their repertories.

" Now, what deviltry are you up to? " I asked of O'Keefe when there were a table and things in glasses between us.

O'Keefe wiped his heated face and instigated a commotion among the floating ice in his glass before he chose to answer.

" I am assisting at the wake," said he, " of the only nation on earth that ever did me a good turn. As one gentleman to another, I am ratifying and celebrating the foreign

289

policy of the late Jefferson Davis, as fine a statesman as
ever settled the financial question of a country. Equal ratio
— that was his platform — a barrel of money for a barrel of
flour — a pair of $20 bills for a pair of boots — a hatful of
currency for a new hat — say, ain't that simple compared
with W. J. B.'s little old oxidized plank?"

"What talk is this?" I asked. "Your financial digres-
sion is merely a subterfuge. Why were you marching in the
ranks of the Confederate Veterans?"

"Because, my lad," answered O'Keefe, "the Confederate
Government in its might and power interposed to protect and
defend Barnard O'Keefe against immediate and dangerous
assassination at the hands of a blood-thirsty foreign country
after the United States of America had overruled his appeal
for protection, and had instructed Private Secretary Cortelyou
to reduce his estimate of the Republican majority for 1905 by
one vote."

"Come, Barney," said I, "the Confederate States of
America has been out of existence nearly forty years. You
do not look older yourself. When was it that the deceased
government exerted its foreign policy in your behalf?"

"Four months ago," said O'Keefe promptly. "The infamous foreign power I alluded to is still staggering from
the official blow dealt it by Mr. Davis's contraband aggregation of states. That's why you see me cake-walking with
the ex-rebs to the illegitimate tune about 'simmon-seeds and
cotton. I vote for the Great Father in Washington, but I
am not going back on Mars' Jeff. You say the Confederacy
has been dead forty years? Well, if it hadn't been for it,
I'd have been breathing to-day with soul so dead I couldn't
have whispered a single cuss-word about my native land. The
O'Keefes are not overburdened with ingratitude."

I must have looked bewildered. "The war was over," I
said vacantly, "in —"

O'Keefe laughed loudly, scattering my thoughts."

" Ask old Doc Millikin if the war is over! " he shouted, hugely diverted. " Oh, no! Doc hasn't surrendered yet. And the Confederate States! Well, I just told you they bucked officially and solidly and nationally against a foreign government four months ago and kept me from being shot. Old Jeff's country stepped in and brought me off under its wing while Roosevelt was having a gunboat repainted and waiting for the National Campaign Committee to look up whether I had ever scratched the ticket."

" Isn't there a story in this, Barney? " I asked.

" No," said O'Keefe; " but I'll give you the facts. You know I went down to Panama when this irritation about a canal began. I thought I'd get in on the ground floor. I did, and had to sleep on it, and drink water with little zoos in it; so, of course, I got the Chagres fever. That was in a little town called San Juan on the coast.

" After I got the fever hard enough to kill a Port-au-Prince nigger, I had a relapse in the shape of Doc Millikin.

" There was a doctor to attend a sick man! If Doc Millikin had your case, he made the terrors of death seem like an invitation to a donkey-party. He had the bedside manners of a Piute medicine-man and the soothing presence of a dray loaded with iron bridge-girders. When he laid his hand on your fevered brow you felt like Cap John Smith just before Pocahontas went his bail.

" Well, this old medical outrage floated down to my shack when I sent for him. He was built like a shad, and his eyebrows was black, and his white whiskers trickled down from his chin like milk coming out of a sprinkling-pot. He had a nigger boy along carrying an old tomato-can full of calomel, and a saw.

" Doc felt my pulse, and then he began to mess up some

calomel with an agricultural implement that belonged to the trowel class.

" ' I don't want any death-mask made yet, Doc,' I says, ' nor my liver put in a plaster-of-Paris cast. I'm sick; and it's medicine I need, not frescoing.'

" ' You're a blame Yankee, ain't you? ' asked Doc, going on mixing up his Portland cement.

" ' I'm from the North,' says I, ' but I'm a plain man, and don't care for mural decorations. When you get the Isthmus all asphalted over with that boll-weevil prescription, would you mind giving me a dose of pain-killer, or a little strychnine on toast to ease up this feeling of unhealthiness that I have got? ' "

" ' They was all sassy, just like you,' says old Doc, ' but we lowered their temperature considerable. Yes, sir, I reckon we sent a good many of ye over to old *mortuis nisi bonum.* Look at Antietam and Bull Run and Seven Pines and around Nashville! There never was a battle where we didn't lick ye unless you was ten to our one. I knew you were a blame Yankee the minute I laid eyes on you.'

" ' Don't reopen the chasm, Doc,' I begs him. ' Any Yankeeness I may have is geographical; and, as far as I am concerned, a Southerner is as good as a Filipino any day. I'm feeling too bad to argue. Let's have secession without misrepresentation, if you say so; but what I need is more laudanum and less Lundy's Lane. If you're mixing that compound gefloxide of gefloxicum for me, please fill my ears with it before you get around to the battle of Gettysburg, for there is a subject full of talk.'

" By this time Doc Millikin had thrown up a line of fortifications on square pieces of paper; and he says to me: ' Yank, take one of these powders every two hours. They won't kill you. I'll be around again about sundown to see if you're alive.'

"Old Doc's powders knocked the chagres. I stayed in San Juan, and got to knowing him better. He was from Mississippi, and the red-hottest Southerner that ever smelled mint. He made Stonewall Jackson and R. E. Lee look like Abolitionists. He had a family somewhere down near Yazoo City; but he stayed away from the States on account of an uncontrollable liking he had for the absence of a Yankee government. Him and me got as thick personally as the Emperor of Russia and the dove of peace, but sectionally we didn't amalgamate.

" 'Twas a beautiful system of medical practice introduced by old Doc into that isthmus of land. He'd take that bracket-saw and the mild chloride and his hypodermic, and treat anything from yellow fever to a personal friend.

"Besides his other liabilities Doc could play a flute for a minute or two. He was guilty of two tunes —'Dixie' and another one that was mighty close to the 'Suwanee River'— you might say one of its tributaries. He used to come down and sit with me while I was getting well, and aggrieve his flute and say unreconstructed things about the North. You'd have thought the smoke from the first gun at Fort Sumter was still floating around in the air.

"You know that was about the time they staged them property revolutions down there, that wound up in the fifth act with the thrilling canal scene where Uncle Sam has nine curtain-calls holding Miss Panama by the hand, while the bloodhounds keep Senator Morgan treed up in a cocoanut-palm.

"That's the way it wound up; but at first it seemed as if Colombia was going to make Panama look like one of the $3.98 kind, with dents made in it in the factory, like they wear at North Beach fish fries. For mine, I played the straw-hat crowd to win; and they gave me a colonel's commission over a brigade of twenty-seven men in the left wing and second joint of the insurgent army.

" The Colombian troops were awfully rude to us. One day when I had my brigade in a sandy spot, with its shoes off doing a battalion drill by squads, the Government army rushed from behind a bush at us, acting as noisy and disagreeable as they could.

" My troops enfiladed, left-faced, and left the spot. After enticing the enemy for three miles or so we struck a brier-patch and had to sit down. When we were ordered to throw up our toes and surrender we obeyed. Five of my best staff-officers fell, suffering extremely with stone-bruised heels.

" Then and there those Colombians took your friend Barney, sir, stripped him of the insignia of his rank, consisting of a pair of brass knuckles and a canteen of rum, and dragged him before a military court. The presiding general went through the usual legal formalities that sometimes cause a case to hang on the calendar of a South American military court as long as ten minutes. He asked me my age, and then sentenced me to be shot.

" They woke up the court interpreter, an American named Jenks, who was in the rum business and vice versa, and told him to translate the verdict.

" Jenks stretched himself and took a morphine tablet.

" ' You've got to back up against th' 'dobe, old man,' says he to me. ' Three weeks, I believe, you get. Haven't got a chew of fine-cut on you, have you? '

" ' Translate that again, with foot-notes and a glossary,' says I. ' I don't know whether I'm discharged, condemned, or handed over to the Gerry Society.'

" ' Oh,' says Jenks, ' don't you understand? You're to be stood up against a 'dobe wall and shot in two or three weeks — three, I think, they said.'

" ' Would you mind asking 'em which? ' says I. ' A week don't amount to much after you are dead, but it seems a real nice long spell while you are alive.'

" ' It's two weeks,' says the interpreter, after inquiring in Spanish of the court. ' Shall I ask 'em again? '

" ' Let be,' says I. ' Let's have a stationary verdict. If I keep on appealing this way they'll have me shot about ten days before I was captured. No, I haven't got any fine-cut.'

" They sends me over to the *calaboza* with a detachment of coloured postal-telegraph boys carrying Enfield rifles, and I am locked up in a kind of brick bakery. The temperature in there was just about the kind mentioned in the cooking recipes that call for a quick oven.

" Then I gives a silver dollar to one of the guards to send for the United States consul. He comes around in pajamas, with a pair of glasses on his nose and a dozen or two inside of him.

" ' I'm to be shot in two weeks,' says I. ' And although I've made a memorandum of it, I don't seem to get it off my mind. You want to call up Uncle Sam on the cable as quick as you can and get him all worked up about it. Have 'em send the *Kentucky* and the *Kearsarge* and the *Oregon* down right away. That'll be about enough battleships; but it wouldn't hurt to have a couple of cruisers and a torpedo-boat destroyer, too. And — say, if Dewey isn't busy, better have him come along on the fastest one of the fleet.'

" ' Now, see here, O'Keefe,' says the consul, getting the best of a hiccup, ' what do you want to bother the State Department about this matter for? '

" ' Didn't you hear me? ' says I; ' I'm to be shot in two weeks. Did you think I said I was going to a lawn-party? And it wouldn't hurt if Roosevelt could get the Japs to send down the *Yellowyamtiskookum* or the *Ogotosingsing* or some other first-class cruisers to help. It would make me feel safer.'

" ' Now, what you want,' says the consul, ' is not to get

excited. I'll send you over some chewing tobacco and some banana fritters when I go back. The United States can't interfere in this. You know you were caught insurging against the government, and you're subject to the laws of this country. Tell you the truth, I've had an intimation from the State Department — unofficially, of course — that whenever a soldier of fortune demands a fleet of gunboats in a case of revolutionary *katzenjammer,* I should cut the cable, give him all the tobacco he wants, and after he's shot take his clothes, if they fit me, for part payment of my salary.'

" ' Consul,' says I to him, ' this is a serious question. You are representing Uncle Sam. This ain't any little international tomfoolery, like a universal peace congress or the christening of the *Shamrock IV.* I'm an American citizen and I demand protection. I demand the Mosquito fleet, and Schley, and the Atlantic squadron, and Bob Evans, and General E. Byrd Grubb, and two or three protocols. What are you going to do about it? '

" ' Nothing doing,' says the consul.

" ' Be off with you, then,' says I, out of patience with him, ' and send me Doc Milliken. Ask Doc to come and see me.'

" Doc comes and looks through the bars at me, surrounded by dirty soldiers, with even my shoes and canteen confiscated, and he looks mightily pleased.

" ' Hello, Yank,' says he, ' getting a little taste of Johnson's Island, now, ain't ye? '

" ' Doc,' says I, ' I've just had an interview with the U. S. consul. I gather from his remarks that I might just as well have been caught selling suspenders in Kishineff under the name of Rosenstein as to be in my present condition. It seems that the only maritime aid I am to receive from the United States is some navy-plug to chew. Doc,' says I, ' can't you suspend hostilities on the slavery question long enough to do something for me? '

" ' It ain't been my habit,' Doc Millikin answers, ' to do any painless dentistry when I find a Yank cutting an eye-tooth. So the Stars and Stripes ain't landing any marines to shell the huts of the Colombian cannibals, hey? Oh, say, can you see by the dawn's early light the star-spangled banner has fluked in the fight? What's the matter with the War Department, hey? It's a great thing to be a citizen of a gold-standard nation, ain't it? '

" ' Rub it in, Doc, all you want,' says I. ' I guess we're weak on foreign policy.'

" ' For a Yank,' says Doc, putting on his specs and talking more mild, ' you ain't so bad. If you had come from below the line I reckon I would have liked you right smart. Now since your country has gone back on you, you have to come to the old doctor whose cotton you burned and whose mules you stole and whose niggers you freed to help you. Ain't that so, Yank? '

" ' It is,' says I heartily, ' and let's have a diagnosis of the case right away, for in two weeks' time all you can do is to hold an autopsy and I don't want to be amputated if I can help it.'

" ' Now,' says Doc, business-like, ' it's easy enough for you to get out of this scrape. Money'll do it. You've got to pay a long string of 'em from General Pomposo down to this anthropoid ape guarding your door. About $10,000 will do the trick. Have you got the money? '

" ' Me? ' says I. ' I've got one Chili dollar, two *real* pieces, and a *medio*.'

" ' Then if you've any last words, utter 'em,' says that old reb. ' The roster of your financial budget sounds quite much to me like the noise of a requiem.'

" ' Change the treatment,' says I. ' I admit that I'm short. Call a consultation or use radium or smuggle me in some saws or something.'

"'Yank,' says Doc Millikin, 'I've a good notion to help you. There's only one government in the world that can get you out of this difficulty; and that's the Confederate States of America, the grandest nation that ever existed.'

"Just as you said to me I says to Doc; 'Why, the Confederacy ain't a nation. It's been absolved forty years ago.'

"'That's a campaign lie,' says Doc. 'She's running along as solid as the Roman Empire. She's the only hope you've got. Now, you, being a Yank, have got to go through with some preliminary obsequies before you can get official aid. You've got to take the oath of allegiance to the Confederate Government. Then I'll guarantee she does all she can for you. What do you say, Yank? — it's your last chance.'

"'If you're fooling with me, Doc,' I answers, 'you're no better than the United States. But as you say it's the last chance, hurry up and swear me. I always did like corn whisky and 'possum anyhow. I believe I'm half Southerner by nature. I'm willing to try the Ku-klux in place of the khaki. Get brisk.'

"Doc Millikin thinks awhile, and then he offers me this oath of allegiance to take without any kind of a chaser:

"'I, Barnard O'Keefe, Yank, being of sound body but a Republican mind, hereby swear to transfer my fealty, respect, and allegiance to the Confederate States of America, and the government thereof in consideration of said government, through its official acts and powers, obtaining my freedom and release from confinement and sentence of death brought about by the exuberance of my Irish proclivities and my general pizenness as a Yank.'

"I repeated these words after Doc, but they seemed to me a kind of hocus-pocus; and I don't believe any life-insurance company in the country would have issued me a policy on the strength of 'em.

" Doc went away saying he would communicate with his government immediately.

" Say — you can imagine how I felt — me to be shot in two weeks and my only hope for help being in a government that's been dead so long that it isn't even remembered except on Decoration Day and when Joe Wheeler signs the voucher for his pay-check. But it was all there was in sight; and somehow I thought Doc Millikin had something up his old alpaca sleeve that wasn't all foolishness.

" Around to the jail comes old Doc again in about a week. I was flea-bitten, a mite sarcastic, and fundamentally hungry.

" ' Any Confederate ironclads in the offing? ' I asks. ' Do you notice any sounds resembling the approach of Jeb Stewart's cavalry overland or Stonewall Jackson sneaking up in the rear? If you do, I wish you'd say so.'

" ' It's too soon yet for help to come,' says Doc.

" ' The sooner the better,' says I. ' I don't care if it gets in fully fifteen minutes before I am shot; and if you happen to lay eyes on Beauregard or Albert Sidney Johnston or any of the relief corps, wig-wag 'em to hike along.'

" ' There's been no answer received yet,' says Doc.

" ' Don't forget,' says I, ' that there's only four days more. I don't know how you propose to work this thing, Doc,' I says to him; ' but it seems to me I'd sleep better if you had got a government that was alive and on the map — like Afghanistan or Great Britain, or old man Kruger's kingdom, to take this matter up. I don't mean any disrespect to your Confederate States, but I can't help feeling that my chances of being pulled out of this scrape was decidedly weakened when General Lee surrendered.'

" ' It's your only chance,' said Doc; ' don't quarrel with it. What did your own country do for you? '

" It was only two days before the morning I was to be shot, when Doc Millikin came around again.

"'All right, Yank,' says he. 'Help's come. The Confederate States of America is going to apply for your release. The representatives of the government arrived on a fruit-steamer last night.'

"'Bully!' says I —'bully for you, Doc! I suppose it's marines with a Gatling. I'm going to love your country all I can for this.'

"'Negotiations,' says old Doc, 'will be opened between the two governments at once. You will know later on to-day if they are successful.'

"About four in the afternoon a soldier in red trousers brings a paper round to the jail, and they unlocks the door and I walks out. The guard at the door bows and I bows, and I steps into the grass and wades around to Doc Millikin's shack.

"Doc was sitting in his hammock playing 'Dixie,' soft and low and out of tune, on his flute. I interrupted him at 'Look away! look away!' and shook his hand for five minutes.

"'I never thought,' says Doc, taking a chew fretfully, 'that I'd ever try to save any blame Yank's life. But, Mr. O'Keefe, I don't see but what you are entitled to be considered part human, anyhow. I never thought Yanks had any of the rudiments of decorum and laudability about them. I reckon I might have been too aggregative in my tabulation. But it ain't me you want to thank — it's the Confederate States of America.'

"'And I'm much obliged to 'em,' says I. 'It's a poor man that wouldn't be patriotic with a country that's saved his life. I'll drink to the Stars and Bars whenever there's a flagstaff and a glass convenient. But where,' says I, 'are the rescuing troops? If there was a gun fired or a shell burst, I didn't hear it.'

"Doc Millikin raises up and points out the window with his flute at the banana-steamer loading with fruit.

"'Yank,' says he, 'there's a steamer that's going to sail in the morning. If I was you, I'd sail on it. The Confederate Government's done all it can for you. There wasn't a gun fired. The negotiations was carried on secretly between the two nations by the purser of that steamer. I got him to do it because I didn't want to appear in it. Twelve thousand dollars was paid to the officials in bribes to let you go.'

"'Man!' says I, sitting down hard —'twelve thousand — how will I ever — who could have — where did the money come from?'

"'Yazoo City,' says Doc Millikin: 'I've got a little saved up there. Two barrels full. It looks good to these Colombians. 'Twas Confederate money, every dollar of it. Now do you see why you'd better leave before they try to pass some of it on an expert?'

"'I do,' says I.

"'Now let's hear you give the password,' says Doc Millikin.

"'Hurrah for Jeff Davis!' says I.

"'Correct,' says Doc. 'And let me tell you something: The next tune I learn on my flute is going to be "Yankee Doodle." I reckon there's some Yanks that are not so pizen. Or, if you was me, would you try "The Red, White, and Blue"?'"

XXII

THE LONESOME ROAD

BROWN as a coffee-berry, rugged, pistoled, spurred, wary, indefeasible, I saw my old friend, Deputy-Marshal Buck Caperton, stumble, with jingling rowels, into a chair in the marshal's outer office.

And because the court-house was almost deserted at that hour, and because Buck would sometimes relate to me things that were out of print, I followed him in and tricked him into talk through knowledge of a weakness he had. For, cigarettes rolled with sweet corn husk were as honey to Buck's palate; and though he could finger the trigger of a forty-five with skill and suddenness, he never could learn to roll a cigarette.

It was through no fault of mine (for I rolled the cigarettes tight and smooth), but the upshot of some whim of his own, that instead of to an Odyssey of the chaparral, I listened to — a dissertation upon matrimony! This from Buck Caperton! But I maintain that the cigarettes were impeccable, and crave absolution for myself.

"We just brought in Jim and Bud Granberry," said Buck. "Train robbing, you know. Held up the Aransas Pass last month. We caught 'em in the Twenty-Mile pear flat, south of the Nueces."

"Have much trouble corralling them?" I asked, for here was the meat that my hunger for epics craved.

"Some," said Buck; and then, during a little pause, his thoughts stampeded off the trail. "It's kind of queer about women," he went on, "and the place they're supposed to occupy in botany. If I was asked to classify them I'd say they was a human loco weed. Ever see a bronc that had been chewing loco? Ride him up to a puddle of water two feet wide, and he'll give a snort and fall back on you. It looks as big as the Mississippi River to him. Next trip he'd walk into a cañon a thousand feet deep thinking it was a prairie-dog hole. Same way with a married man.

" I was thinking of Perry Rountree, that used to be my sidekicker before he committed matrimony. In them days me and Perry hated indisturbances of any kind. We roamed around considerable, stirring up the echoes and making 'em attend to business. Why, when me and Perry wanted to have some fun in a town it was a picnic for the census takers. They just counted the marshal's posse that it took to subdue us, and there was your population. But then there came along this Mariana Goodnight girl and looked at Perry sideways, and he was all bridle-wise and saddle-broke before you could skin a yearling.

" I wasn't even asked to the wedding. I reckon the bride had my pedigree and the front elevation of my habits all mapped out, and she decided that Perry would trot better in double harness without any unconverted mustang like Buck Caperton whickering around on the matrimonial range. So it was six months before I saw Perry again.

" One day I was passing on the edge of town, and I see something like a man in a little yard by a little house with a sprinkling-pot squirting water on a rose-bush. Seemed to me, I'd seen something like it before, and I stopped at the gate, trying to figure out its brands. 'Twas not Perry Rountree, but 'twas the kind of a curdled jellyfish matrimony had made out of him.

" Homicide was what that Mariana had perpetrated. He was looking well enough, but he had on a white collar and shoes, and you could tell in a minute that he'd speak polite and pay taxes and stick his little finger out while drinking, just like a sheep man or a citizen. Great skyrockets! but I hated to see Perry all corrupted and Willie-ized like that.

"He came out to the gate, and shook hands; and I says, with scorn, and speaking like a paroquet with the pip: 'Beg pardon — Mr. Rountree, I believe. Seems to me I sagatiated in your associations once, if I am not mistaken.'

"'Oh, go to the devil, Buck,' says Perry, polite, as I was afraid he'd be.

"'Well, then,' says I, 'you poor, contaminated adjunct of a sprinkling-pot and degraded household pet, what did you go and do it for? Look at you, all decent and unriotous, and only fit to sit on juries and mend the wood-house door. You was a man once. I have hostility for all such acts. Why don't you go in the house and count the tidies or set the clock, and not stand out here in the atmosphere? A jack-rabbit might come along and bite you.'

"'Now, Buck,' says Perry, speaking mild, and some sorrowful, 'you don't understand. A married man has got to be different. He feels different from a tough old cloudburst like you. It's sinful to waste time pulling up towns just to look at their roots, and playing faro and looking upon red liquor, and such restless policies as them.'

"'There was a time,' I says, and I expect I sighed when I mentioned it, 'when a certain domesticated little Mary's lamb I could name was some instructed himself in the line of pernicious sprightliness. I never expected, Perry, to see you reduced down from a full-grown pestilence to such a frivolous fraction of a man. Why,' says I, 'you've got a necktie on; and you speak a senseless kind of indoor drivel that reminds me of a storekeeper or a lady. You look to me like you might tote an umbrella and wear suspenders, and go home of nights.'

" ' The little woman,' says Perry, ' has made some improvements, I believe. You can't understand, Buck. I haven't been away from the house at night since we was married.'

" We talked on a while, me and Perry, and, as sure as I live, that man interrupted me in the middle of my talk to tell me about six tomato plants he had growing in his garden. Shoved his agricultural degradation right up under my nose while I was telling him about the fun we had tarring and feathering that faro dealer at California Pete's layout! But by and by Perry shows a flicker of sense.

" ' Buck,' says he, ' I'll have to admit that it is a little dull at times. Not that I'm not perfectly happy with the little woman, but a man seems to require some excitement now and then. Now, I'll tell you: Mariana's gone visiting this afternoon, and she won't be home till seven o'clock. That's the limit for both of us — seven o'clock. Neither of us ever stays out a minute after that time unless we are together. Now, I'm glad you came along, Buck,' says Perry, ' for I'm feeling just like having one more rip-roaring razoo with you for the sake of old times. What you say to us putting in the afternoon having fun — I'd like it fine,' says Perry.

" I slapped that old captive range-rider half across his little garden.

" ' Get your hat, you old dried-up alligator,' I shouts, ' you ain't dead yet. You're part human, anyhow, if you did get all bogged up in matrimony. We'll take this town to pieces and see what makes it tick. We'll make all kinds of profligate demands upon the science of cork pulling. You'll grow horns yet, old muley cow,' says I, punching Perry in the ribs, ' if you trot around on the trail of vice with your Uncle Buck.'

" ' I'll have to be home by seven, you know,' says Perry again.

" ' Oh, yes,' says I, winking to myself, for I knew the kind of seven o'clocks Perry Rountree got back by after he once got to passing repartee with the bartenders.

" We goes down to the Gray Mule saloon — that old 'dobe building by the depot.

" ' Give it a name,' says I, as soon as we got one hoof on the foot-rest.

" ' Sarsaparilla,' says Perry.

" You could have knocked me down with a lemon peeling.

" ' Insult me as much as you want to,' I says to Perry, ' but don't startle the bartender. He may have heart-disease. Come on, now; your tongue got twisted.   The tall glasses,' I orders, ' and the bottle in the left-hand corner of the ice-chest.'

" ' Sarsaparilla,' repeats Perry, and then his eyes get animated, and I see he's got some great scheme in his mind he wants to emit.

" ' Buck,' he says, all interested, ' I'll tell you what! I want to make this a red-letter day. I've been keeping close at home, and I want to turn myself a-loose. We'll have the highest old time you ever saw. We'll go in the back room here and play checkers till half-past six.'

" I leaned against the bar, and I says to Gotch-eared Mike, who was on watch:

" ' For God's sake don't mention this. You know what Perry used to be. He's had the fever, and the doctor says we must humour him.'

" ' Give us the checker-board and the men, Mike,' says Perry. ' Come on, Buck, I'm just wild to have some excitement.'

" ' I went in the back room with Perry. Before we closed the door, I says to Mike:

" ' Don't ever let it straggle out from under your hat that you seen Buck Caperton fraternal with sarsaparilla or

persona grata with a checker-board, or I'll make a swallow-
fork in your other ear.'

" I locked the door and me and Perry played checkers. To
see that poor old humiliated piece of household bric-a-brac
sitting there and sniggering out loud whenever he jumped
a man, and all obnoxious with animation when he got into
my king row, would have made a sheep-dog sick with mortification. Him that was once satisfied only when he was peg-
ging six boards at keno or giving the faro dealers nervous
prostration — to see him pushing them checkers about like
Sally Louisa at a school-children's party — why, I was all
smothered up with mortification.

" And I sits there playing the black men, all sweating for
fear somebody I knew would find it out. And I thinks to
myself some about this marrying business, and how it seems
to be the same kind of a game as that Mrs. Delilah played.
She give her old man a hair cut, and everybody knows what
a man's head looks like after a woman cuts his hair. And
then when the Pharisees came around to guy him he was so
'shamed he went to work and kicked the whole house down
on top of the whole outfit. 'Them married men,' thinks I,
' lose all their spirit and instinct for riot and foolishness.
They won't drink, they won't buck the tiger, they won't even
fight. What do they want to go and stay married for?' I
asks myself.

" But Perry seems to be having hilarity in considerable
quantities.

" ' Buck old hoss,' says he, ' isn't this just the hell-roar-
ingest time we ever had in our lives? I don't know when I've
been stirred up so. You see, I've been sticking pretty close
to home since I married, and I haven't been on a spree in a
long time.'

" ' Spree!' Yes, that's what he called it. Playing checkers in the back room of the Gray Mule! I suppose it did seem to him a little more immoral and nearer to a prolonged debauch than standing over six tomato plants with a sprinkling-pot.

"Every little bit Perry looks at his watch and says:

"'I got to be home, you know, Buck, at seven.'

"'All right,' I'd say. 'Romp along and move. This here excitement's killing me. If I don't reform some, and loosen up the strain of this checkered dissipation I won't have a nerve left.'

"It might have been half-past six when commotions began to go on outside in the street. We heard a yelling and a six-shootering, and a lot of galloping and manœuvres.

"'What's that?' I wonders.

"'Oh, some nonsense outside,' says Perry. 'It's your move. We just got time to play this game.'

"'I'll just take a peep through the window,' says I, 'and see. You can't expect a mere mortal to stand the excitement of having a king jumped and listen to an unidentified conflict going on at the same time.'

"'The Gray Mule saloon was one of them old Spanish 'dobe buildings, and the back room only had two little windows a foot wide, with iron bars in 'em. I looked out one, and I see the cause of the rucus.

"There was the Trimble gang — ten of 'em — the worst outfit of desperadoes and horse-thieves in Texas, coming up the street shooting right and left. They was coming right straight for the Gray Mule. Then they got past the range of my sight, but we heard 'em ride up to the front door, and then they socked the place full of lead. We heard the big looking-glass behind the bar knocked all to pieces and the bottles crashing. We could see Gotch-eared Mike in his apron running across the plaza like a coyote, with the bullets puffing up the dust all around him. Then the gang went to work in the saloon, drinking what they wanted and smashing what they didn't.

"Me and Perry both knew that gang, and they knew us. The year before Perry married, him and me was in the same ranger company — and we fought that outfit down on the San Miguel, and brought back Ben Trimble and two others for murder.

"'We can't get out,' says I. "We'll have to stay in here till they leave.'

Perry looked at his watch.

"'Twenty-five to seven,' says he. 'We can finish that game. I got two men on you. It's your move, Buck. I got to be home at seven, you know.'

"We sat down and went on playing. The Trimble gang had a roughhouse for sure. They were getting good and drunk. They'd drink a while and holler a while, and then they'd shoot up a few bottles and glasses. Two or three times they came and tried to open our door. Then there was some more shooting outside, and I looked out the window again. Ham Gossett, the town marshal, had a posse in the houses and stores across the street, and was trying to bag a Trimble or two through the windows.

"I lost that game of checkers. I'm free in saying that I lost three kings that I might have saved if I had been corralled in a more peaceful pasture. But that drivelling married man sat there and cackled when he won a man like an unintelligent hen picking up a grain of corn.

"When the game was over Perry gets up and looks at his watch.

"'I've had a glorious time, Buck,' says he, 'but I'll have to be going now. It's a quarter to seven, and I got to be home by seven, you know.'

"I thought he was joking.

"'They'll clear out or be dead drunk in half an hour or an

hour,' says I. 'You ain't that tired of being married that you want to commit any more sudden suicide, are you?' says I, giving him the laugh.

"'One time,' says Perry, 'I was half an hour late getting home. I met Mariana on the street looking for me. If you could have seen her, Buck — but you don't understand. She knows what a wild kind of a snoozer I've been, and she's afraid something will happen. I'll never be late getting home again. I'll say good-bye to you now, Buck.'

"I got between him and the door.

"'Married man,' says I, 'I know you was christened a fool the minute the preacher tangled you up, but don't you never sometimes think one little think on a human basis? There's ten of that gang in there, and they're pizen with whiskey and desire for murder. They'll drink you up like a bottle of booze before you get half-way to the door. Be intelligent, now, and use at least wild-hog sense. Sit down and wait till we have some chance to get out without being carried in baskets.'

"'I got to be home by seven, Buck,' repeats this hen-pecked thing of little wisdom, like an unthinking poll parrot. 'Mariana,' says he, ''ll be looking out for me.' And he reaches down and pulls a leg out of the checker table. 'I'll go through this Trimble outfit,' says he, 'like a cottontail through a brush corral. I'm not pestered any more with a desire to engage in rucuses, but I got to be home by seven. You lock the door after me, Buck. And don't you forget — I won three out of them five games. I'd play longer, but Mariana —'

"'Hush up, you old locoed road runner,' I interrupts. 'Did you ever notice your Uncle Buck locking doors against trouble? I'm not married,' says I, 'but I'm as big a d——n fool as any Mormon. One from four leaves three,' says I, and I gathers out another leg of the table. 'We'll get home by seven,' says I, 'whether it's the heavenly one or the other. May I see you home?' says I, 'you sarsaparilla-drinking, checker-playing glutton for death and destruction.'

"We opened the door easy, and then stampeded for the front. Part of the gang was lined up at the bar; part of 'em was passing over the drinks, and two or three was peeping out the door and window taking shots at the marshal's crowd. The room was so full of smoke we got half-way to the front door before they noticed us. Then I heard Berry Trimble's voice somewhere yell out:

"'How'd that Buck Caperton get in here?' and he skinned the side of my neck with a bullet. I reckon he felt bad over that miss, for Berry's the best shot south of the Southern Pacific Railroad. But the smoke in the saloon was some too thick for good shooting.

"Me and Perry smashed over two of the gang with our table legs, which didn't miss like the guns did, and as we run out the door I grabbed a Winchester from a fellow who was watching the outside, and I turned and regulated the account of Mr. Berry.

"Me and Perry got out and around the corner all right. I never much expected to get out, but I wasn't going to be intimidated by that married man. According to Perry's idea, checkers was the event of the day, but if I am any judge of gentle recreations that little table-leg parade through the Gray Mule saloon deserved the head-lines in the bill of particulars.

"'Walk fast,' says Perry, 'it's two minutes to seven, and I got to be home by —'

"'Oh, shut up,' says I. 'I had an appointment as chief performer at an inquest at seven, and I'm not kicking about not keeping it.'

"I had to pass by Perry's little house. His Mariana was standing at the gate. We got there at five minutes past seven.

She had on a blue wrapper, and her hair was pulled back smooth like little girls do when they want to look grown-folksy. She didn't see us till we got close, for she was gazing up the other way. Then she backed around, and saw Perry, and a kind of a look scooted around over her face — danged if I can describe it. I heard her breathe long, just like a cow when you turn her calf in the lot, and she says: 'You're late, Perry.'

" 'Five minutes,' says Perry, cheerful. 'Me and old Buck was having a game of checkers.'

" Perry introduces me to Mariana, and they ask me to come in. No, sir-ee. I'd had enough truck with married folks for that day. I says I'll be going along, and that I've spent a very pleasant afternoon with my old partner —'especially,' says I, just to jostle Perry, 'during that game when the table legs came all loose.' But I'd promised him not to let her know anything.

" I've been worrying over that business ever since it happened," continued Buck. " There's one thing about it that's got me all twisted up, and I can't figure it out."

" What was that? " I asked, as I rolled and handed Buck the last cigarette.

" Why, I'll tell you. When I saw the look that little woman give Perry when she turned round and saw him coming back to the ranch safe — why was it I got the idea all in a minute that that look of hers was worth more than the whole caboodle of us — sarsaparilla, checkers, and all, and that the d—n fool in the game wasn't named Perry Rountree at all? "

THE END